IMAGES
of Rail

Delaware and Hudson Railway

ON THE COVER: **THE HUMP CREW.** "Humping" cars (featured on page 82) involves pushing a string of cars from a receiving yard track over a hump at the entrance of a "classification" yard into a different track to make up varied trains. It would take many men to accomplish this in the days of steam locomotives. (Author's collection.)

IMAGES
of Rail

Delaware and Hudson Railway

Marilyn E. Dufresne

ARCADIA
PUBLISHING

ISBN 978-0-7385-7390-8

Published by Arcadia Publishing
Charleston, South Carolina

Printed in the United States of America

Library of Congress Control Number: 2010929509

For all general information, please contact Arcadia Publishing:
Telephone 843-853-2070
Fax 843-853-0044
E-mail sales@arcadiapublishing.com
For customer service and orders:
Toll-Free 1-888-313-2665

Visit us on the Internet at www.arcadiapublishing.com

I would like to dedicate this book to the members of the Bridge Line Historical Society in Albany and all others who strive to keep the memories of the Delaware and Hudson Railway alive.

CONTENTS

ACKNOWLEDGMENTS

This book is based on the vintage postcard collection I've assembled over a 10-year period. I have added other memorabilia and photographs along the way. Special thanks to my daughter Debbie Dufresne and her husband, Michael Woods, for their unique insight into this undertaking. Debbie also helped with the task of typing while I was recuperating from a broken finger. I would also like to thank Brad Peterson, a D&H (Bridge Line) engineer and historian of the Bridge Line Historical Society in Albany. He is from Porter Corners, New York, and his answers to my questions helped with the success of this book. Dick Weidman of Worcester, a former D&H employee, was also a source of information on railway stations. Many thanks go to the Worcester Historical Society and the New York State Historical Society in Cooperstown for the use of their materials. Unless otherwise noted, all images come from the author's collection.

INTRODUCTION

The Delaware and Hudson Railway was born in the early 1800s when the Delaware and Hudson Canal Company had its eye on the coal mines of Pennsylvania and sought a way to ship the black coal by railroad, as well as canal, for a larger market to increase business.

In 1814, William and Maurice Wurts, dry good merchants in Philadelphia, opened a coal mine in the area of Carbondale and began to transport the "black gold" over the Moosic mountains and construct a canal connecting the Hudson and Delaware Rivers. The Wurts brothers purchased all available stock in the D&H Canal Company.

The *Stourbridge Lion*, the first steam engine to run on U.S. rails, could only chug along at 10 miles per hour. It ran between Carbondale and Honesdale, Pennsylvania, on August 8, 1829. In that year, the Delaware and Hudson Canal Company imported this little engine from England with a delivery price of $2,914.90. The track was laid on 6-inch-by-9-inch hemlock ties placed 10 feet apart with 2.25-inch-wide iron straps fastened to the inside track edges to provide extra wear.

The canal company prospered, but after the Civil War the company realized it had to expand. About this time, plans were under way to construct a railroad line from Albany to Binghamton and the southern tier with the name Albany and Susquehanna (A&S).

On July 17, 1865, the first train steamed down the tracks as far as Worcester, stopping at all the little towns along the way amid cheers and bands as folks gathered to witness the wonder of this new mode of transportation. Although the railroad was chartered in 1851, financial difficulties and postponements delayed completion of it until 1868. The Delaware and Hudson Canal Company managers negotiated a deal with the A&S to move anthracite over their tracks. The D&H Canal Company also, along with the expansion program, petitioned New York State in 1867 for permission for railroad rights. The decision was formidable. The D&H Canal Company felt the Albany and Susquehanna tracks would serve as a means of reaching small towns along the route to Binghamton, so it offered to help financially with the purchase of $500,000 worth of A&S bonds to keep a deal for completion of the railroad line from Albany to Ninevah. The line opened January 14, 1869, after fulfillment of the entire project.

In 1868, Oneonta was chosen to be the home for an old structure moved from Harpursville to serve as a shelter for engines until something more permanent could be built. In October 1870, work on a roundhouse was well underway. This was followed by several enlargements and construction projects, including a second engine house.

A massive new roundhouse was opened in Oneonta in May 1906, with plans designed by the American Railway Master Mechanics Association. This new roundhouse, for 25 years regarded as the largest of its kind in the world, had 52 stalls for locomotives and four pits where engines could dump their ashes. Eventually the yards at Oneonta became the main center for the D&H system.

The gravity railroad closed January 3, 1899, and on April 28, 1899, changed its name to the Delaware and Hudson Company. Over the next few years, the Delaware and Hudson incorporated several railways, forming a long branch west from Plattsburg south to Lake Placid. It incorporated Napierville Junction Railway, from St. Constant Junction near Montreal, now Delson (Delaware and Hudson) to Rouses Point and Wilkes-Barre, Pennsylvania, with an interchange at Hanover Township, Pennsylvania, for the connecting railroads. The property of the Delaware and Hudson Company was transferred to the Delaware and Hudson Railroad Corporation on April 1, 1930.

As the line began to grow, so did repair shops including those in Oneonta, Green Island, and Carbondale, Pennsylvania. The D&H prospered in the 1920s, and during that time 12 passenger trains ran from Albany to Binghamton on a daily schedule. The D&H began to act as a "bridge" in 1938, spanning the gap between other railroads by carrying large amounts of freight. Thus historians know it as the "bridge line" today.

Over the years, growth in the D&H system was inevitable. As a result, small towns grew. Oneonta was known as "Rail City, U.S.A." as everyone thought passenger service was here to stay. The D&H Company has a long, rich history in the Oneonta area. In 1924, it installed a 105-foot turntable in the roundhouse and two years later undertook replacement of the old machine shop. An employee locker room was the result of a conversion of the machine shop.

The 1930s proved to be the heyday of the D&H, and as an added benefit to beautify the area employees took time to maintain flower gardens around the complex and station.

In the 1940s, the Oneonta roundhouse underwent changes to keep up with the introduction of the J class Challenger, locomotives able to reach speeds of up to 70 miles per hour because of unique balancing rods. Steam locomotives were on their way out in 1944 when the D&H purchased two diesels.

On March 13, 1946, a devastating fire took place in the coal pocket at the Oneonta yard. Flames destroyed eight fully loaded coal cars, each holding 50 tons of coal. Two men lost their lives in this out-of-control blaze.

The year 1954 saw the demise of the roundhouse when D&H officials announced that it would close immediately. In December, the Schesser Demolition Company of Scranton, Pennsylvania, began to dismantle the structure. The D&H was losing money every day it stayed in business. Things went from bad to worse for the D&H, when in 1968 the railroad was reorganized as the Delaware and Hudson Railway and placed under the control of Norfolk and Western via Dereco, a holding company that also owned the Erie-Lackawanna Railroad. Damages following Hurricane Agnes put Erie-Lackawanna into receivership and the D&H back on its own.

In 1984, Guilford Rail System purchased the D&H with the prospect of operating a regional railroad from Maine in the east to New York and Montreal. The purchase price was $500,000, reflecting bad financial shape. Guilford Transportation later put the D&H into bankruptcy.

Since 1991, the Delaware and Hudson Railway has been a subsidiary of Canadian Pacific Railroad, with the latter assuming total operations. It is now called Canadian Pacific System, Northeast U.S. Service, Bridge Line Division. The D&H has very few engines and railcars left.

Today D&H rails still provide an important link between shippers and receivers to and from eastern Canada, New England, and points south, thus establishing itself as a high-speed "bridge line" moving freight between important connections with other railroads. It will be remembered for its part in ushering in the great railroad era.

For those who have always fancied railroads like the D&H, such as Jim Shaughnessy, Jim Loudon, and John Taibi to name a few, they are reminded that passenger service, steam locomotives, and those great billows of smoke floating against a blue sky are long gone. In their place are lengthy freight, some over 100 cars long, pulled by high-speed, sleek diesels sounding their warning whistles at all the crossings, assuring everyone that the Delaware and Hudson Railway—now know as the "bridge line"—and memories of it are alive and well.

One

In the Beginning

In the beginning, it was the appreciation of steam power in the 1800s that led everyone to believe coal would be the source to provide this. The Wurts brothers became pioneers in the coal business by purchasing coal-bearing land. They continued their search for anthracite and ways to market the coal. Their pioneering spirit grew, and in 1822 one of their new mines produced over 1,000 tons of anthracite. In the early days, the D&H Canal Company and their gravity railroad provided the means of moving coal to markets like New York City. Once in New York state, the canal company set its sights on a new, little railroad called the Albany and Susquehanna (A&S). It was soon acquired by lease and would prove to be the perfect means of marketing coal along all the stations from Binghamton to Albany and points north and east. The Wurts brothers soon abandoned the canal and gravity railroad and changed the corporate title to the Delaware and Hudson Company on April 28, 1899.

Locomotive built in 1860 at Dickson shops, Scranton, Pa. for D & H Canal Co. R. R.

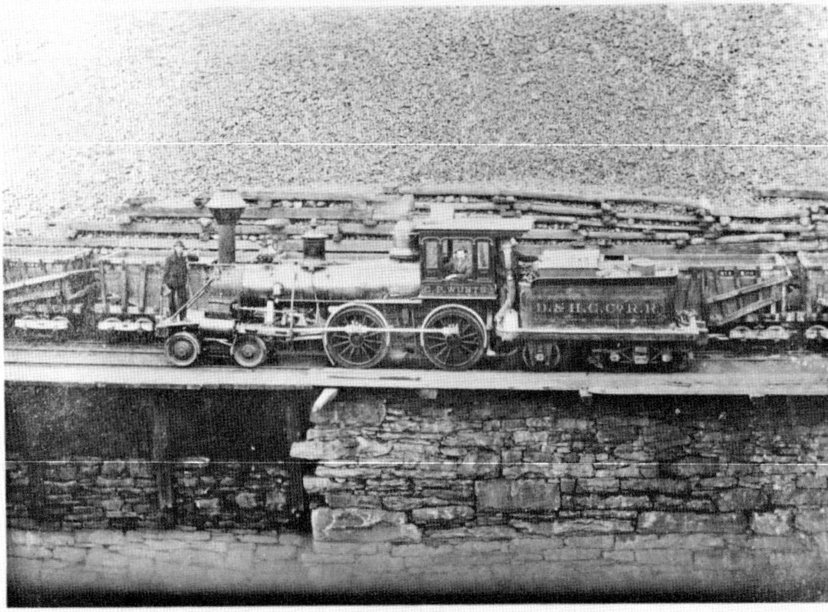

D&H Canal Company. The D&H Canal Company used locomotives built in the 1860s at Dickson Shops in Scranton, Pennsylvania. In those early days, the Honesdale area was a wilderness. Once coal was being shipped by canal, everything changed and the area began to grow.

"The Lackawanna," built in 1862 at Dickson shops, Scranton, Pa. for D & H Canal Co.

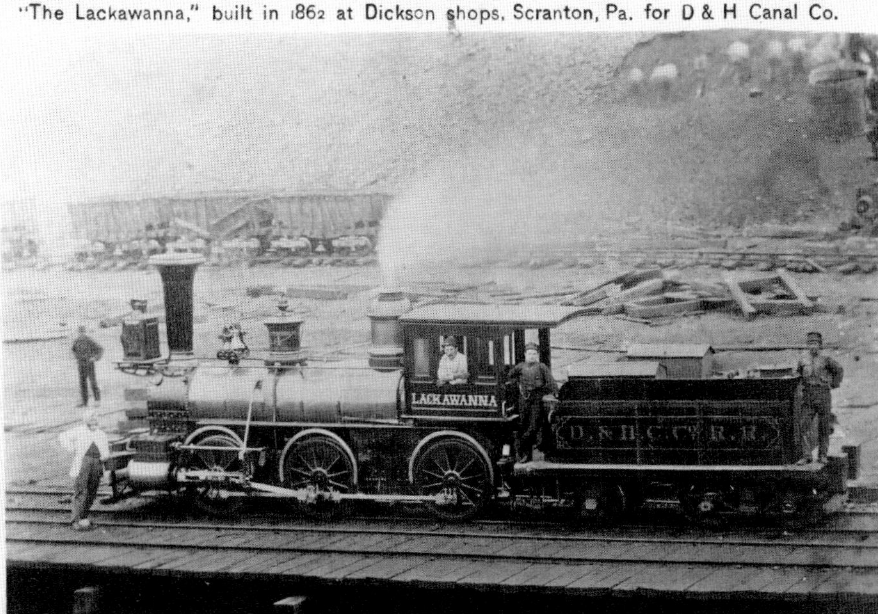

The Lackawanna. Another style of steam locomotive, Lackawanna Engine No. 4, was built in 1862 at the Dickson shops in Scranton, Pennsylvania. The gravity railroad used a cable on which cars descended on a slope by gravity. The second track shown in this photograph allows the weight of cars going down to help raise the empty cars going back up. This engine was used for 37 years before being scrapped.

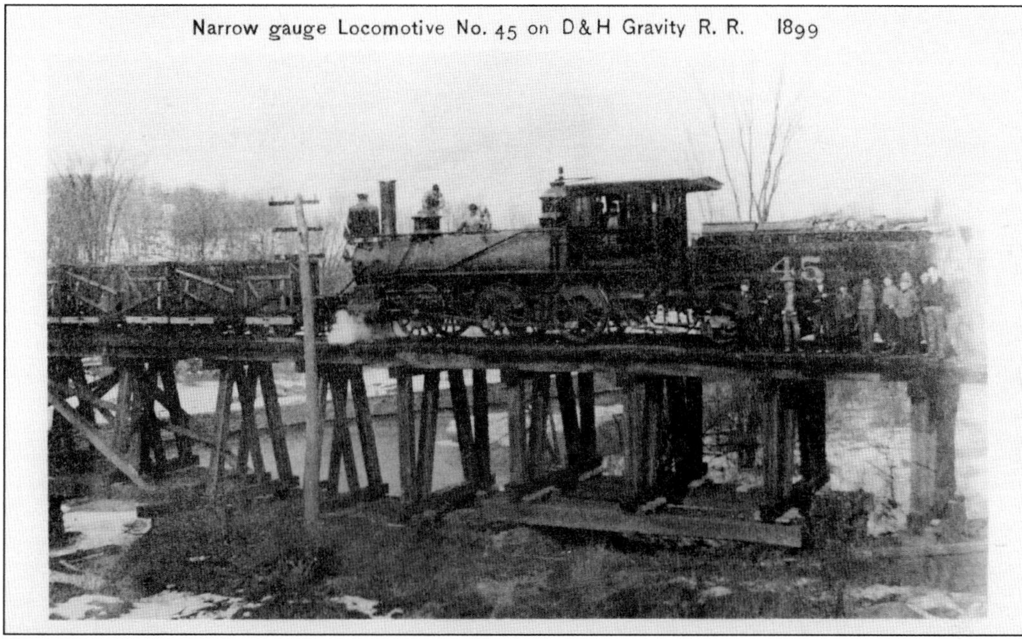

NARROW GAUGE. Locomotive No. 45 traveled on narrow-gauge tracks. Workers stand to the right in the picture. The train is crossing over a river by means of a wooden trestle. The D&H Canal closed January 3, 1899, but it had carried the bulk of New York City's coal until after the Civil War.

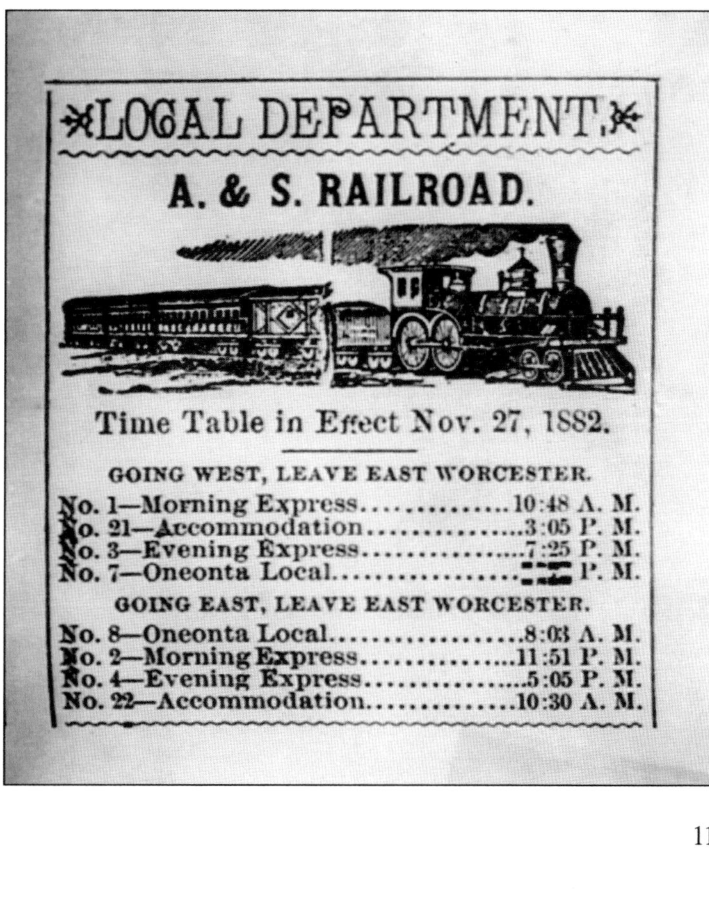

LOCAL DEPARTMENT.

A. & S. RAILROAD.

Time Table in Effect Nov. 27, 1882.

GOING WEST, LEAVE EAST WORCESTER.

No. 1—Morning Express..............10:48 A. M.
No. 21—Accommodation..............3:05 P. M.
No. 3—Evening Express..............7:25 P. M.
No. 7—Oneonta Local..............[illegible] P. M.

GOING EAST, LEAVE EAST WORCESTER.

No. 8—Oneonta Local..............8:03 A. M.
No. 2—Morning Express..............11:51 P. M.
No. 4—Evening Express..............5:05 P. M.
No. 22—Accommodation..............10:30 A. M.

ALBANY AND SUSQUEHANNA. The D&H Canal Company sought to expand and move its anthracite coal over the rails of New York state's fledgling railroad, the Albany and Susquehanna (A&S). When completed on January 14, 1869, locomotives could run from Albany to Ninevah. This A&S timetable is from 1882.

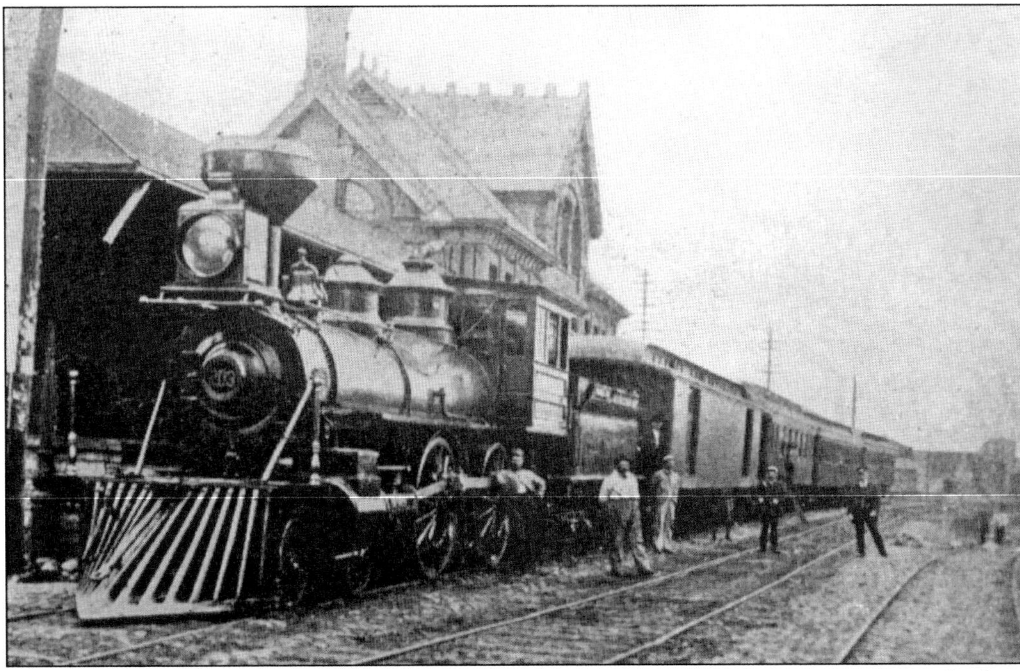

PASSENGER TRAIN. This Dickson-built passenger train waits at Albany station in 1876. The front of the locomotive features what was typically referred to as a "cow catcher," which was used to push debris off the tracks. The crew, from left, are W. H. Ostrander, fireman; H. A. White, engineer; Newton McKebby, baggage man; Fred Condon, brakeman; and Frank Vincent, conductor. (New York State Historical Association collection.)

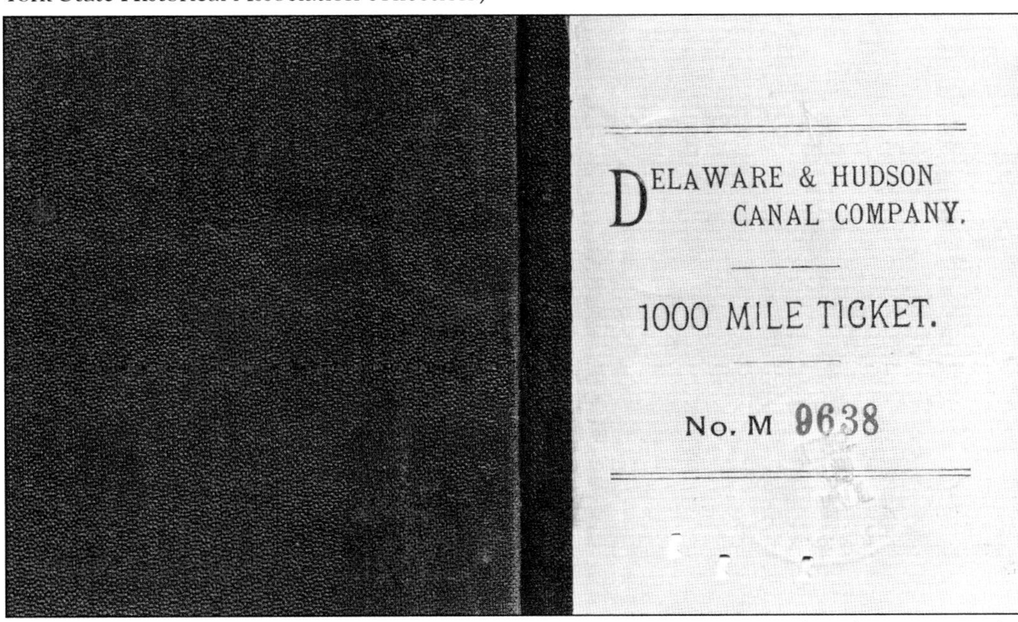

1,000-MILE TICKET. This Delaware and Hudson Canal Company 1,000-mile ticket was issued to C. O. Waterman of Worcester and countersigned by A. L. Emmons, the station agent at Worcester. One of the rules states that 20 coupons in either direction shall be surrendered for passage between Carbondale and Honesdale. (Worcester Historical Society collection.)

Two

D&H STATIONS

At one time, every city or town along the Delaware and Hudson or the old Albany and Susquehanna provided a station for passengers to purchase tickets or have a place to rest while waiting for a train. The station agent and assistants kept busy selling tickets and labeling express packages, as well as sorting baggage and freight parcels.

Night and day, railroad regulation coal-fired stoves had to be kept going during the fall and winter. In warmer weather, the stove needed to be polished.

Every waiting room had a spittoon that had to be clean and handy. Station employees were constantly checking connections and answering questions for prospective passengers.

The telegraph operator was busy with messages from nearby stations to see if the train was on time. The whistle sounded at the crossing, the rails hummed, and the train rolled in amid a cloud of smoke.

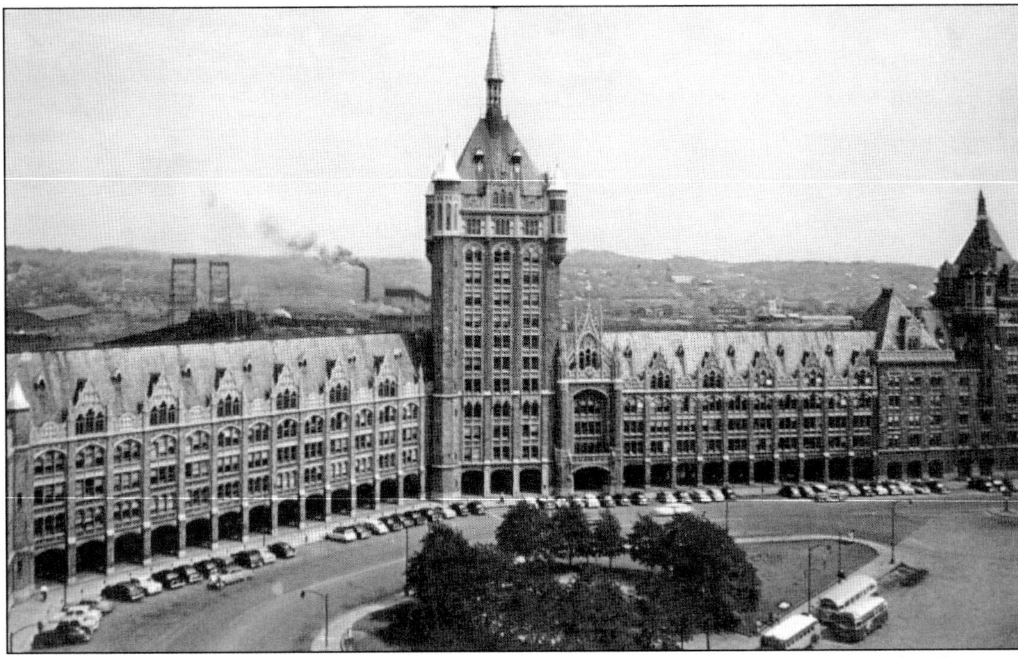

D&H Headquarters. The D&H office building in Albany was the result of a redevelopment project at Steamboat Square in 1913. The Gothic-style structure became the offices for the D&H. A 12-story tower and two five-story wings built at angles give this building its unique features. This structure now provides space for New York State offices.

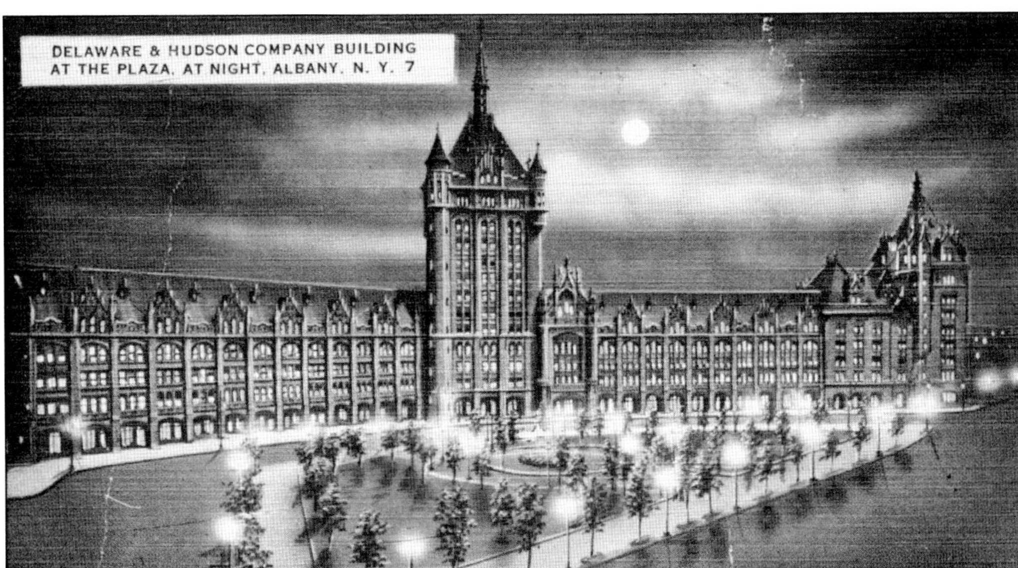

D&H Building. This Delaware and Hudson photograph was taken at night in the plaza. The structure is so imposing in size that it is often mistaken as the state capitol. In the early 1900s, Albany was a busy port for freight and passenger service.

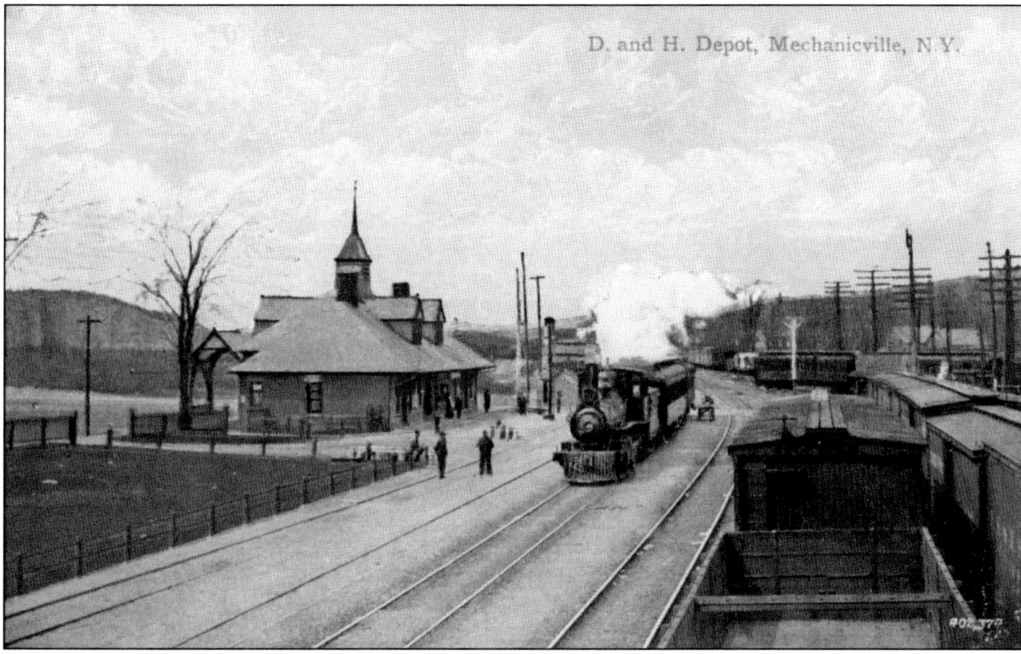

MECHANICVILLE STATION. This 1910 postcard features the rail yard at Mechanicville and the station. Dormer windows, a steeple, and a weather vane highlight the station, while an early steam engine awaits passengers as it prepares to depart.

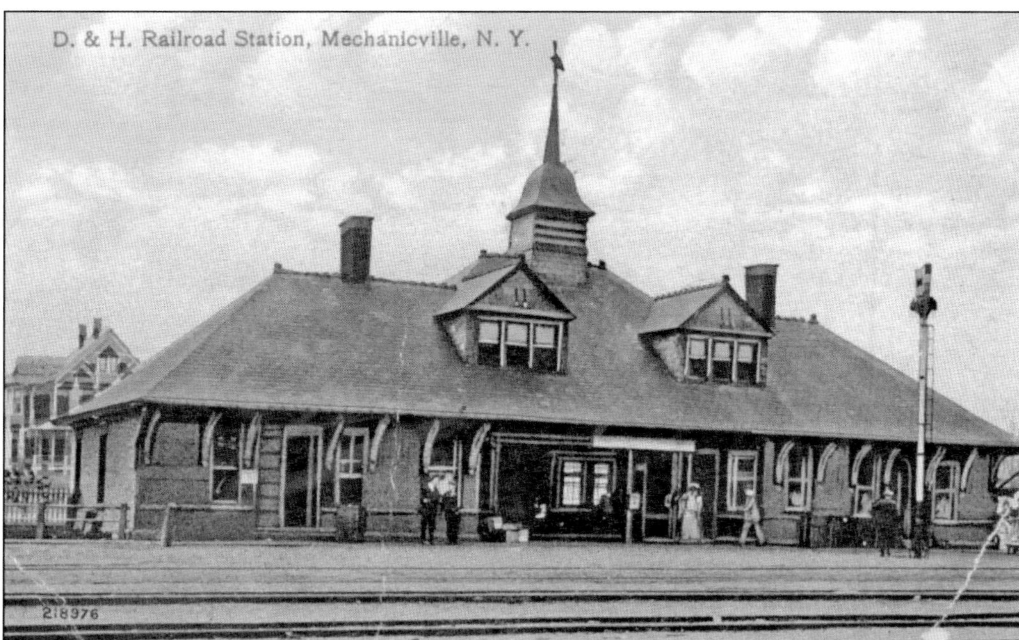

A SECOND VIEW. This D&H station postcard from 1917 shows a front view of the building. The message on the back reads, "Had a companion on the trip yesterday. A boy who was coming home to Decatur, Illinois, on furlough [World War I soldier]."

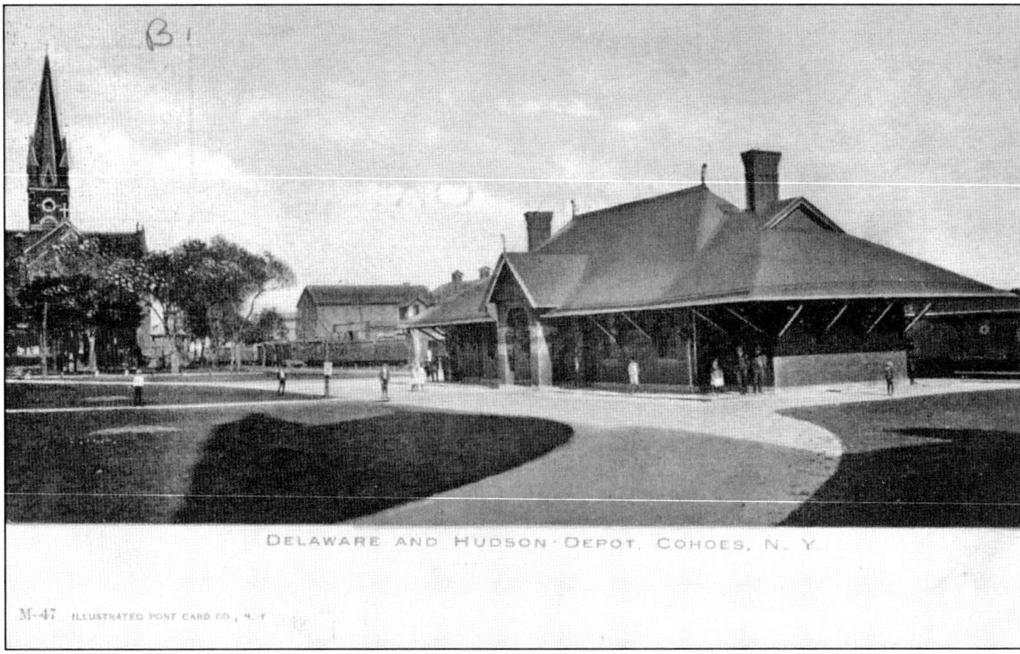

COHOES STATION. The Cohoes D&H station has a style similar to the one in Mechanicville. It is highlighted with a gable roof, eave supports with mounted finials, and a circular driveway in the front. Cohoes, called the "spindle city" because of textile production, also has a 1910 freight house that is in the historic district.

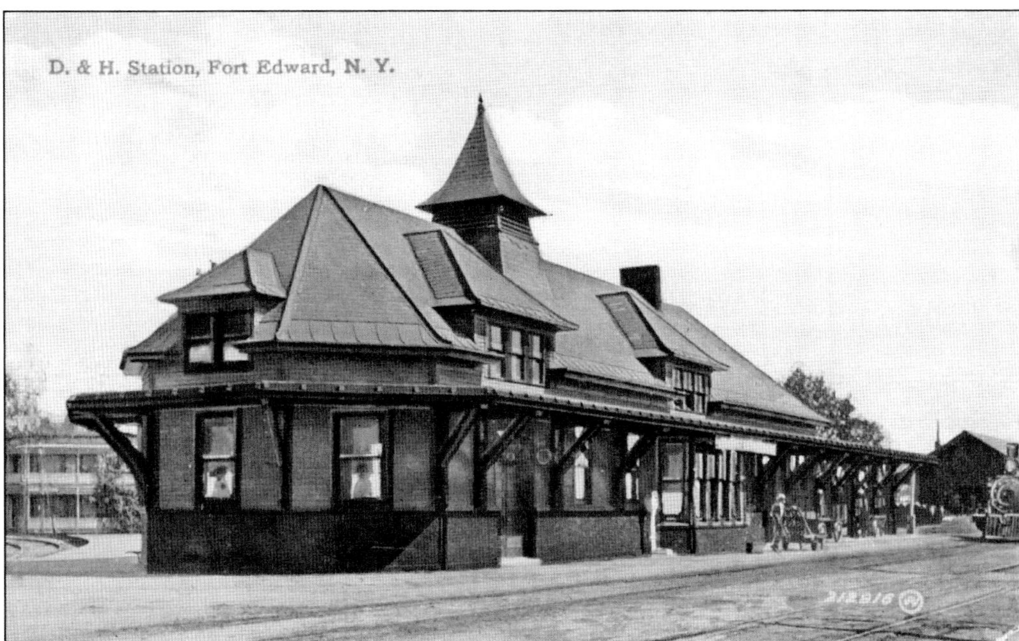

FORT EDWARD. A D&H employee with a baggage cart awaits the arrival of the train. A message on the reverse side of this early postcard states, "Did you go to the Cambridge fair? Cora and John went this morning."

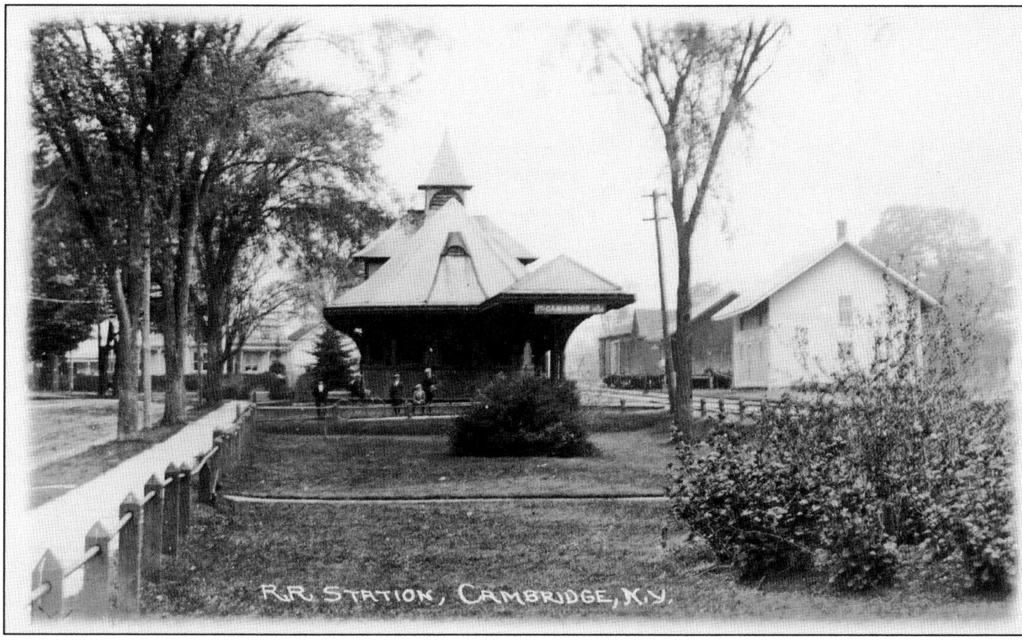

CAMBRIDGE STATION. Cement posts line the walkway leading to the Cambridge, New York, station. A variety of roof peaks, many with "eyebrow" windows, and decorative columns facing the tracks in front of the structure make for interesting architecture. The station and a freight depot still stand. Cambridge is located near the Vermont border.

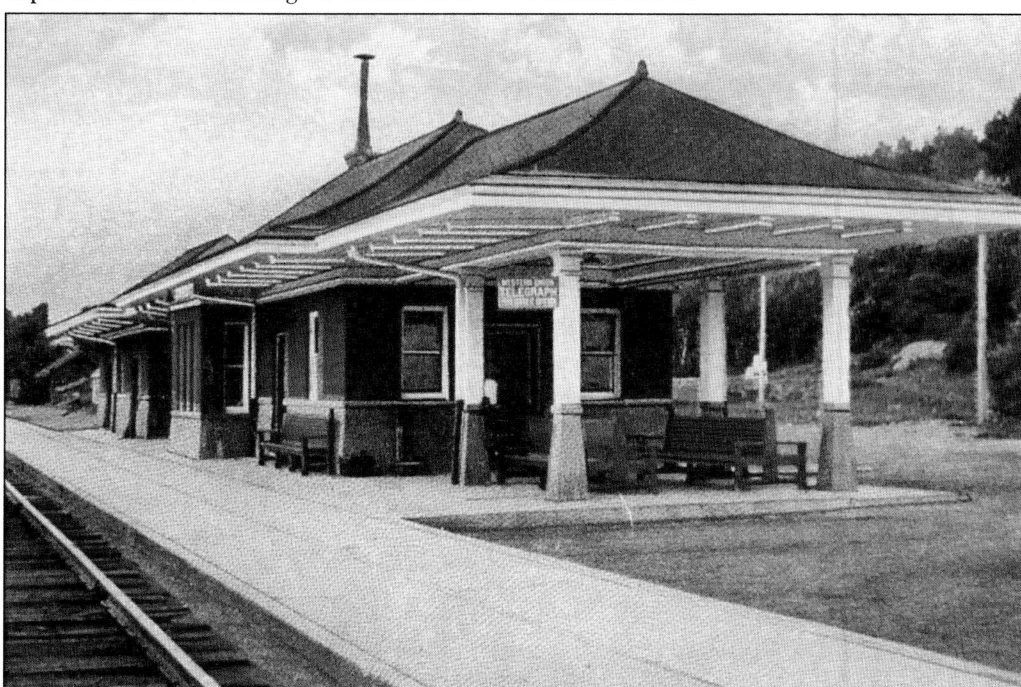

RIPARIUS. This is a postcard of the Riverside train station in Riparius, photographed in 1913. The roof portion to the right is supported by four columns over an open space with benches for passengers waiting to board an incoming train.

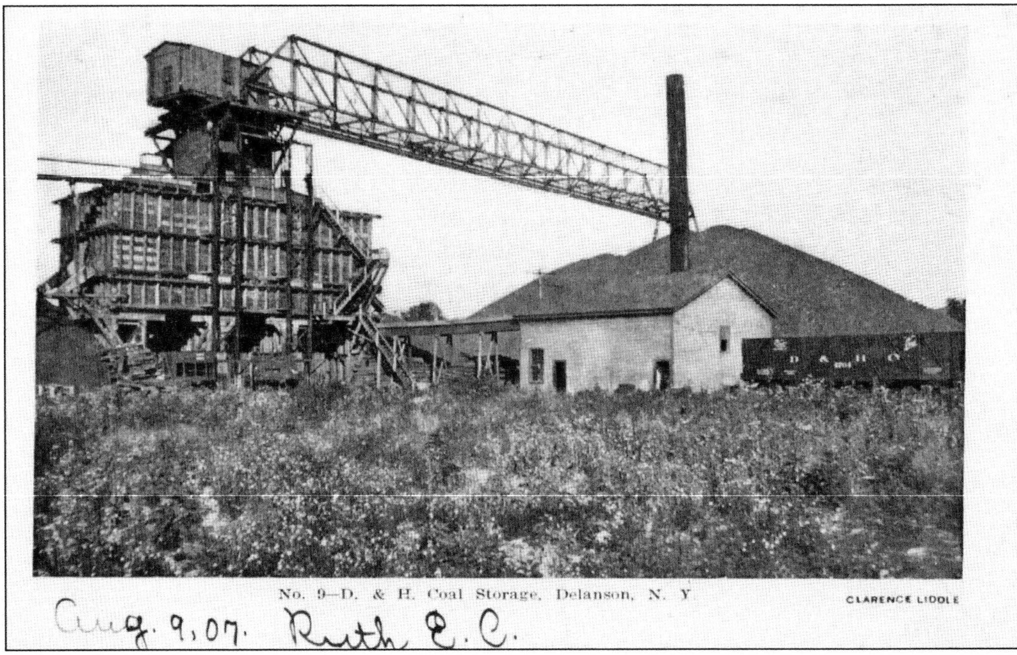

Delanson. This is an early photograph of the D&H coal storage area in Delanson. Anthracite was the main reason the Delaware and Hudson Canal Company chose to market its coal to all the little towns and villages along the original rail lines of the Albany and Susquehanna.

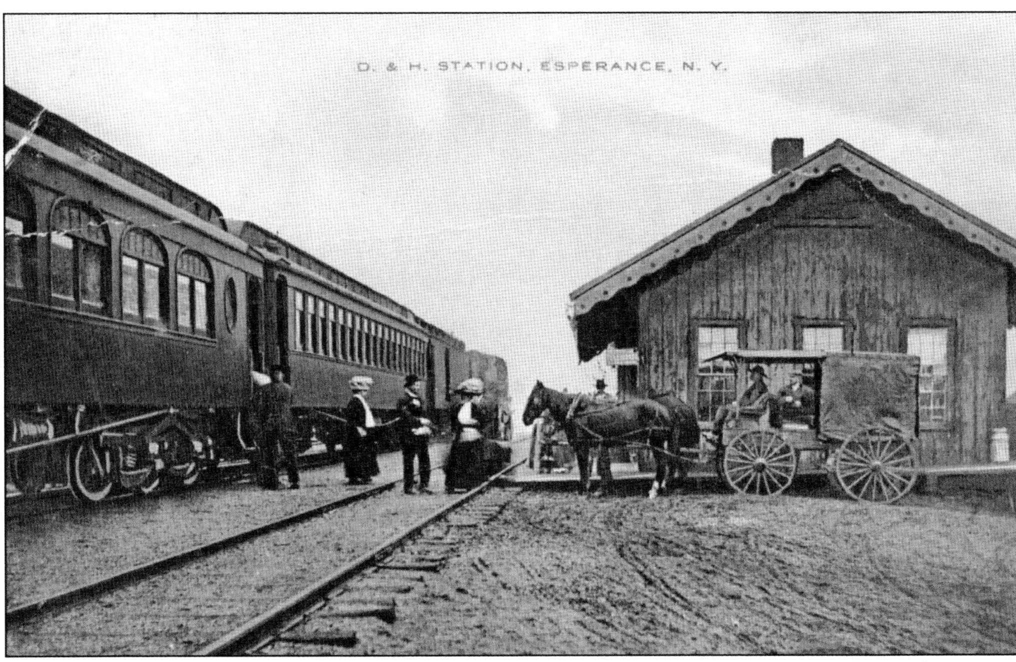

Esperance Station. This 1916 postcard features the D&H station in Esperance, located on Route 20. The station has nine-over-nine-pane windows, board-and-batten siding, and gingerbread-style decoration along the roofline. The horse and wagon livery is on hand to pick up or deliver passengers to the station.

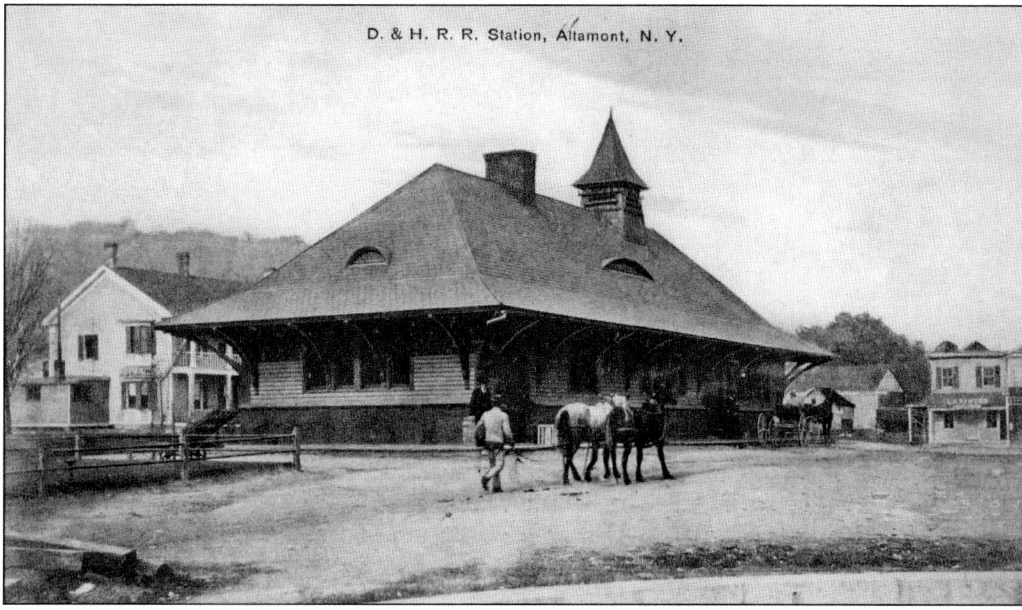

ALTAMONT STATION. This is an early postcard view of the D&H station in Altamont. Two "eyebrow" windows and a cupola adorn the structure. The message on the reverse side reads, "Went to the fair at Altamont yesterday. A big crowd." The first Altamont station was built in 1864 on the site of the present building. The new station was built in 1897, and the old one was moved down the tracks about 150 yards. (Bridge Line Historical Society [BLHS] *Bulletin*, February 2002.)

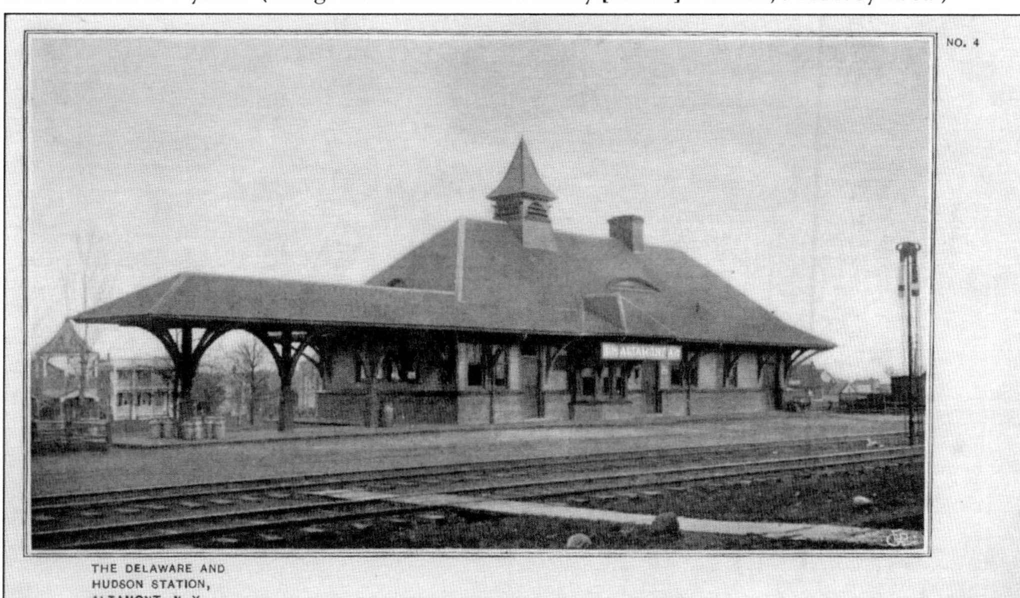

ALTAMONT D&H. This photograph shows at least two tracks running past the station. Milk cans to the left are awaiting pickup on the next train. Notice the "eyebrow" window in the center of the roof. Altamont was once known as Knowersville, a name that was kept until 1887. The remains of a D&H turntable are still visible in a corner of the rail yard. An insurance office has opened in the waiting room of the former station, and a dentist office occupies the earlier baggage area. (BLHS *Bulletin*, February 2002.)

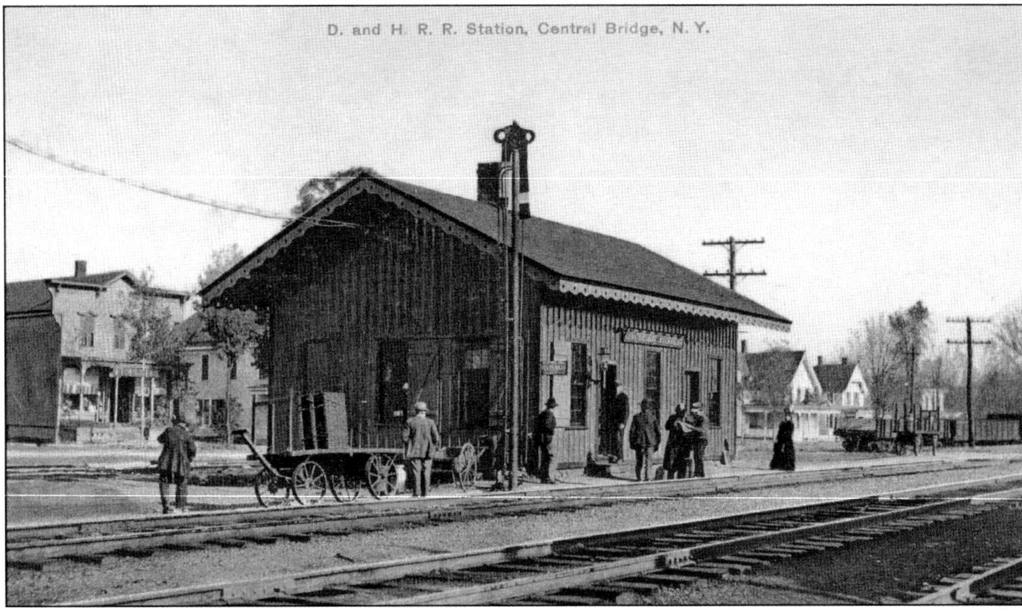

CENTRAL BRIDGE STATION. This D&H station in Central Bridge is smaller than some of the others. Board-and-batten siding and fancy trim along the roofline add character to this building. The baggage cart to the left awaits the arrival of the next train. The message on the back states, "We started over toward Carlisle, got stuck fast in mud. Had to come back toward Central Bridge. Take train tonight."

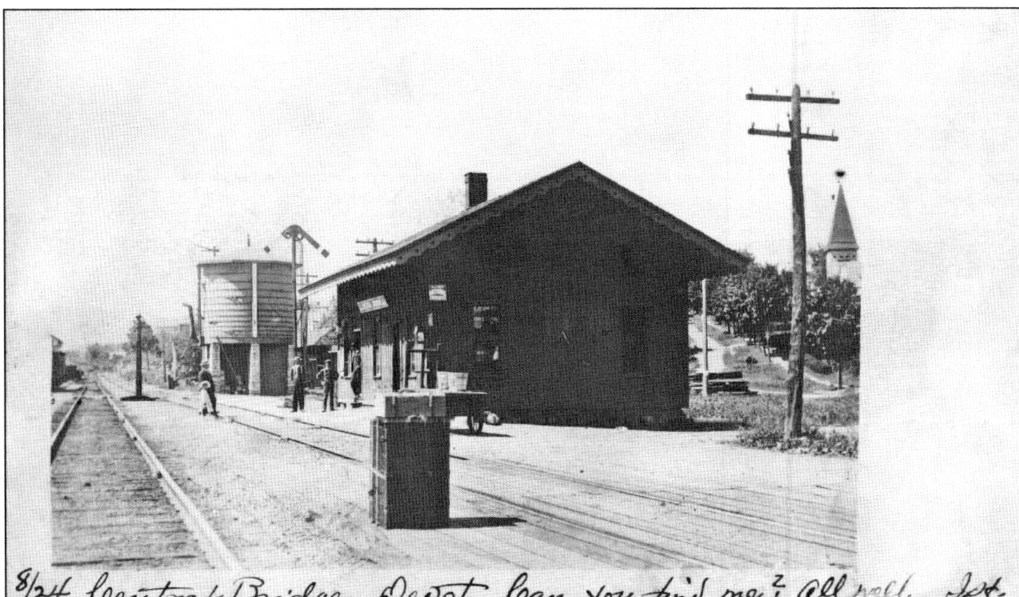

CENTRAL BRIDGE DEPOT. This 1906 postcard shows a great view of the D&H station. An important part of a station stop for a steam locomotive is the water tower, shown here to the center left. The device for trains to pick up mailbags without stopping is shown to the far left. Called a mail catcher, the hook-like device matches up with an arm on a fast train that snatches the mailbag off the post. It would not be necessary for a train to stop if there were no passengers waiting to board or de-board the train.

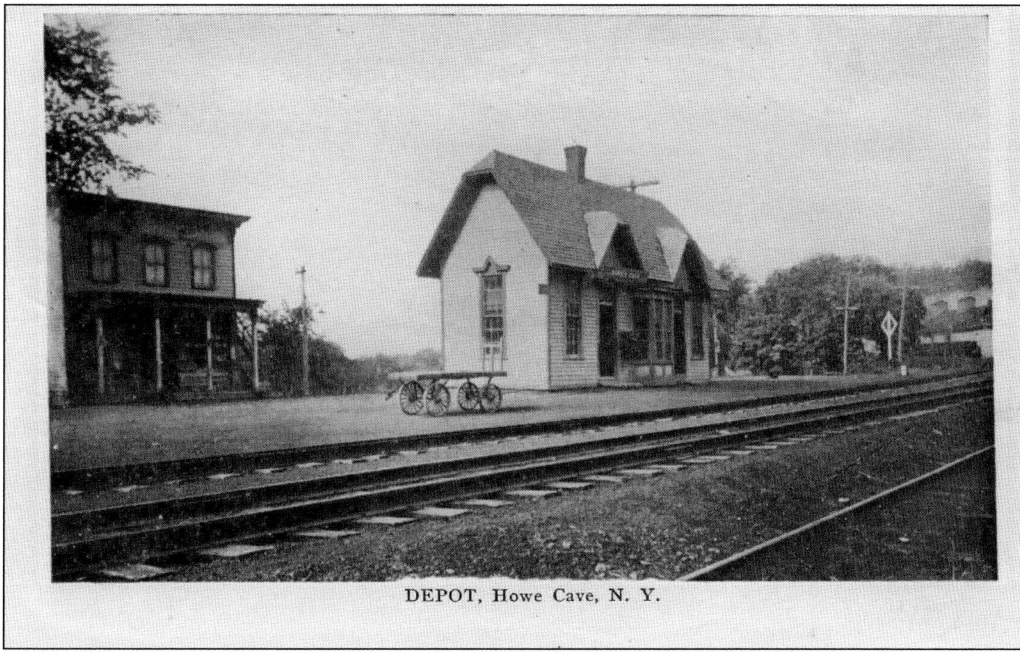

HOWE CAVE. A small D&H depot located a few miles from Cobleskill is shown here. This station has a bay window so the station agent can look out to see incoming locomotives.

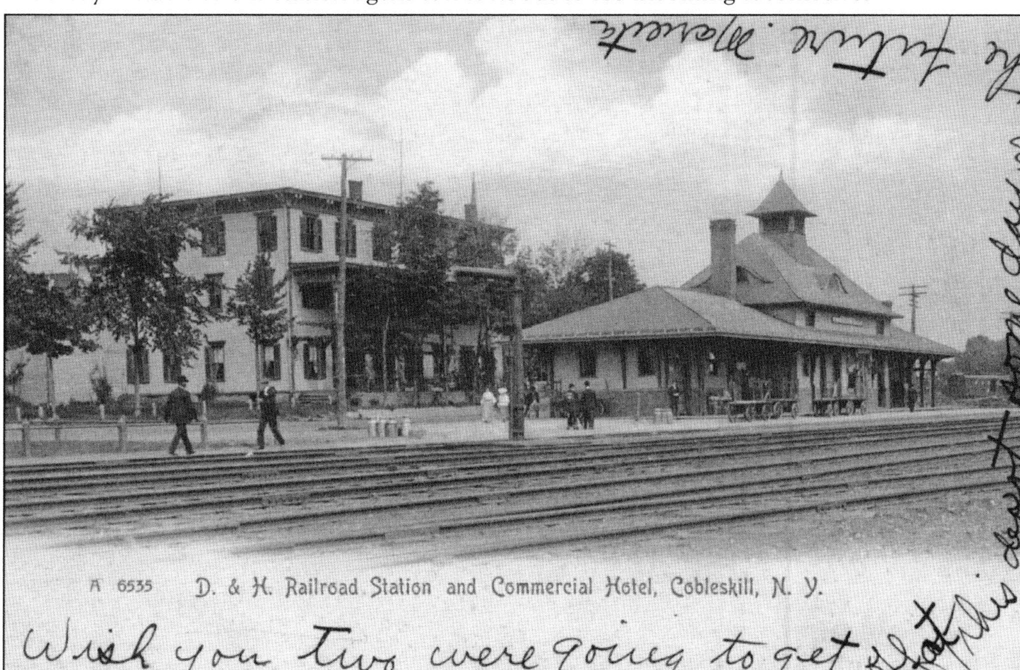

COMMERCIAL HOTEL AND STATION. Local farmer Monroe Shafer opposed the arrival of the railroad and "hoped he would die before he ever saw a train rolling across his farm." His wish came true, as he passed away the day before the first train arrived in the village of Cobleskill. The arrival of the train gave Cobleskill the distinction of becoming the most populous village in Schoharie County.

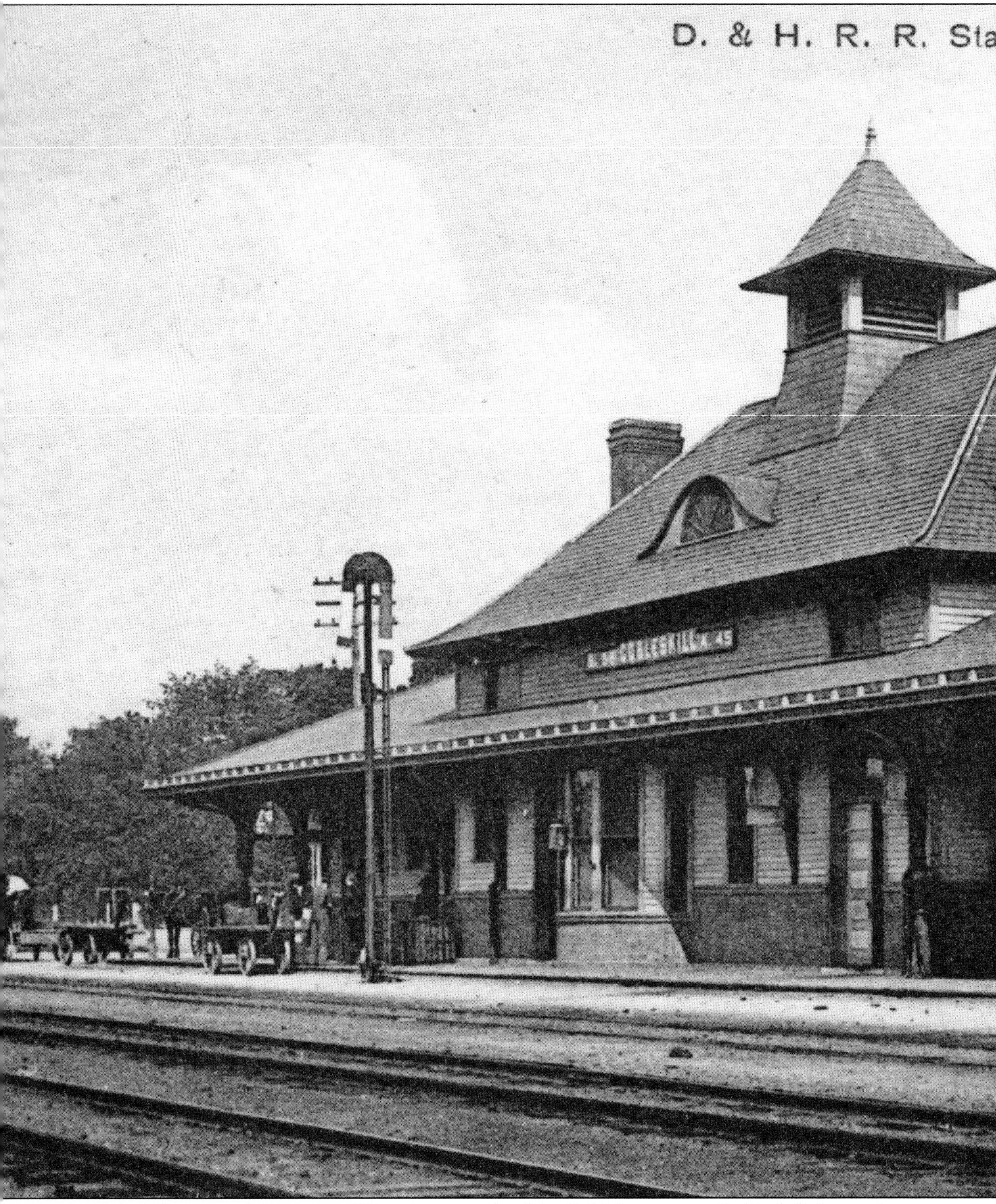

D&H Station, Cobleskill. This photograph of the D&H station in Cobleskill shows the many outstanding features of the building. "Eyebrow" attic windows provide an interesting addition to the many decorative features of the roofline. A wagon full of milk cans awaits pickup by the next train. In 1906, disembarking passengers could cross the street behind the station and enjoy a

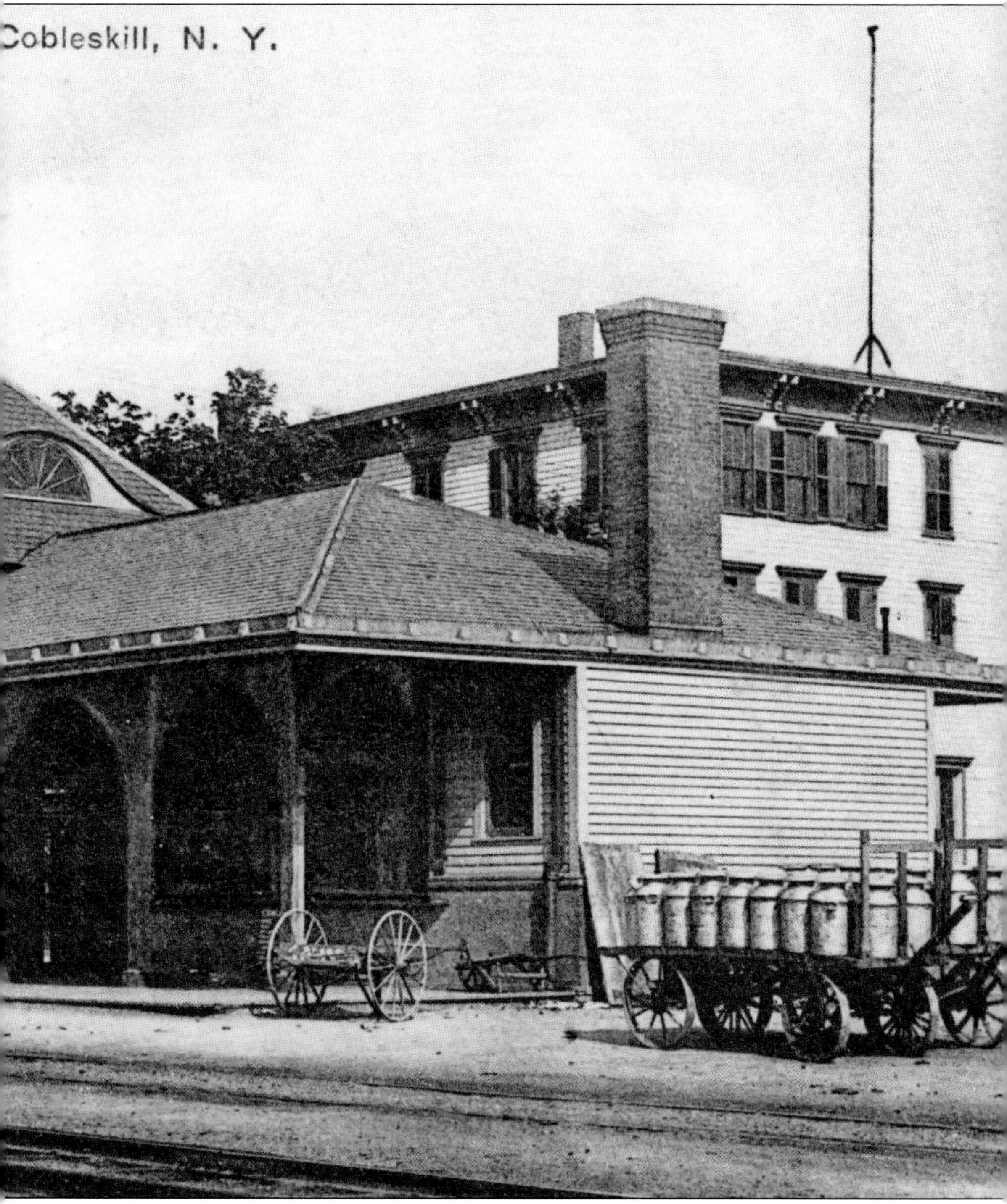

meal at the Commercial Hotel. Jacob H. Mann, senior editor of *The Cobleskill Index*, had a habit of waking early each morning and walking up the tracks to get breakfast at the hotel restaurant. On Wednesday, September 7, 1932, he was killed instantly when a train hit him. The Commercial Hotel is no longer there. The station is most recently a sports bar.

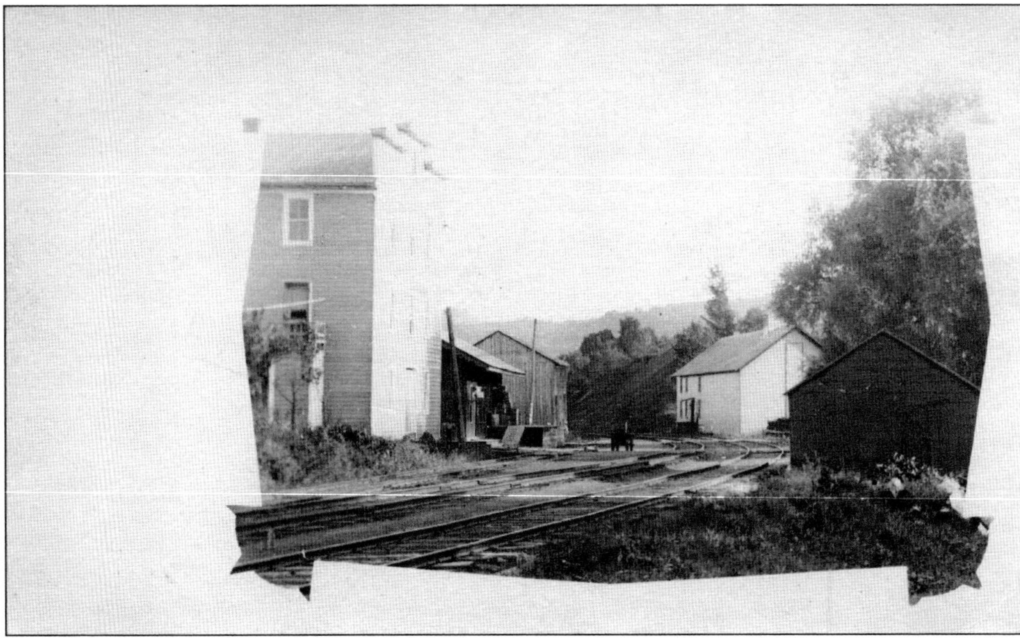

HYNDSVILLE STATION. D&H tracks are shown running through the little hamlet of Hyndsville just a few miles from Cobleskill. The little station is behind the building to the left, and the railroad freight cart sits in front of the station near the tracks. Trains brought in coal to Hyndsville on the Cherry Valley branch. The last passenger train was run in 1931. One year later, the station was torn down.

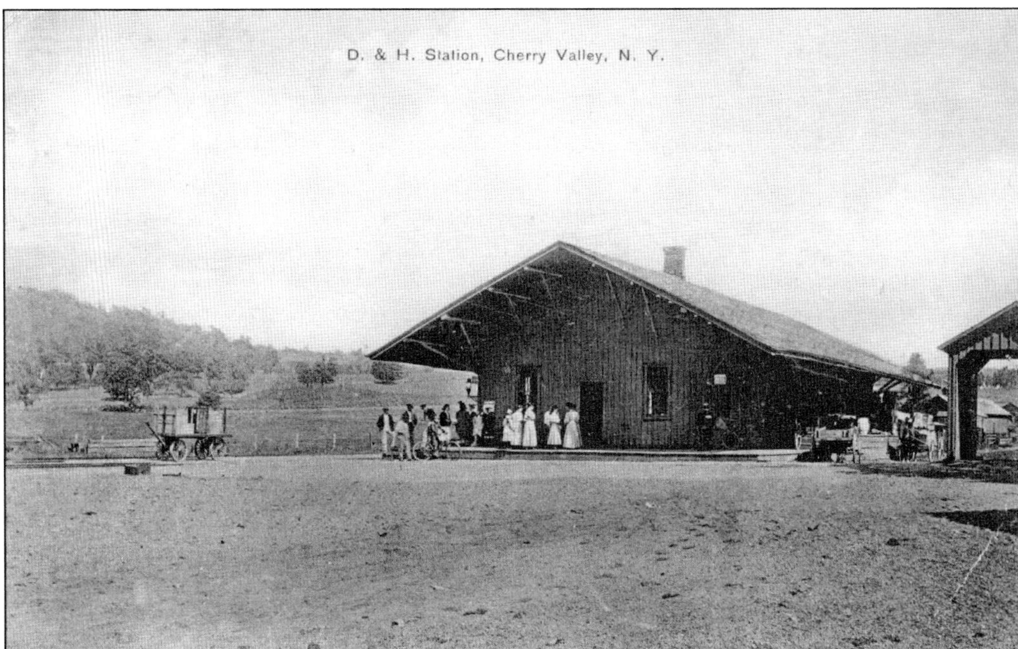

CHERRY VALLEY STATION. The D&H Cherry Valley station is shown here. The train provided the transportation of coal, milk, and people to and from Cherry Valley to Cobleskill. Today the building is home to the Cherry Valley Fire Department. Tracks no longer go past this building.

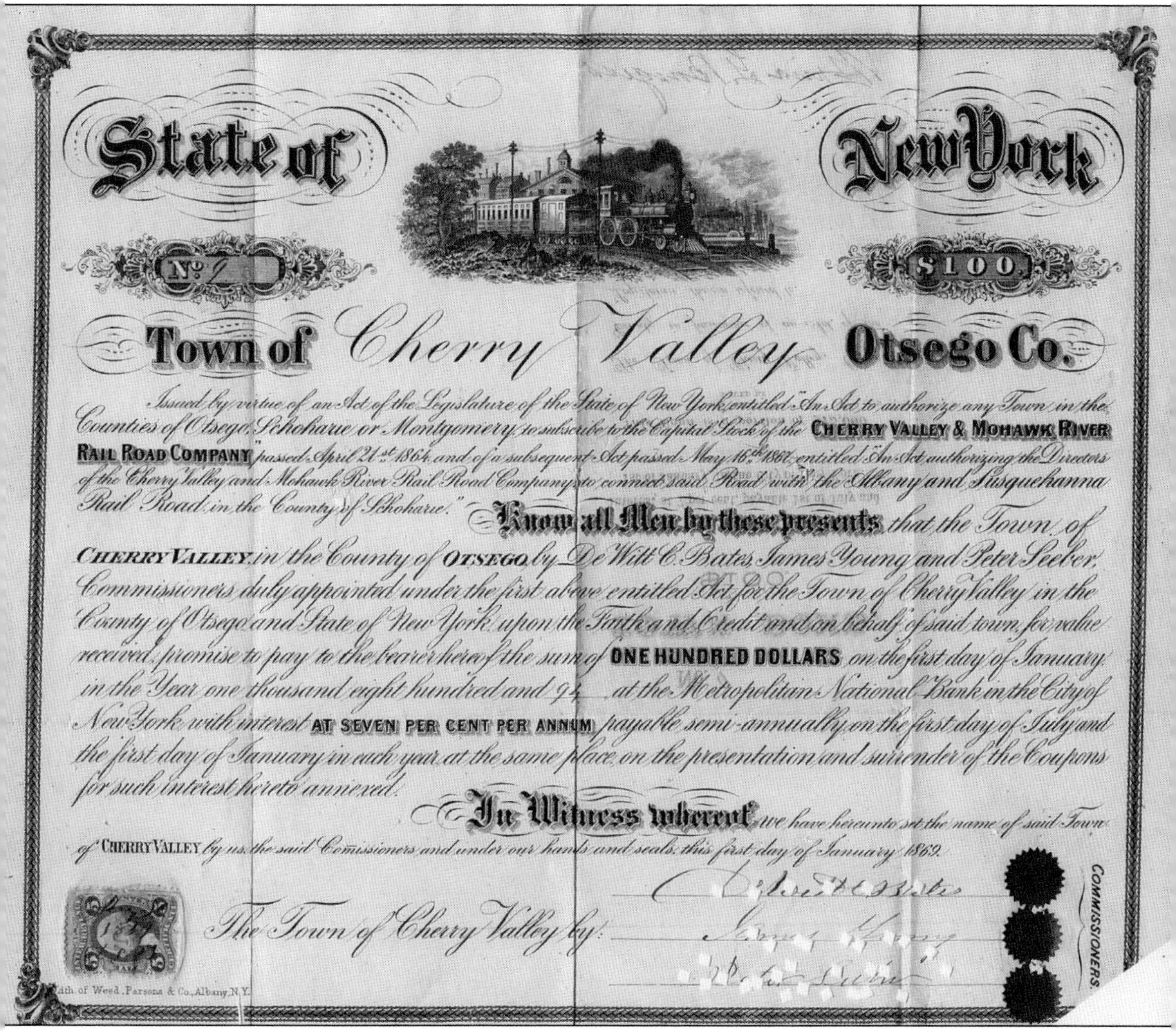

State of New York

No. $100

Town of Cherry Valley Otsego Co.

Issued by virtue of an Act of the Legislature of the State of New York entitled "An Act to authorize any Town in the Counties of Otsego, Schoharie or Montgomery to subscribe to the Capital Stock of the CHERRY VALLEY & MOHAWK RIVER RAIL ROAD COMPANY" passed April 21st 1864 and of a subsequent Act passed May 16th 1867, entitled "An Act authorizing the Directors of the Cherry Valley and Mohawk River Rail Road Company to connect said Road with the Albany and Susquehanna Rail Road in the County of Schoharie." Know all Men by these presents that the Town of CHERRY VALLEY in the County of OTSEGO by DeWitt C. Bates, James Young and Peter Seeber, Commissioners duly appointed under the first above entitled Act for the Town of Cherry Valley in the County of Otsego and State of New York upon the Faith and Credit and on behalf of said town, for value received, promise to pay to the bearer hereof the sum of ONE HUNDRED DOLLARS on the first day of January in the Year one thousand eight hundred and 94 at the Metropolitan National Bank in the City of New York with interest AT SEVEN PER CENT PER ANNUM payable semi-annually on the first day of July and the first day of January in each year at the same place, on the presentation and surrender of the Coupons for such interest hereto annexed.

In Witness whereof we have hereunto set the name of said Town of CHERRY VALLEY by us the said Comissioners and under our hands and seals, this first day of January 1869.

The Town of Cherry Valley by:

COMMISSIONERS

Lith. of Weed, Parsons & Co., Albany, N.Y.

STOCK CERTIFICATE. This certificate, issued in January 1869, provides an interest in the Cherry Valley and Mohawk River Rail Road Company to connect said road with the Albany and Susquehanna Railroad in Schoharie County. This $100 town bond, which paid seven percent interest, is a portion of the $75,000 issued by the Town of Cherry Valley on the first day of January 1869. (Courtesy of Willis Barshied Jr.)

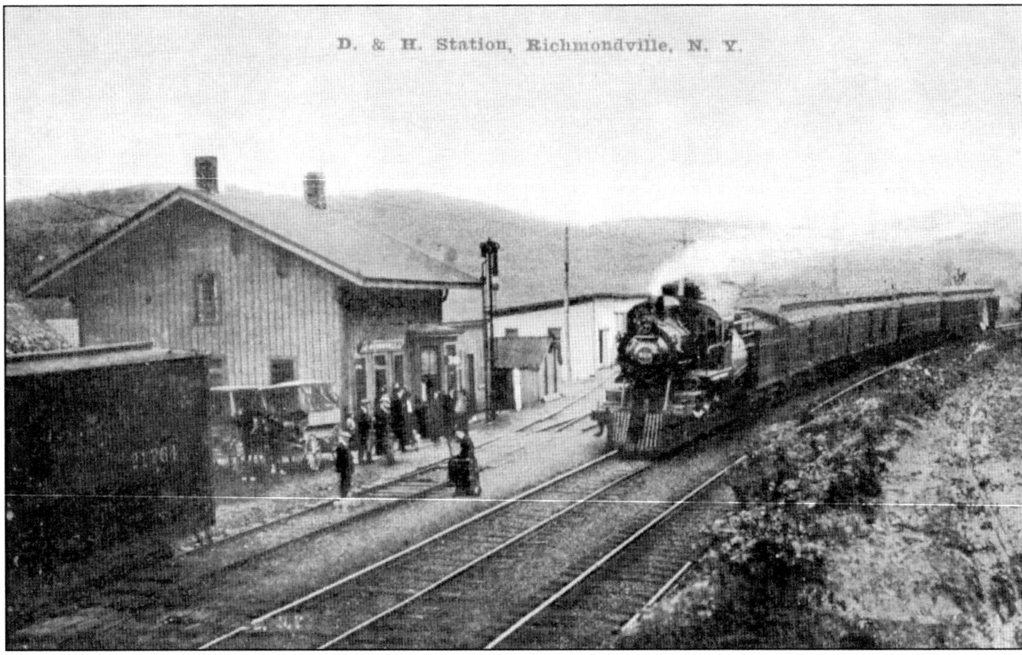

RICHMONDVILLE STATION. Three sets of tracks, one for unloading boxcars, pass in front of Richmondville's D&H station. Several hacks (horses) from a livery are on hand for the convenience of passengers. Board-and-batten (or vertical) siding, two chimneys, and a bay window are some of this station's features.

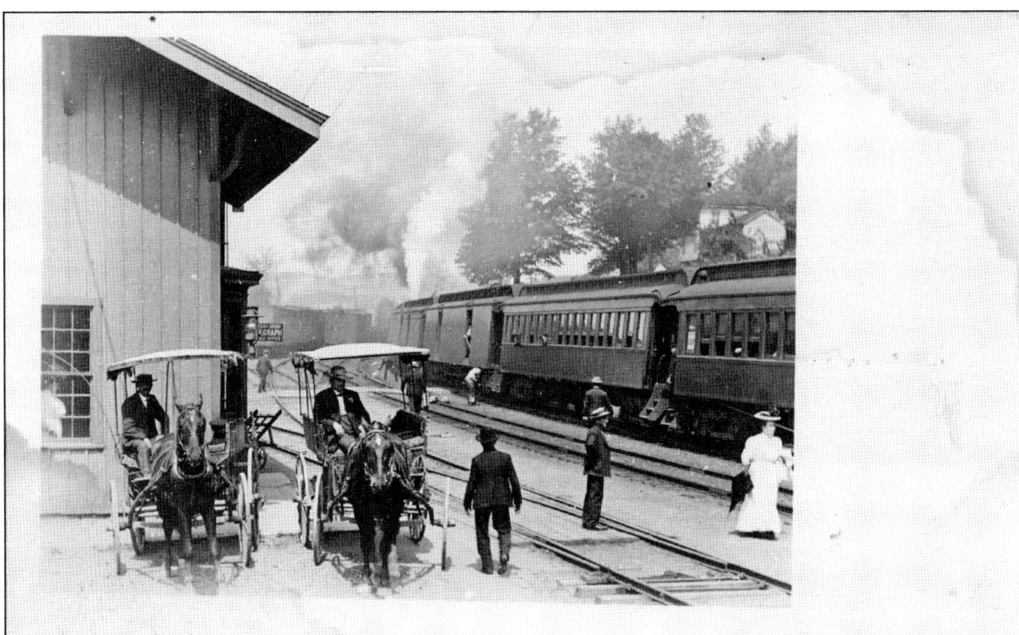

ANOTHER VIEW. A second view of the Richmondville D&H station shows a train stopped for passengers. Board-and-batten siding and nine-over-nine-pane windows date this structure to the 1870s. Railroad hacks stand by to give folks a lift.

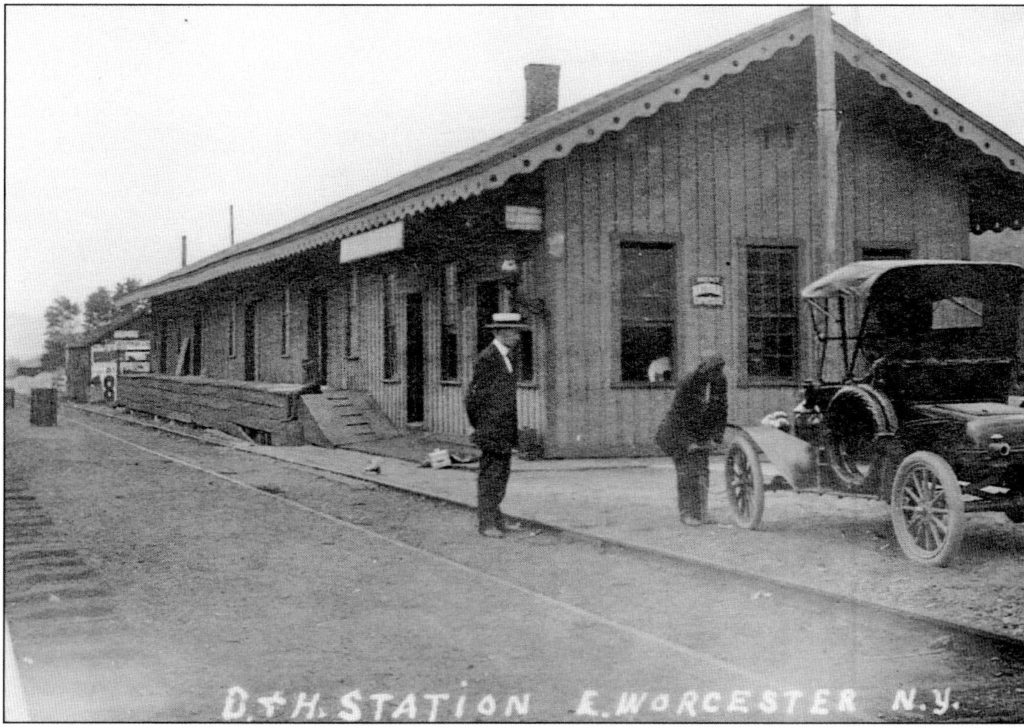

East Worcester Station. The former station, owned by C. Herzog Supply, Inc., burned in 1993. There were 50 hot-water heaters and a carload of General Electric appliances and boilers stored there. The owner said the fire originated from a group of young people using candles during a séance. The original station featured board-and-batten siding and a peaked roof with decorative "gingerbread" trim.

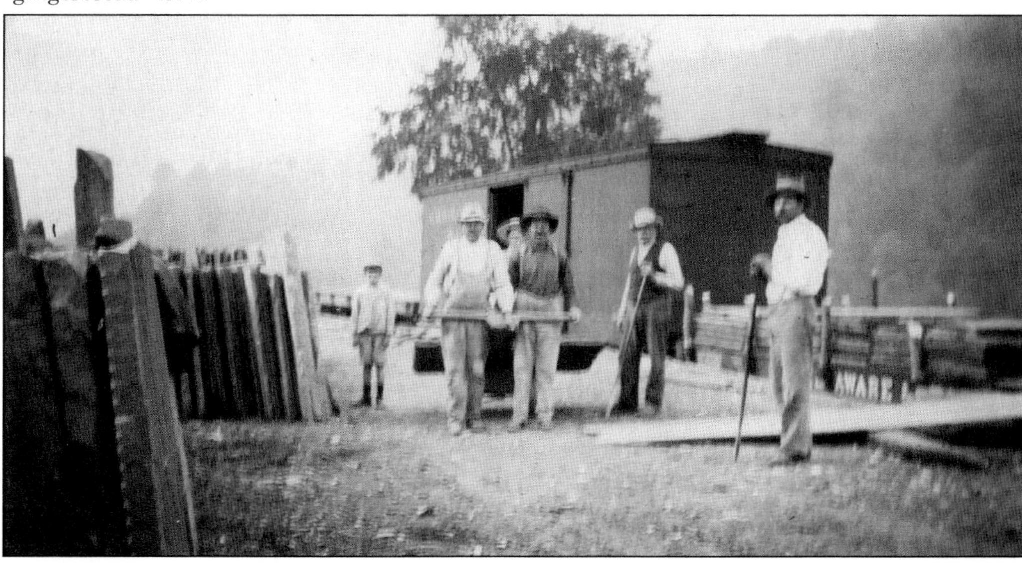

Dante Brothers. In 1889, the Dante brothers of East Worcester shipped 190 carloads of flagstone to city markets such as Schenectady. A stone quarry was located several miles from East Worcester near a duck farm. Workers shown here prepare to load large pieces of flagstone on a waiting D&H boxcar.

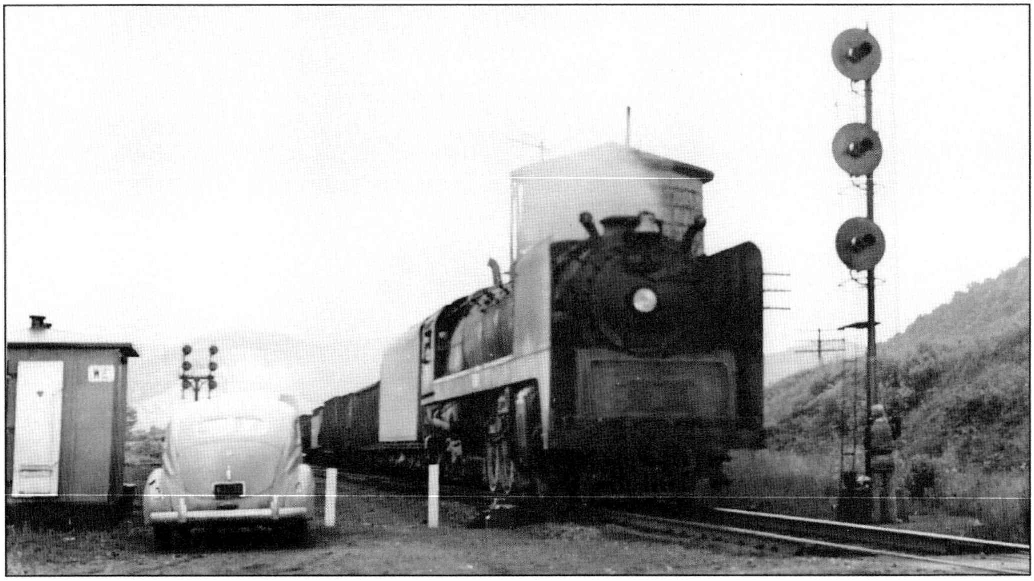

Locomotive No. 303. The No. 303 train is stopped on the tracks outside of East Worcester as a D&H employee works on the signal lights to the right. The picture was taken July 24, 1947. Howard Cooper of East Worcester was the station agent there for a number of years. The water tank behind the engine sits on a base of flagstone from a local stone quarry. When the water tank was dismantled, the flagstone was dumped in the creek behind a local farm.

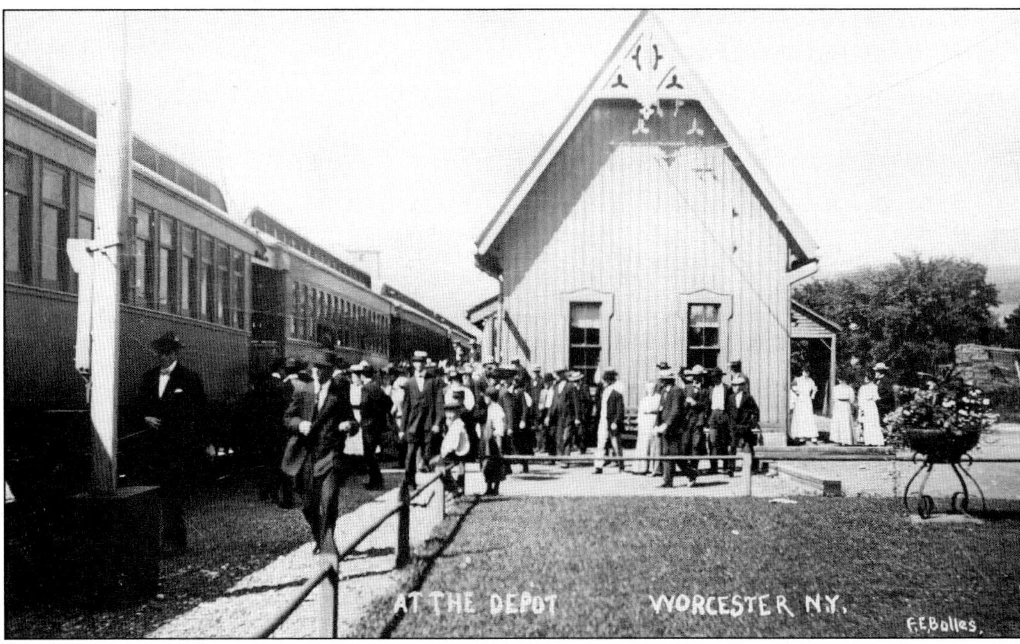

D&H Station, Worcester. This is the second station built in Worcester following the burning of the first one in 1879. The square hotel bus, which had benches along its sides and a rear step entrance, met all the trains. There was a gala day on July 17, 1865, for East Worcester and Worcester when the Albany and Susquehanna made a run on the line completed thus far. The little engine with a bulging smokestack was pulling several brightly painted yellow wooden cars. A new mode of transportation had arrived in the area.

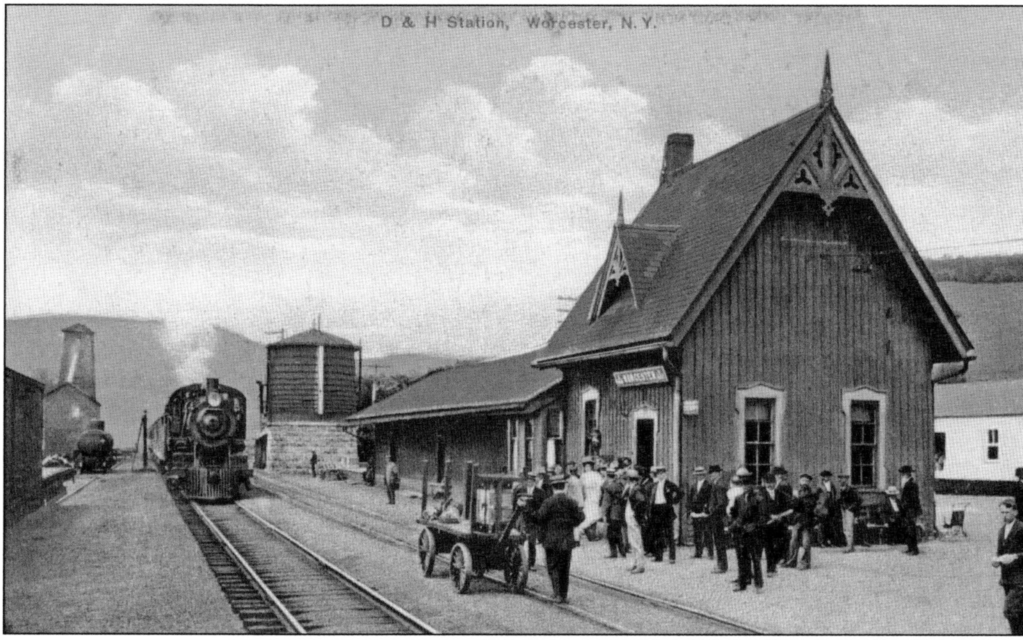

D&H WORCESTER. A busy station in Worcester shows the arrival of a passenger train. In the early days, as many as five passenger trains arrived from each direction daily. The station had board-and-batten siding, a slate roof, and other decorative elements. A storage area for railway express packages was located to the left. Canadian Pacific demolished the station in 1999.

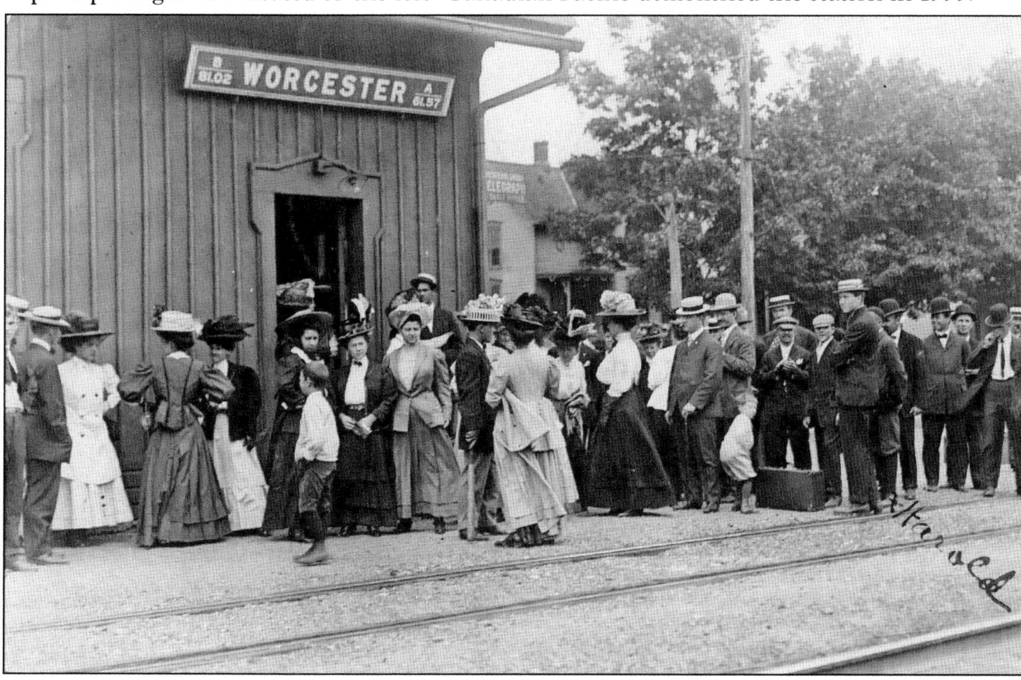

WAITING FOR THE TRAIN. Men, women, and children line up to wait for a D&H train at the Worcester station. The folks might be headed to Cobleskill to watch a baseball game with the home team participating. It is also possible that passengers are headed to "fair week" in either Oneonta or Cobleskill.

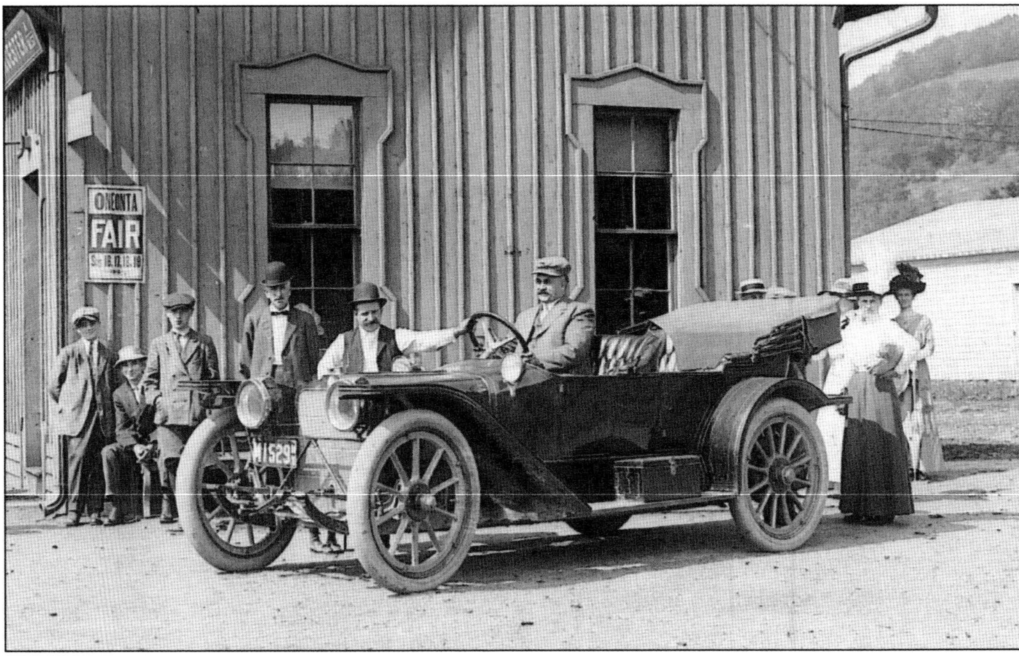

WORCESTER STATION (1912). Omer Sloat's Buick is parked at the Worcester station waiting for an incoming passenger train. Sloat was a proprietor of the Worcester Inn at one time and perhaps was waiting to pick up someone who planned to stay at the inn. The sign on the station advertises the Oneonta Fair.

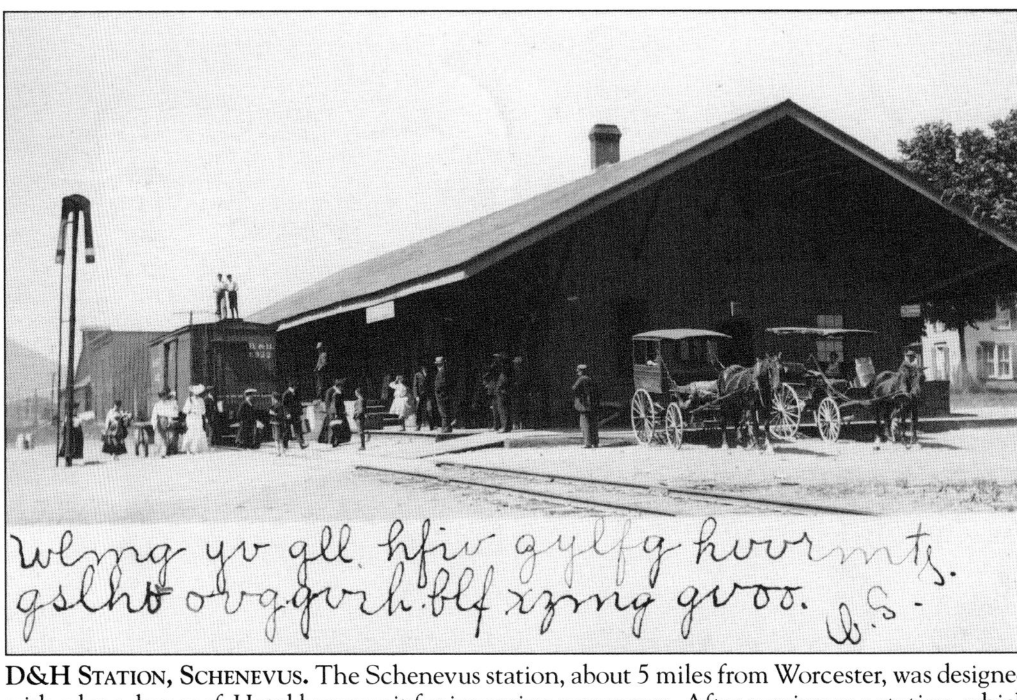

D&H STATION, SCHENEVUS. The Schenevus station, about 5 miles from Worcester, was designed with a long, low roof. Hotel buses wait for incoming passengers. After serving as a station, which was constructed in 1867, the building contained an Agway store for several years but is now vacant. The writing at the bottom must have been a secret code between the sender and receiver.

STATION HEIST. The Schenevus station became a busy place after the railroad arrived, with operators working 24 hours a day. A newspaper item from the *Worcester Times* dated January 28, 1909, stated, "Three masked men armed with revolvers held up the telegraph operator in the Schenevus Station on Saturday at 10:45 p.m. H. N. Bronk was reading a magazine when ordered to hold up his hands. The masked men took $17.75 and left. There were no clews [sic]."

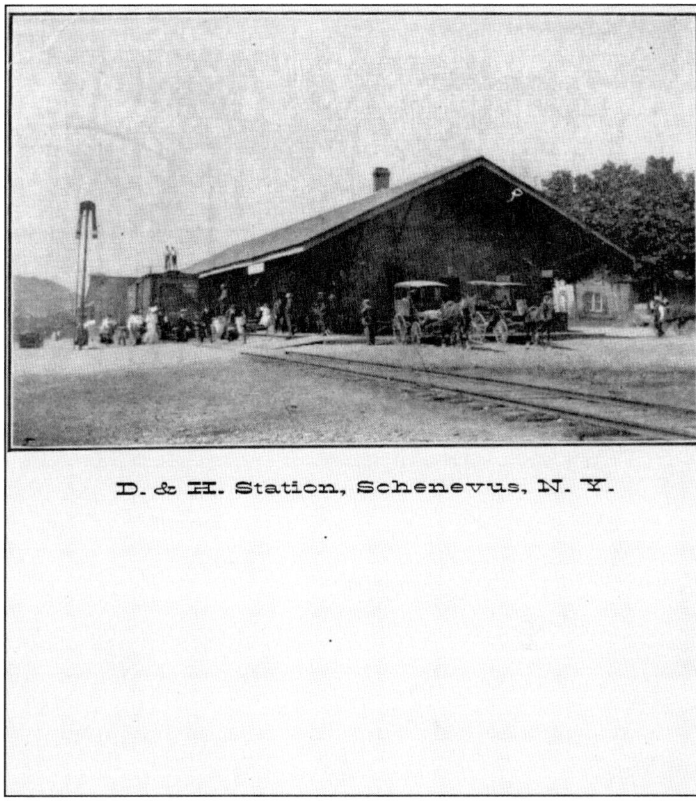

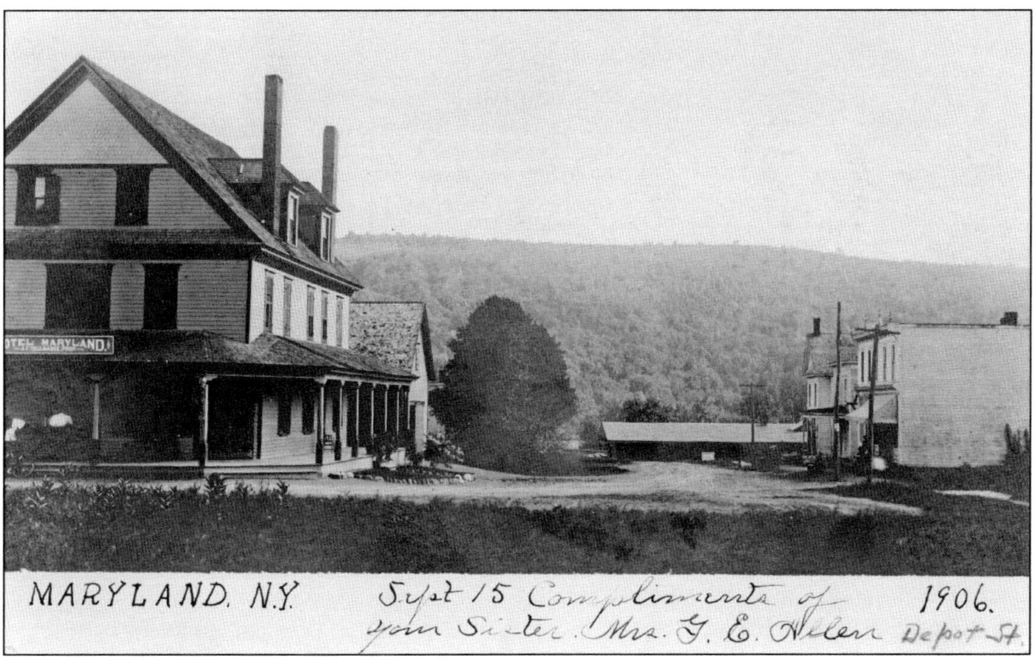

DEPOT STREET, MARYLAND. This is the view of the Maryland D&H station from Depot Street in 1906. Maryland was once called Sperryville before the railroad went through the little hamlet. This was an attractive little station highlighted with gingerbread-style decor.

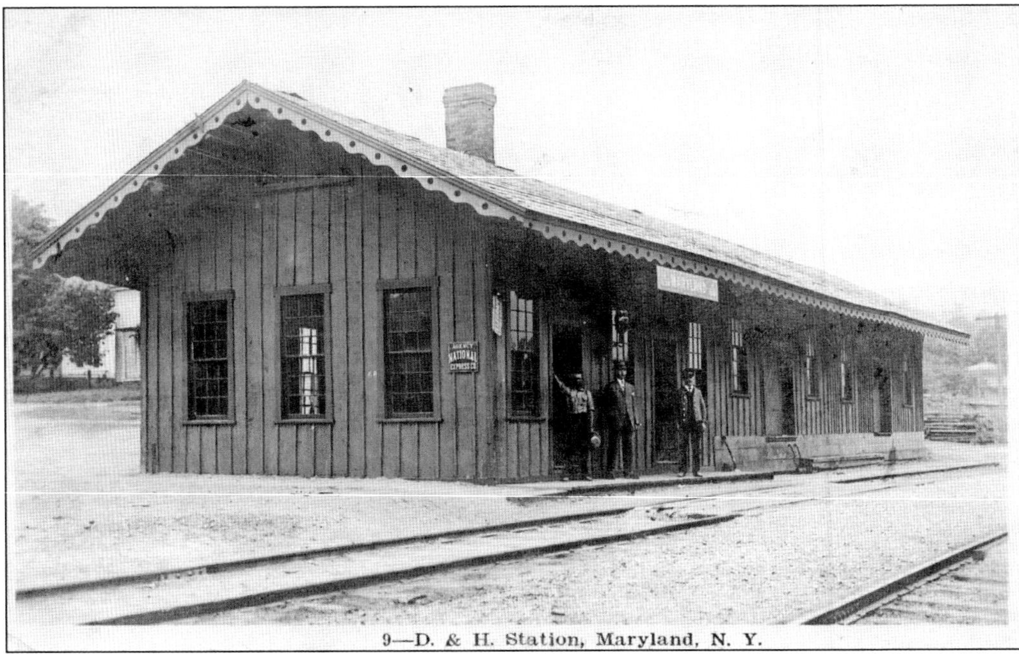

D&H Station, Maryland. All that is left of this once busy little station is its framework and roof. Reportedly used for target practice by a local gun club, the building sits among the weeds without leaving a trace of its former role with the D&H rail system. This station also had board-and-batten siding and gingerbread adornment around the roofline.

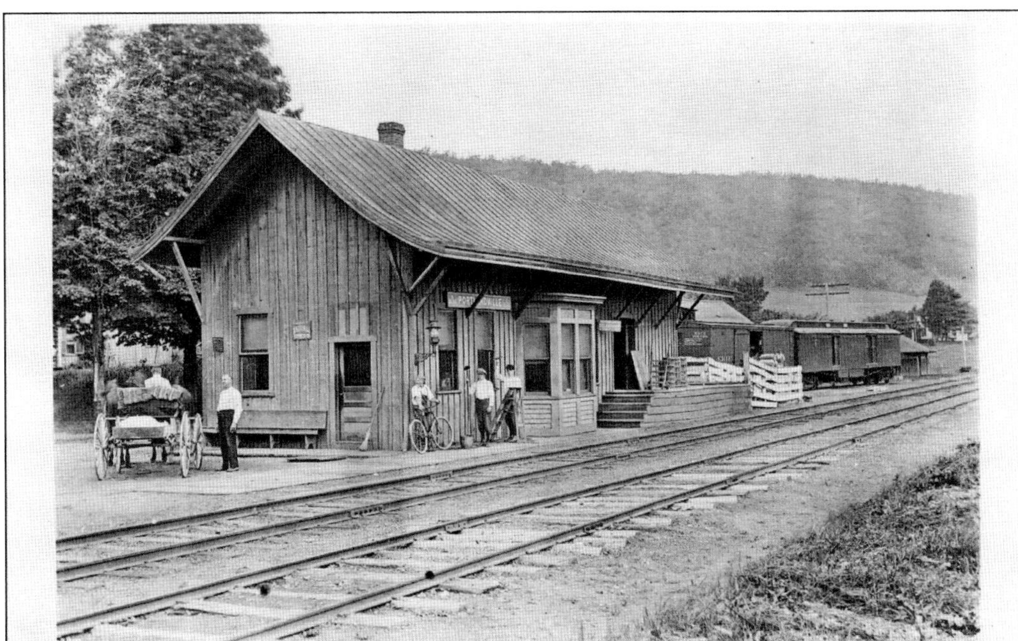

Portlandville Depot. The Portlandville depot, a small station situated along the route to Cooperstown, features traditional board-and-batten siding and a bay window for the stationmaster to spot incoming trains. Boys with a bicycle wait for the next passenger train to stop.

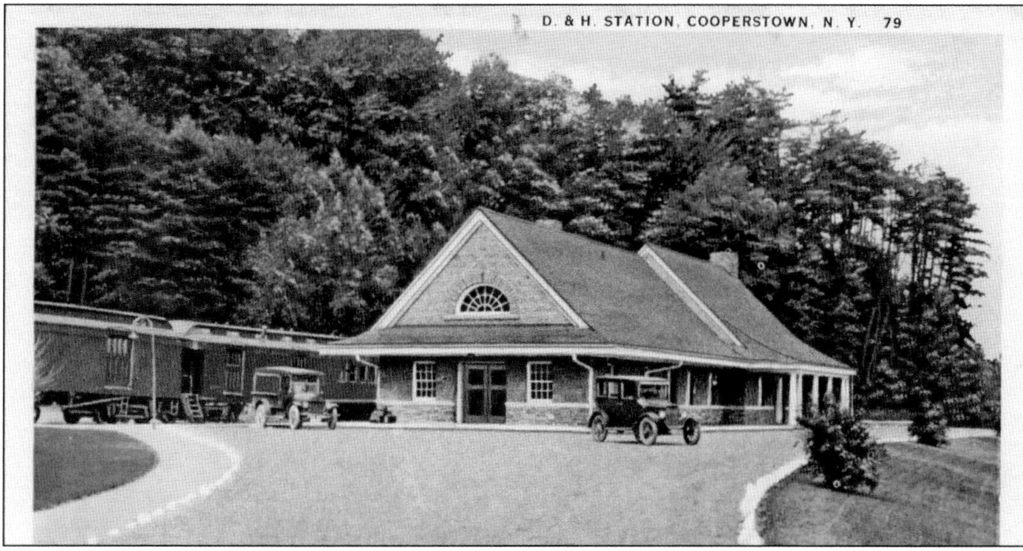

D&H STATION, COOPERSTOWN. On October 8, 1913, the taxpayers of the town of Otsego (Cooperstown), by a vote of 302 to 74, decided to authorize the sale of the Albany and Susquehanna Railroad stock owned by the town. The D&H agreed with the Cooperstown Board of Trade to bid $7,500 for the stock, which originally had a par value of $200,000. If accepted, the D&H Company said it would remove arbitrary freight rates and also erect a new freight and passenger station in character with other town buildings. This attractive stone station, built by the D&H in 1916, is now a private home.

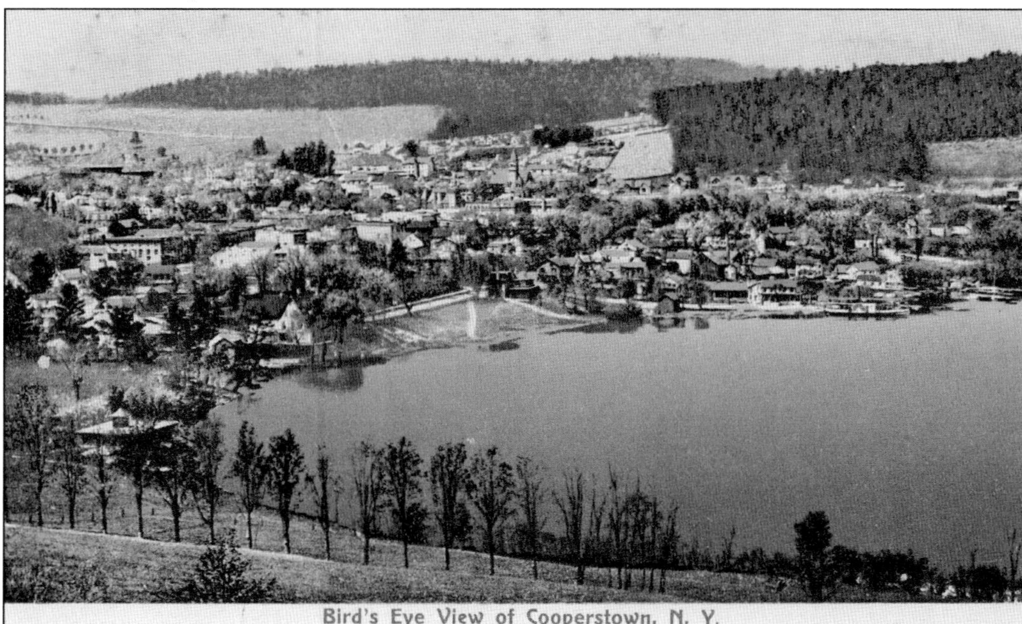

VACATION SPOT. Although Cooperstown cannot be reached by the D&H rails, it is still a wonderful vacation spot. Folks travel from all over the country to vacation here. The photograph shown is of the village at the turn of the 20th century. On July 14, 1869, the Cooperstown and Susquehanna Valley Railroad began operations. In 1903, the D&H purchased the line. In early days, folks could travel to Cooperstown by train; today everyone gets there by car.

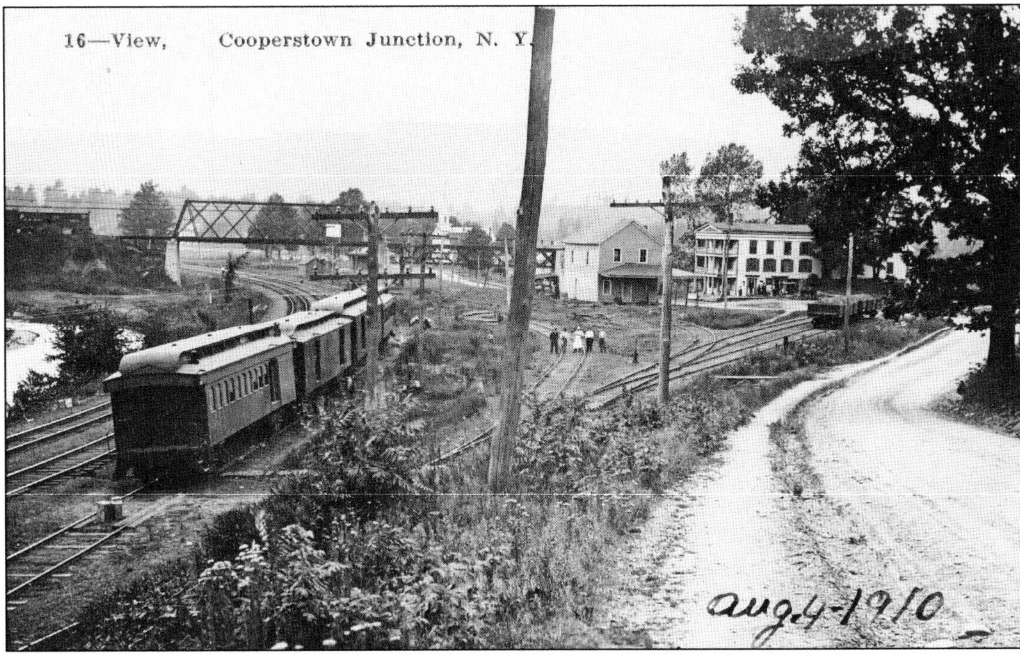

Cooperstown Junction. In 1903, the Delaware and Hudson purchased the Cooperstown and Charlotte Valley Railroad, which crossed the Delaware and Hudson tracks at Cooperstown Junction. The dirt road passing under the trestle is now Route 7. The three tracks led from the junction into the Oneonta rail yard. This August 4, 1910, photograph shows a bustling junction. One train is on the track heading south, while another is passing over the trestle in the distance.

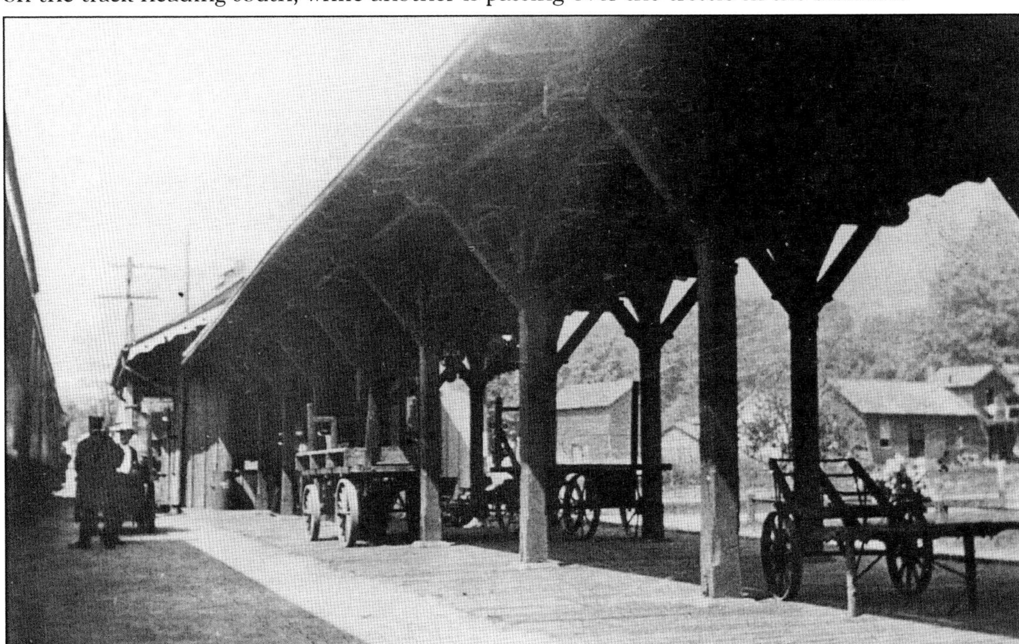

Colliersville Depot. This is a view of the Colliersville station. Local people knew the hamlet as Colliers, named after Isaac Collier in 1785. The Delaware and Hudson called the stop Colliersville on its station map.

Three

Oneonta and the Roundhouse

It was a great day for Oneonta when the Delaware and Hudson management made the decision to come to Oneonta on April 10, 1872, to build its machine shop and eventually the world-famous roundhouse. Two years earlier, on February 24, 1870, the A&S leased its railroad to the D&H Company. This brought the "good old days" to Oneonta via the railroad. Everyone prospered—the people, rail workers, the surrounding area, and the railroad itself. Freight trains hauling coal and other goods chugged up and down the valley, trailed by billowing clouds of smoke that steam locomotives are known for. In 1906, the world's largest roundhouse was built.

Hundreds of railroad positions were available for carpenters, tinsmiths, electricians, plumbers, machinists, upholsterers, and many others. New families arrived by the hundreds seeking security for their future.

Families from many ethnic backgrounds settled in Oneonta. Today a new generation of community leaders and successful businessmen are descendants of the railroad families that continue to touch the lives of this community.

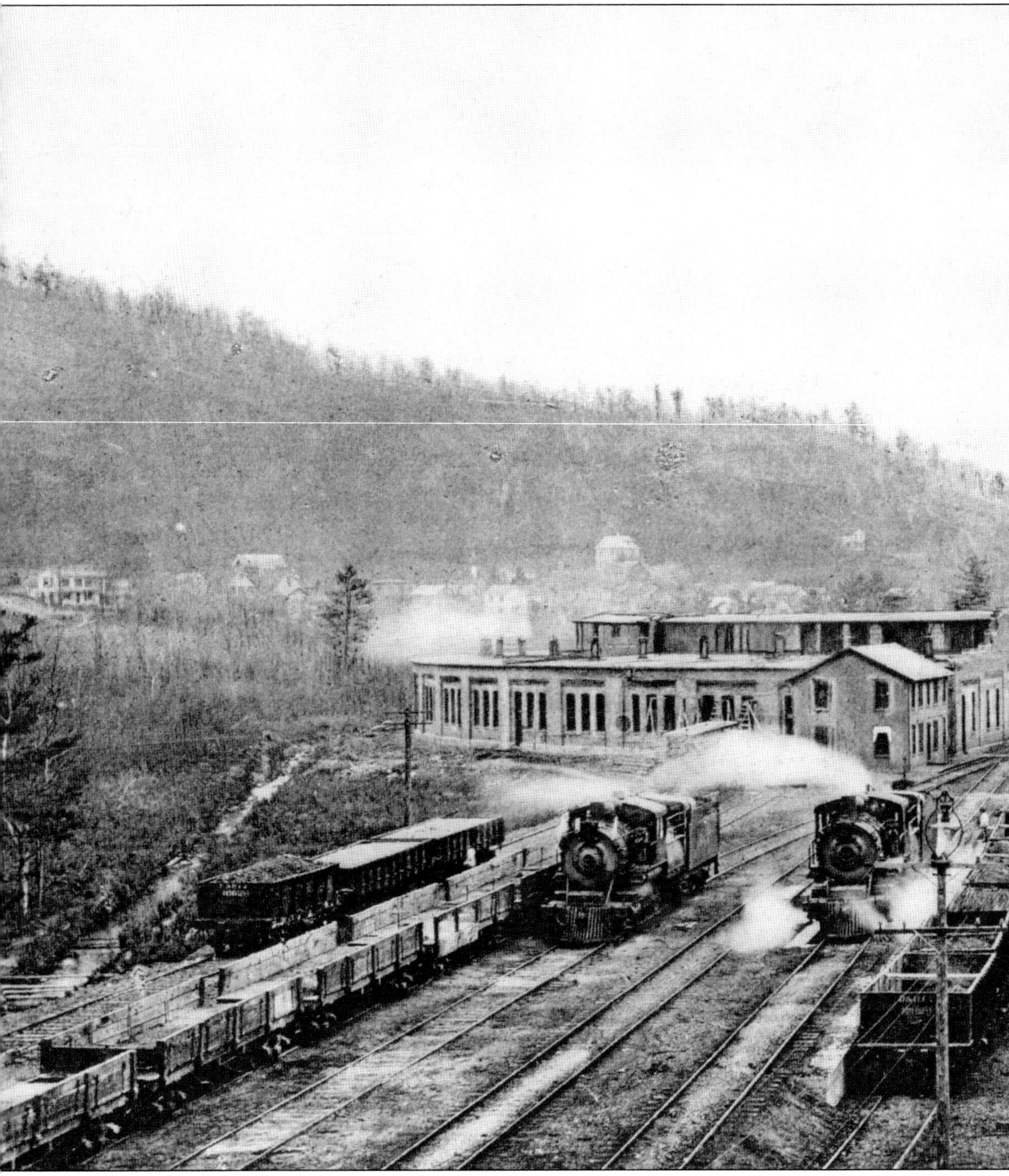

D&H Roundhouse. The new Oneonta roundhouse, featuring 52 stalls, was completed in 1906. The American Railway Master Mechanics Association provided the guidelines for this massive structure. For the next 25 years, Oneonta had the distinction of being home to the world's largest roundhouse. Engines chug in and out of the roundhouse as they stop for repairs and take on water from the two tanks to the right. An electric motor powered the 75-foot-long turntable, and the walls of the structure contained 1.5 million bricks. The final destruction of the roundhouse took

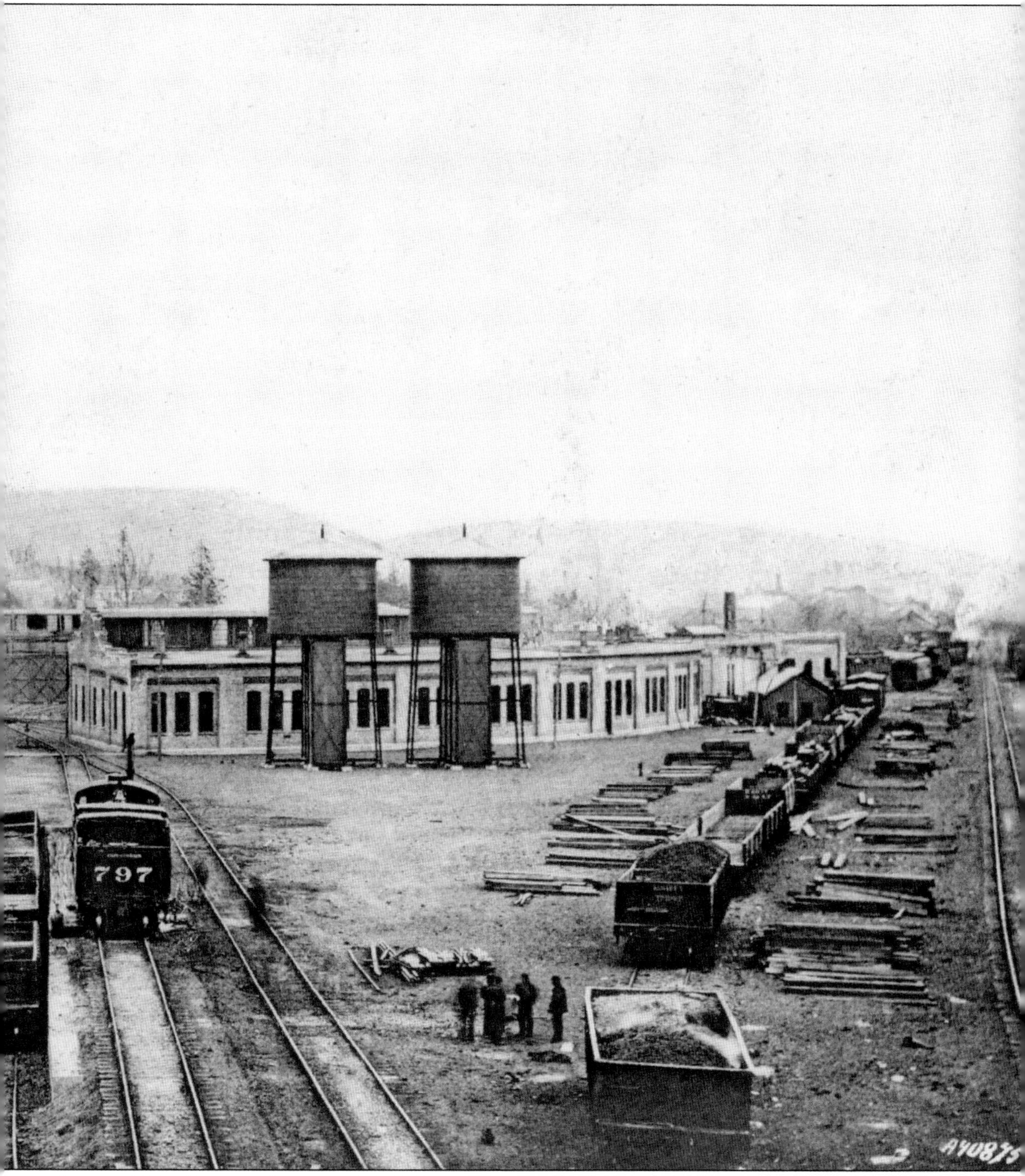

place in 1993. Oneonta historian Mark Simonson reported in his December 9, 2002, column in the *Daily Star* that as a result of being dismantled, 18,000 bricks from the roundhouse were offered by current owners of the property to Hanford Mills Museum in East Meredith to be used as part of a steam boiler restoration project at the museum. The logo on most of the bricks was NEBCo (from the New England Brick Company of Cambridge, Massachusetts).

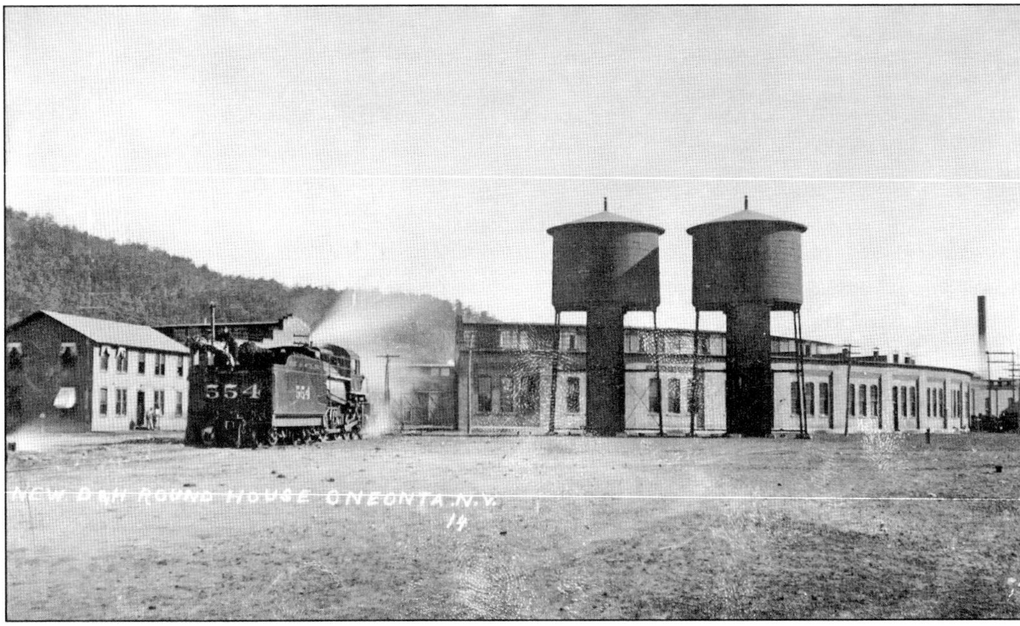

Locomotive No. 554. D&H engine No. 554 prepares to enter Oneonta's roundhouse to undergo certain steps in a procedure that includes filling the tender with coal, taking on sand, and then moving to the ash pit before being hosed down and getting filled with water from the storage tanks.

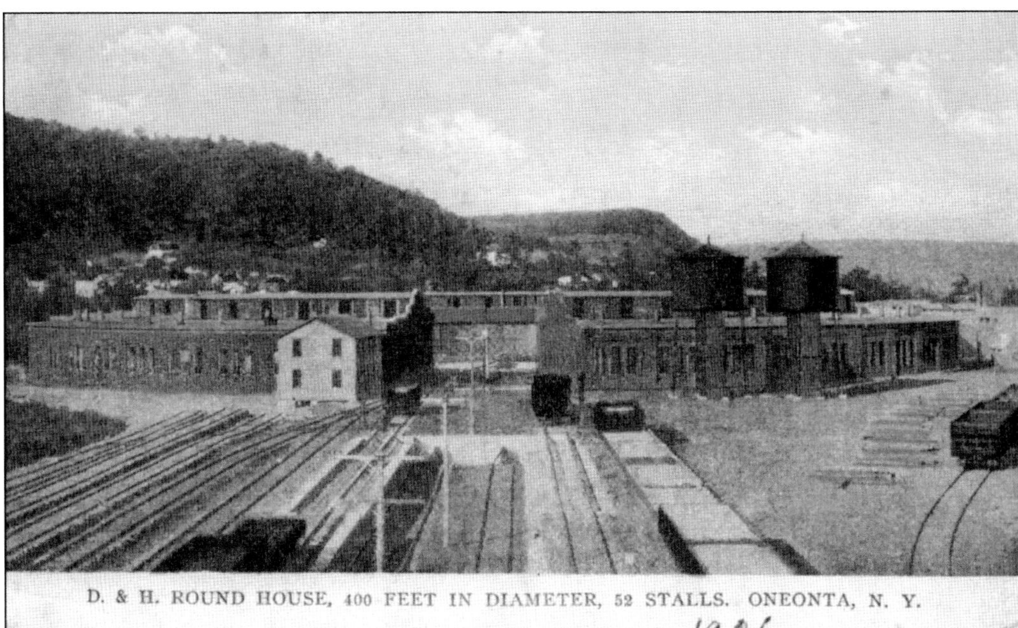

Main Center. The railroad yards in Oneonta provided the main center in the entire D&H system for repairs and distribution. The building of the roundhouse made it necessary to hire hundreds of extra workers, and this, in turn, proved beneficial to Oneonta's economy. A building boom took place as the population increased.

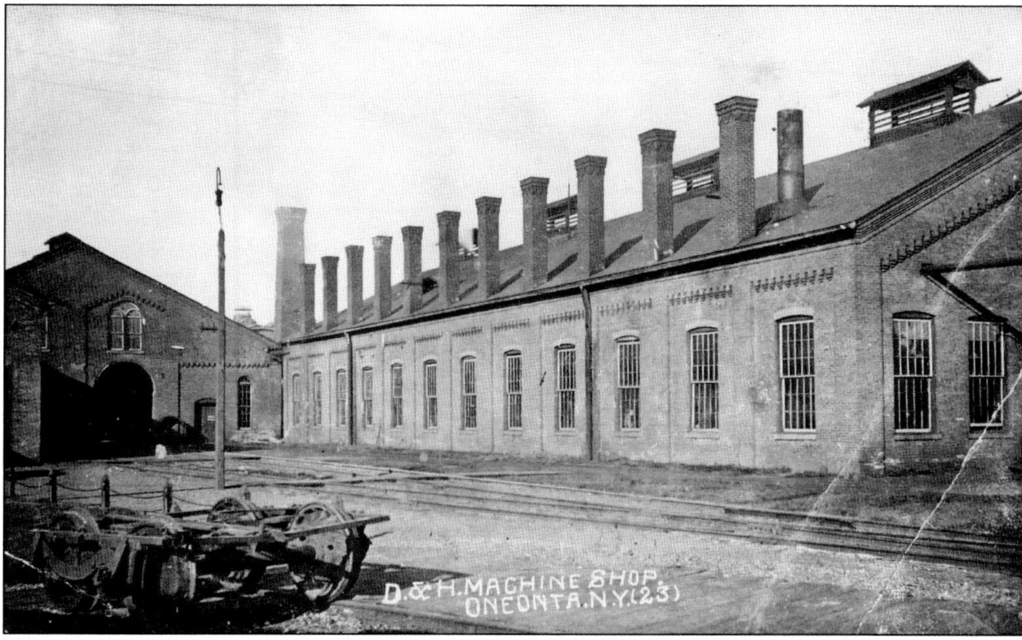

MACHINE SHOP. This 1908 postcard shows an early view of the machine shop at the roundhouse complex. Engine repairs were of the utmost importance and were taken care of after the engineer reported the problem to the necessary department. Note all the chimney stacks along the roof of the shop. In 1927, following the building of a new machine shop, this building was turned into a locker room for employees.

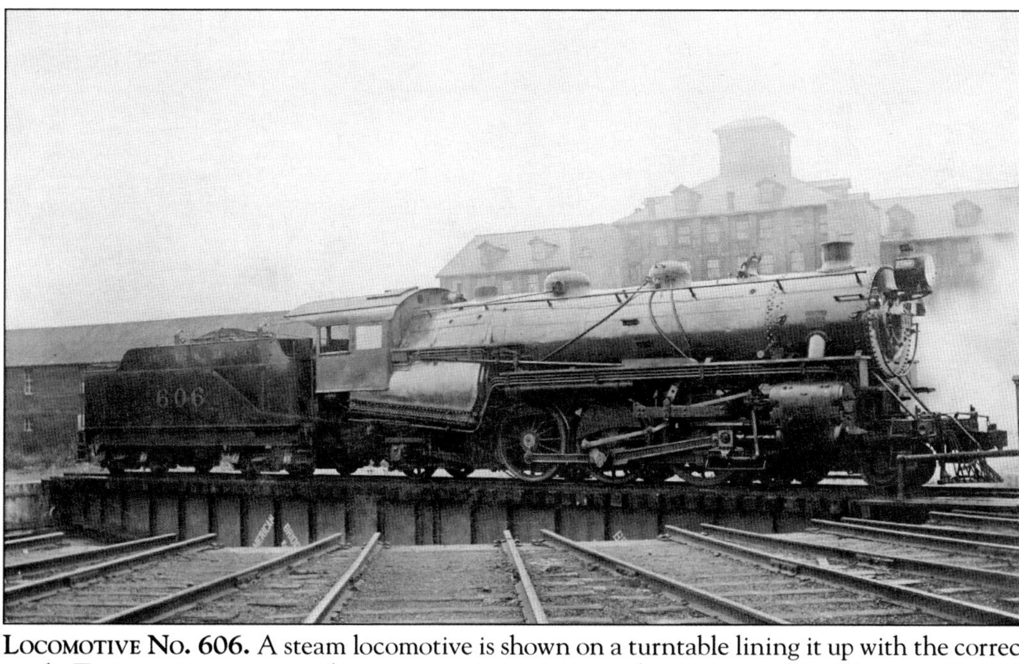

LOCOMOTIVE NO. 606. A steam locomotive is shown on a turntable lining it up with the correct track. Train maintenance and repair were imperative and very systematic. The roundhouse's turntable, which was powered by electricity, totaled 75 feet in length.

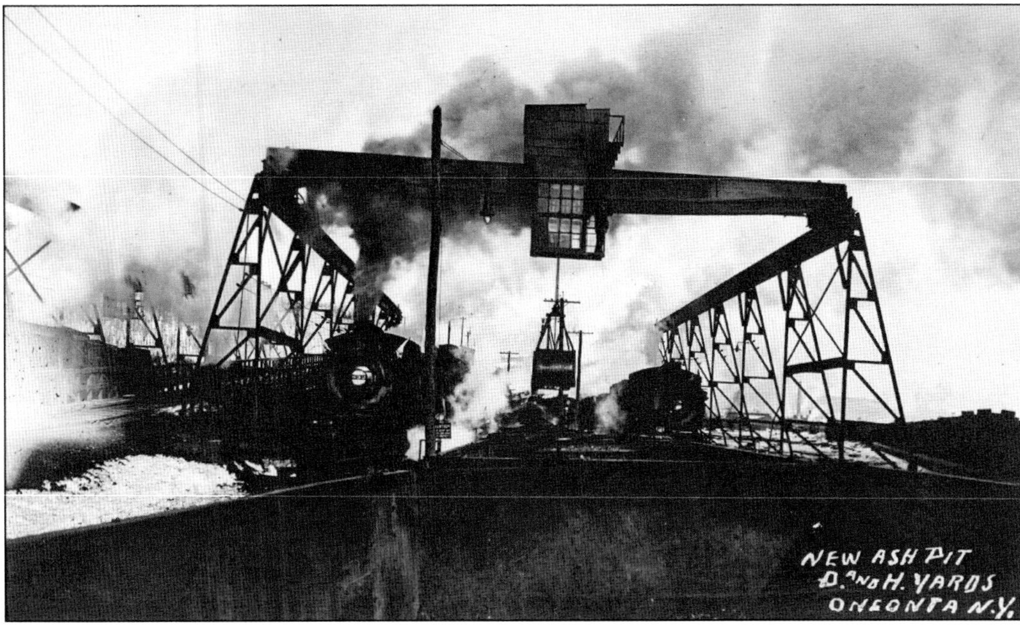

THE NEW ASH PIT. This dramatic photograph shows two locomotives using the ash pit, which was equipped with overhead cranes. Engines entering the area first received coal for the tender, followed by a supply of sand. Ashes would then be dumped into trenches and the fire raked back. The storage tank provided water for the locomotive, after which it would be hosed down. Gondolas wait to be filled with ashes, which will then be hauled away.

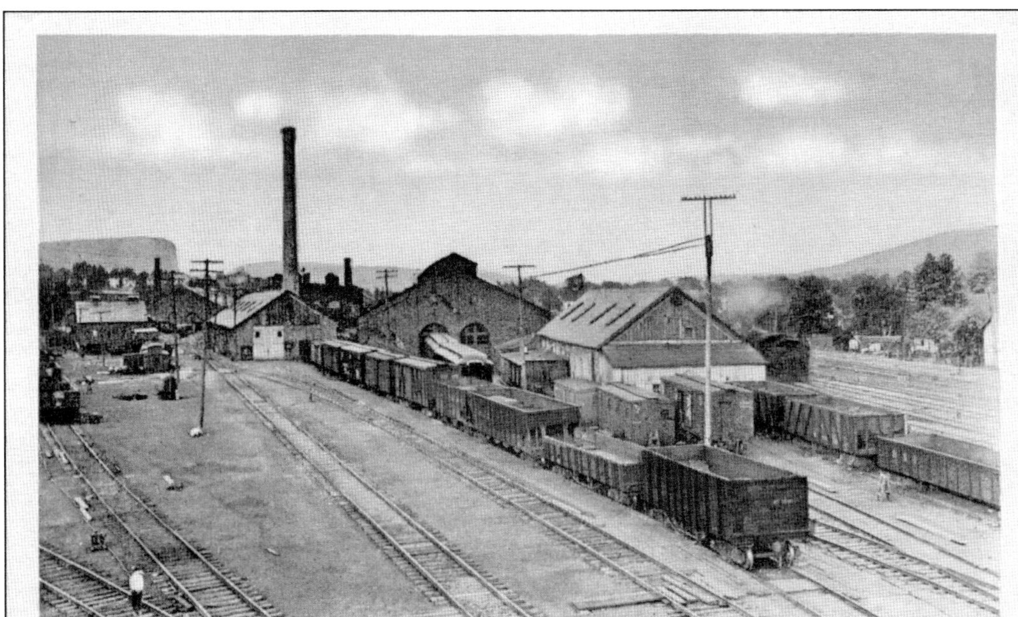

D&H SHOP. This is part of the massive roundhouse complex showing boxcars, coal cars, and gondolas. A severe drought hit the Oneonta area in the summer of 1908. Eventually the D&H was faced with the water shortage problem, which it fixed by using driven wells.

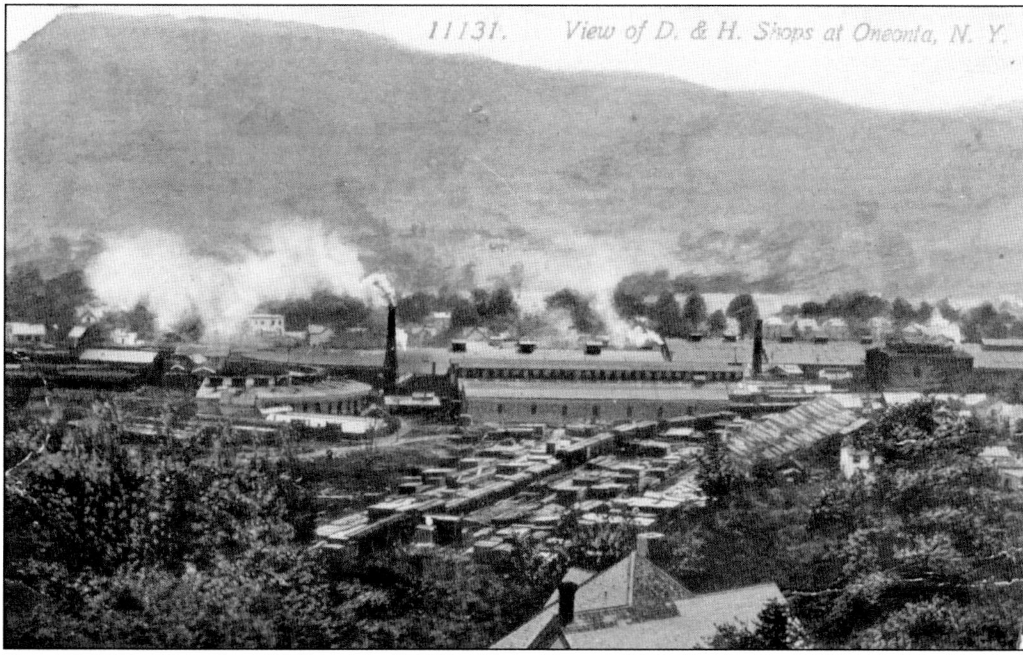

View of D&H Shops. Smokestacks, buildings in the roundhouse complex, rooftops, and railroad car storage all point to Oneonta's distinction as "Rail City."

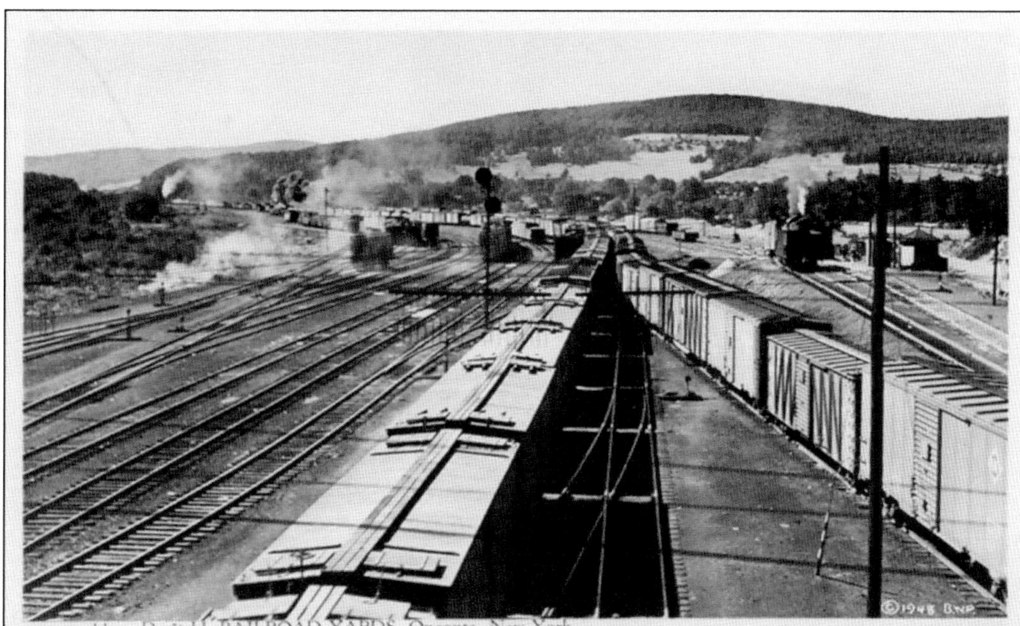

D&H Yards. During the glory days of the D&H in Oneonta, traffic on the rails reached gigantic proportions. At one time, 100 train crews of five men each manned the locomotives in and out of the area.

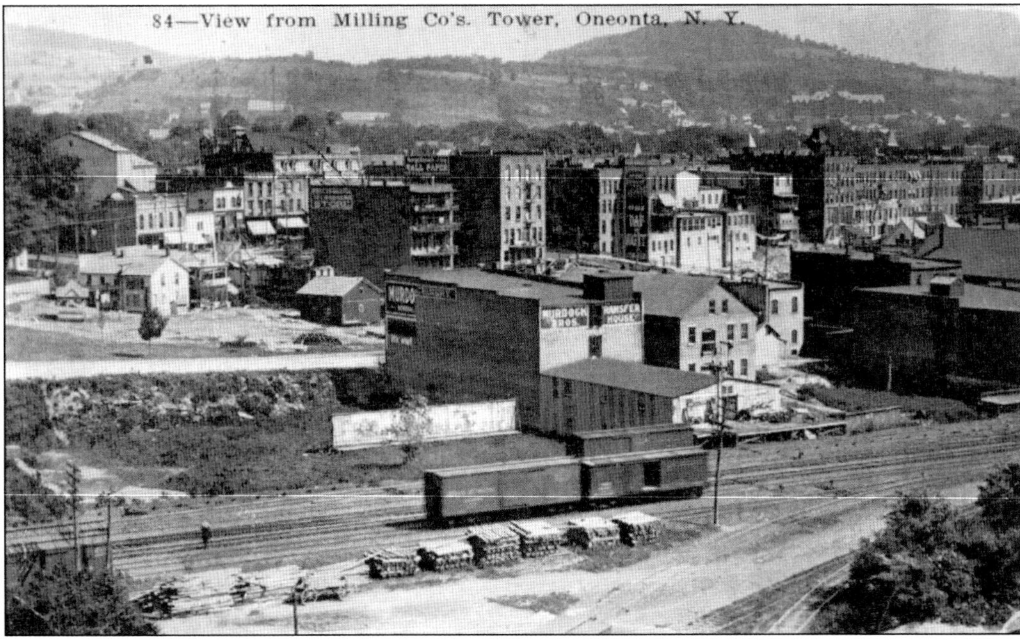

MILLING TOWER VIEW. The roundhouse and rail yards of the D&H, which offered employment to many in the area, contributed to the growth of Oneonta as a city. This view from the Milling Company's tower overlooks a portion of tracks as well as the growing business section of the city.

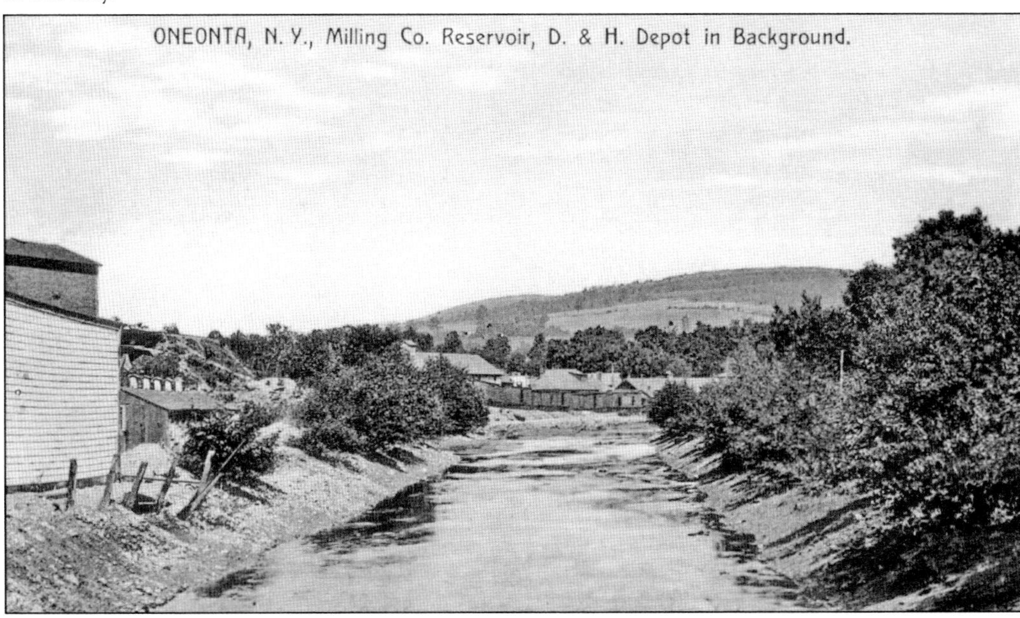

SABOTAGE PLOT. In 1918, a sabotage plot in Oneonta was uncovered when three German spies were caught and sent to jail. A Milling Company employee found a loaded shotgun shell in the grinding machine after a German immigrant went home early. A Delaware and Hudson employee gained information on troop movement and war supply shipments; he was later discovered to be a lieutenant in the Kaiser's Army. A third man, a paymaster who was found to be a German major, also worked locally.

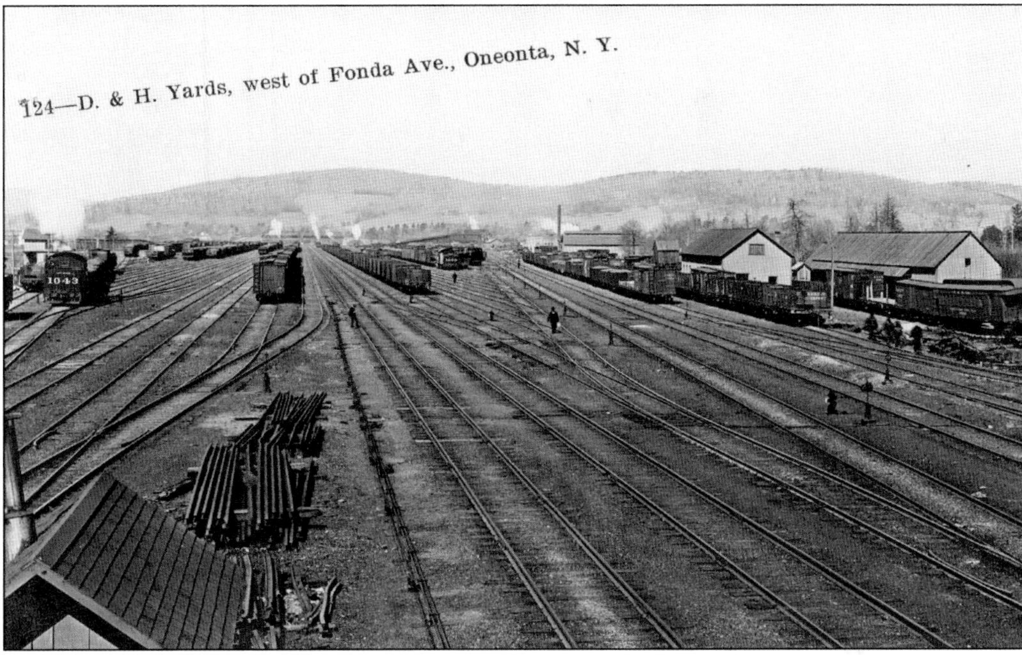

WEST OF FONDA AVENUE. An expanse of tracks as far as the eye can see makes up a portion of the D&H yards west of Fonda Avenue in Oneonta. A supply of new rails is piled up to the left. Switches, signal lights, and boxcars give the viewer an idea of how busy the yard could be on a daily basis.

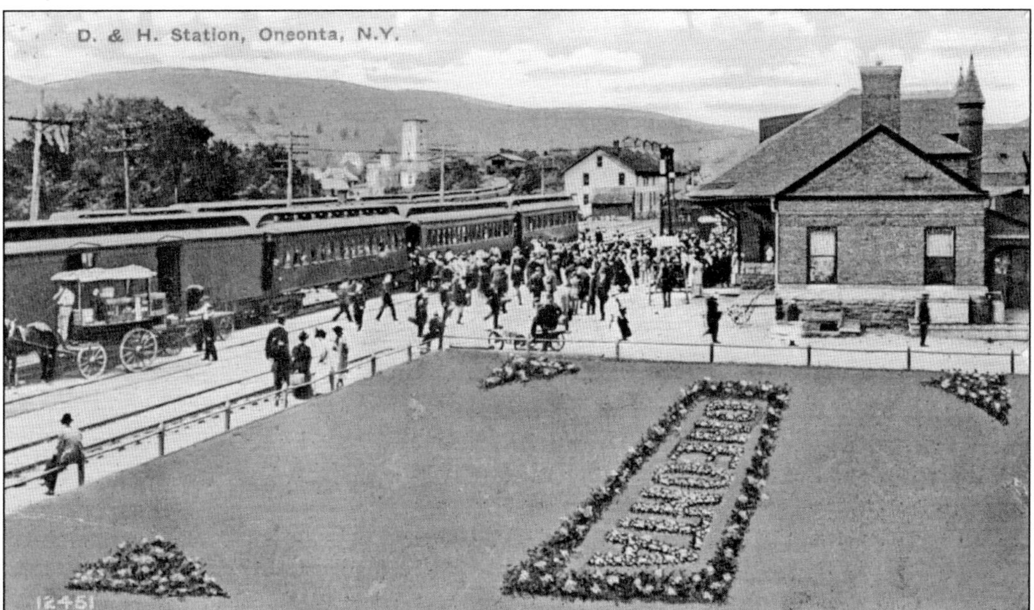

ONEONTA'S D&H STATION. The D&H station in Oneonta was built in 1892 at the foot of Broad Street, giving prospective rail customers a direct route while catching a train. During the heyday of the D&H, female visitors coming to Oneonta were given a bouquet of flowers. The word "Oneonta" was spelled out in large letters in a flower bed near the station. Passenger service ended January 24, 1963, and the station is now an upscale restaurant.

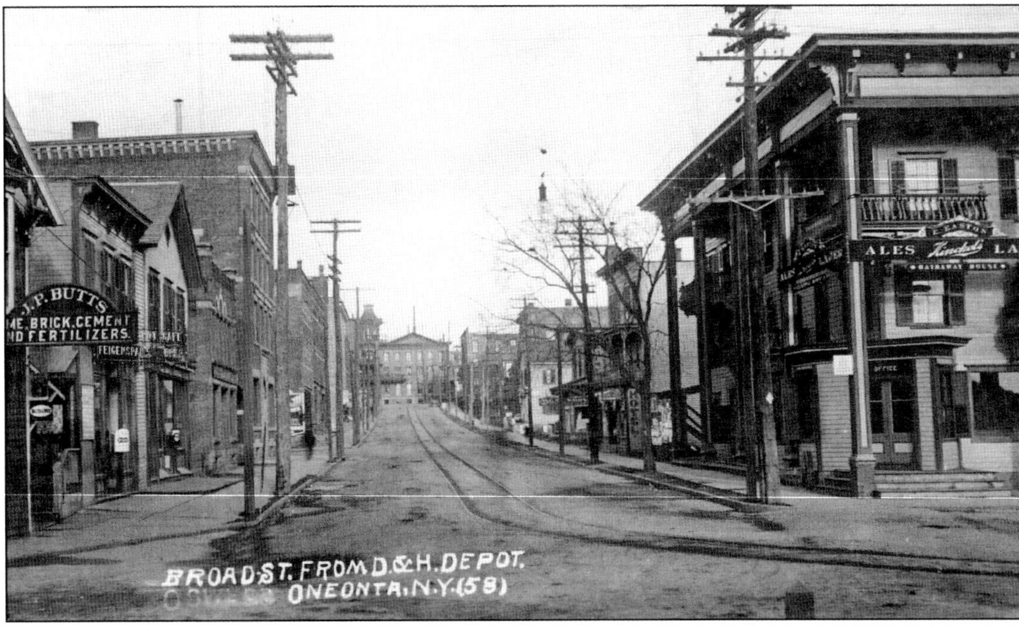

BROAD STREET. Oneonta's Broad Street, once an important thoroughfare to the D&H station and the buildings around it, has been completely demolished to make way for a modern hotel and other upgrades. Among the businesses no longer there are Bern Furniture; L. P. Butts, which moved to new quarters on Market Street; the Hathaway House; and a cigar factory.

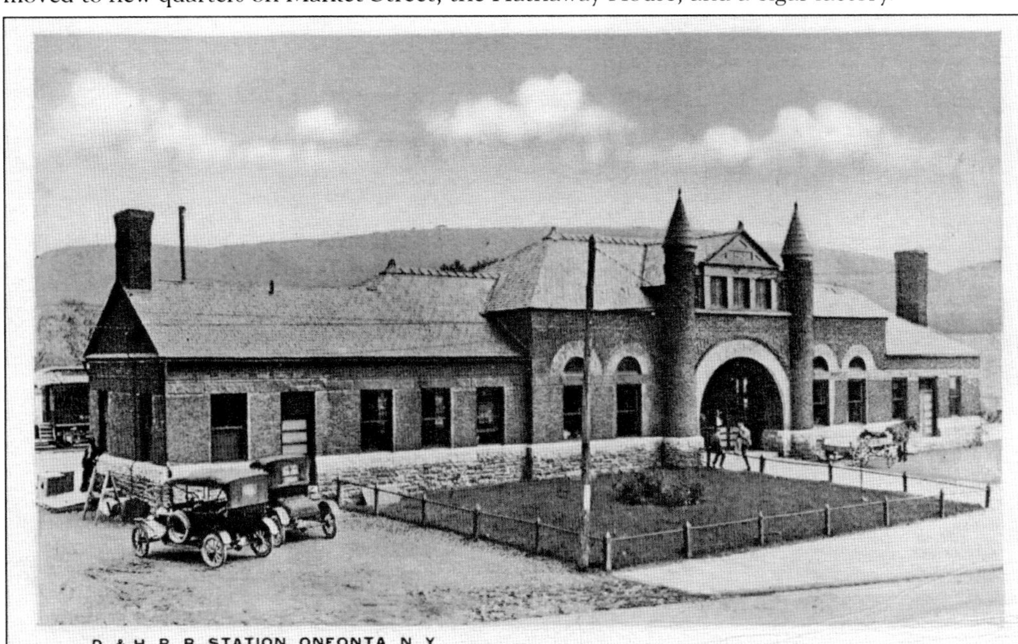

STATION FRONT VIEW. Oneonta's beautiful station still stands as a tribute to the D&H Railway's glory days. Each day, five to six passenger trains—both incoming and outgoing—traveled the 142 miles from Albany to Binghamton. The Albany and Susquehanna train first arrived in Oneonta on August 29,1865. The locomotive *E. R. Ford* arrived, pulling four coaches, three baggage cars, and two platform cars. There was much celebrating until the train left at 4:00 p.m. for Albany.

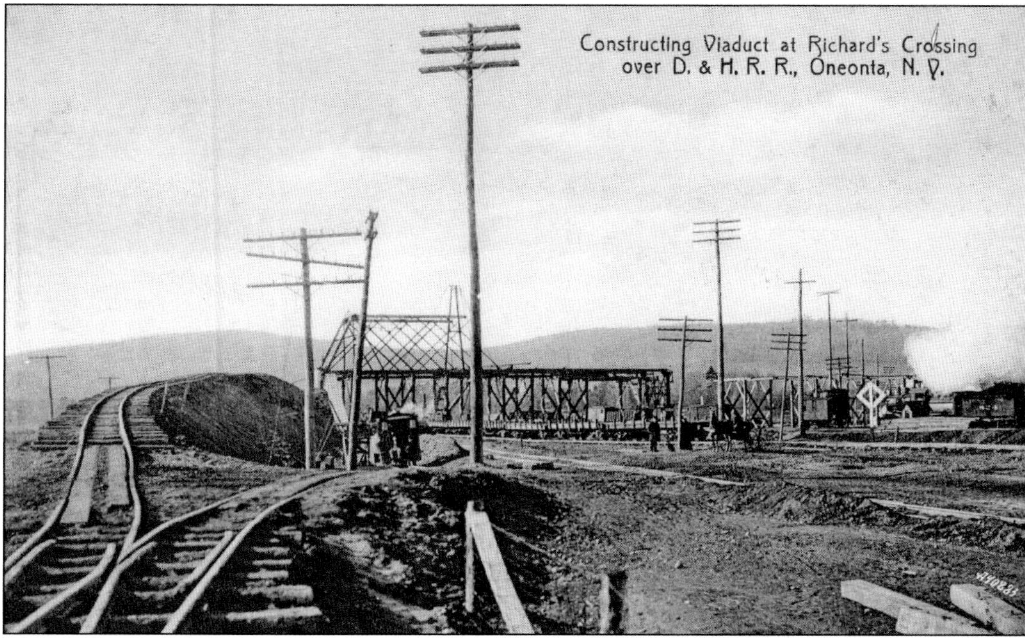

RICHARD'S CROSSING CONSTRUCTION. A viaduct was constructed at Richard's Crossing over the D&H tracks to ensure that travelers would not have to wait at least two hours to cross over the rails. Heavy train traffic, along with protests by village trustees, convinced D&H management in Albany that a viaduct was needed.

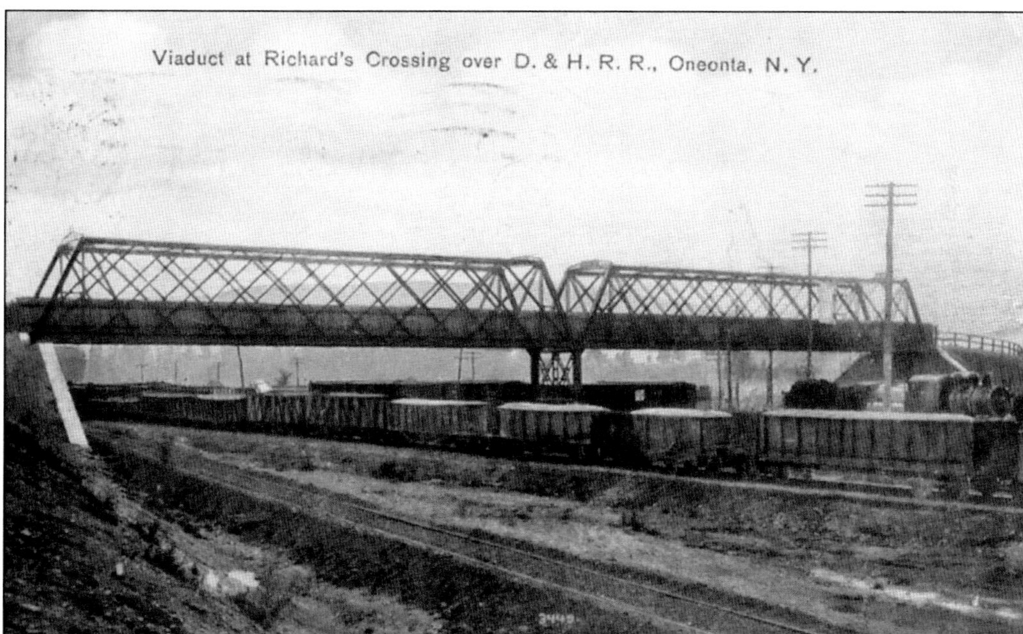

COMPLETED VIADUCT. The viaduct at Richard's Crossing was built by the D&H and completed in 1906. Pedestrians and other travelers were able to safely cross over the tracks. Heavy rail traffic continued for many years.

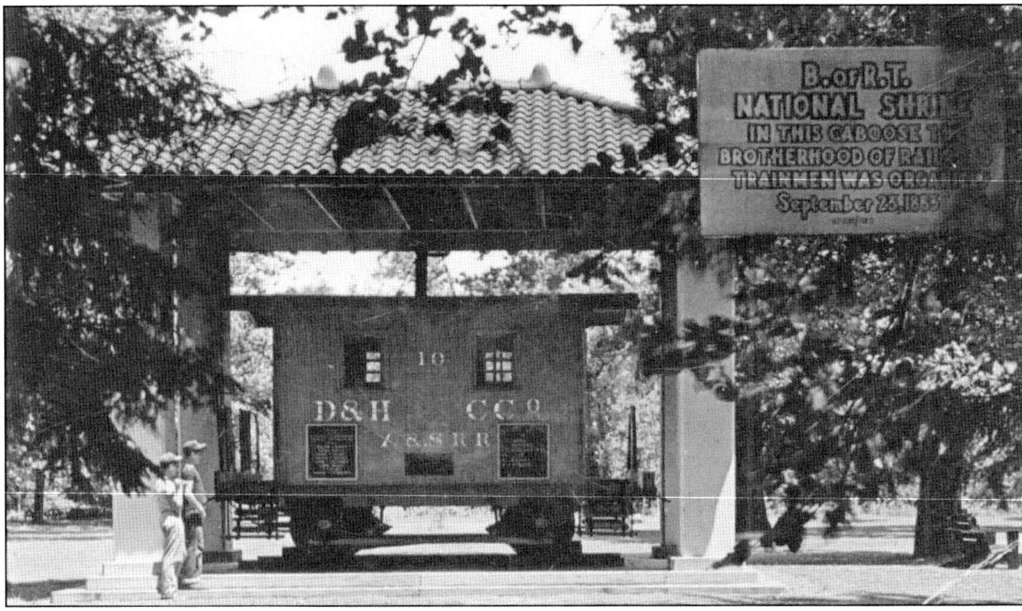

HISTORIC CABOOSE. Neahwa Park is the final resting place for Oneonta's "little red caboose." In 1883, eight Delaware and Hudson Railway brakemen met in the caboose to express their views on working conditions, salaries, and safety issues in the hopes of making improvements to their lives as D&H employees.

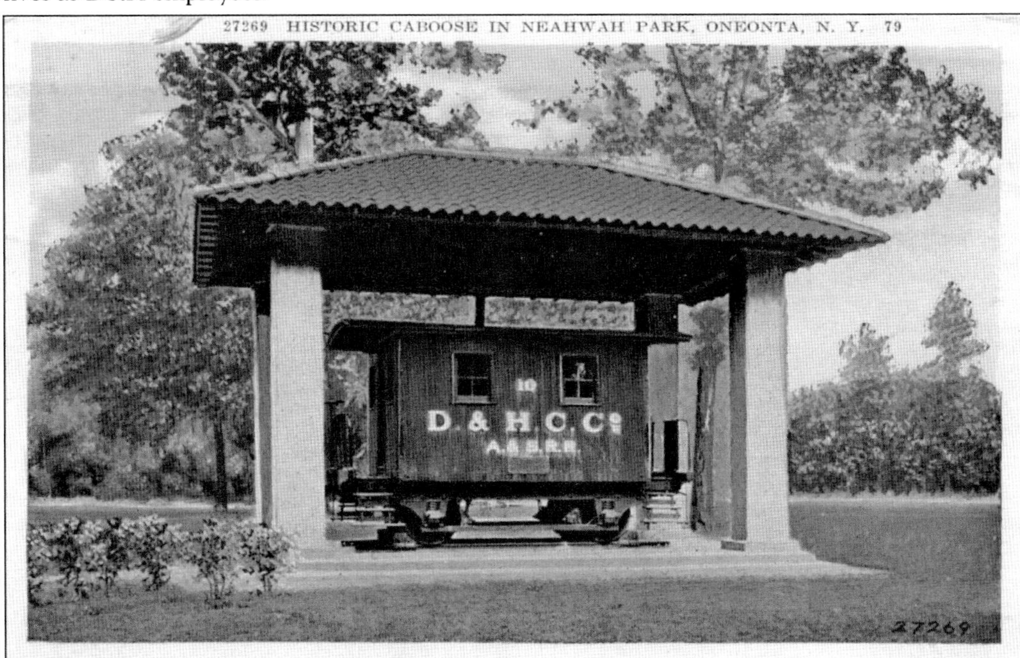

D&H CABOOSE. Eight railroad employees laid the groundwork for the Brotherhood of Railroad Brakemen union while meeting in this caboose. The name was later changed to Brotherhood of Railroad Trainmen, now a national railroad union. In the 1980s, the Smithsonian Institution tried in vain to have the caboose moved to its museum in Washington, D.C., but Oneonta won out. The caboose has been restored and is now preserved in an enclosed area for all to see.

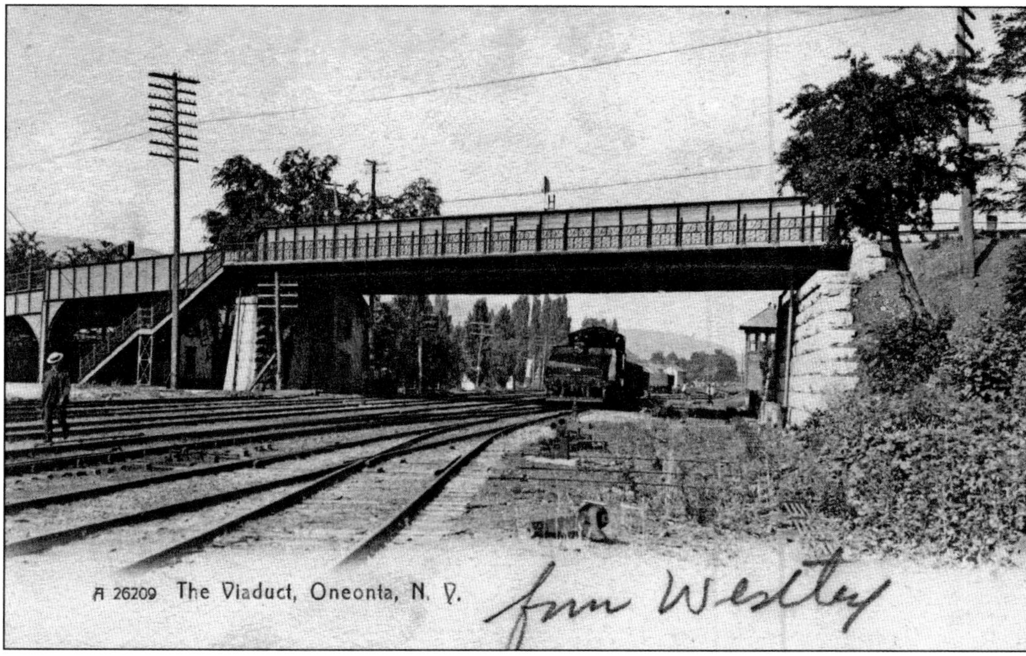

1907 VIEW. This is a view of the tracks running under a Main Street viaduct in Oneonta. In the early 20th century, riding the cars became a popular pastime, and rail traffic was available to travel just about anywhere. Several viaducts were needed in the Oneonta area because of the abundance of rails in the D&H yard.

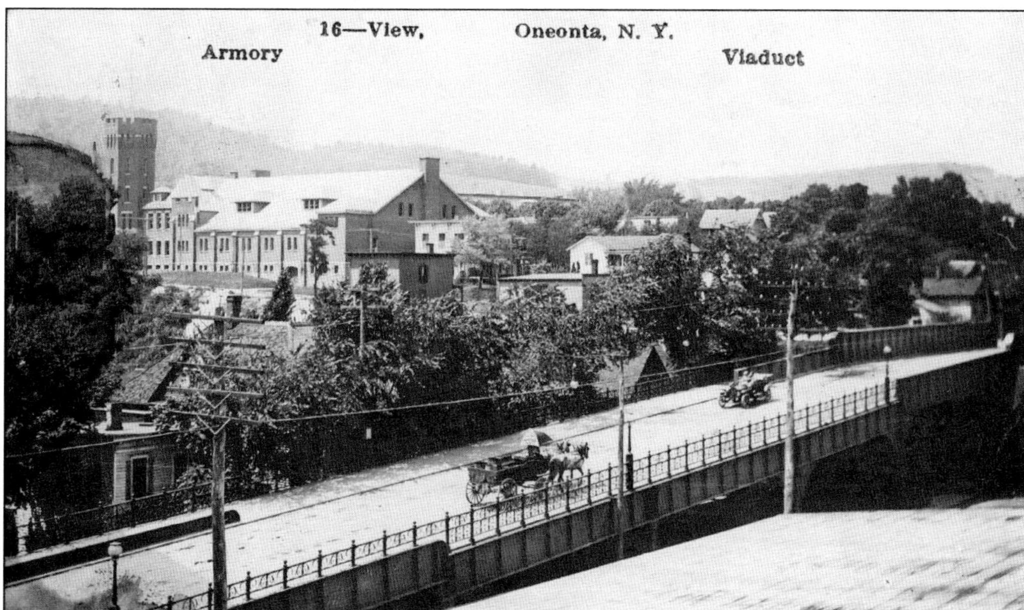

MAIN STREET VIADUCT. The Main Street viaduct opened in 1904. This view shows the armory in the background. Before then, vehicles and pedestrians used the dangerous grade crossing over the D&H tracks. Half the cost, $125,000, was paid by the D&H. The state and Oneonta each paid a fourth. Samuel Coon, a longtime D&H employee, and his wife, Augusta, were the first to cross the viaduct—in a horse and buggy.

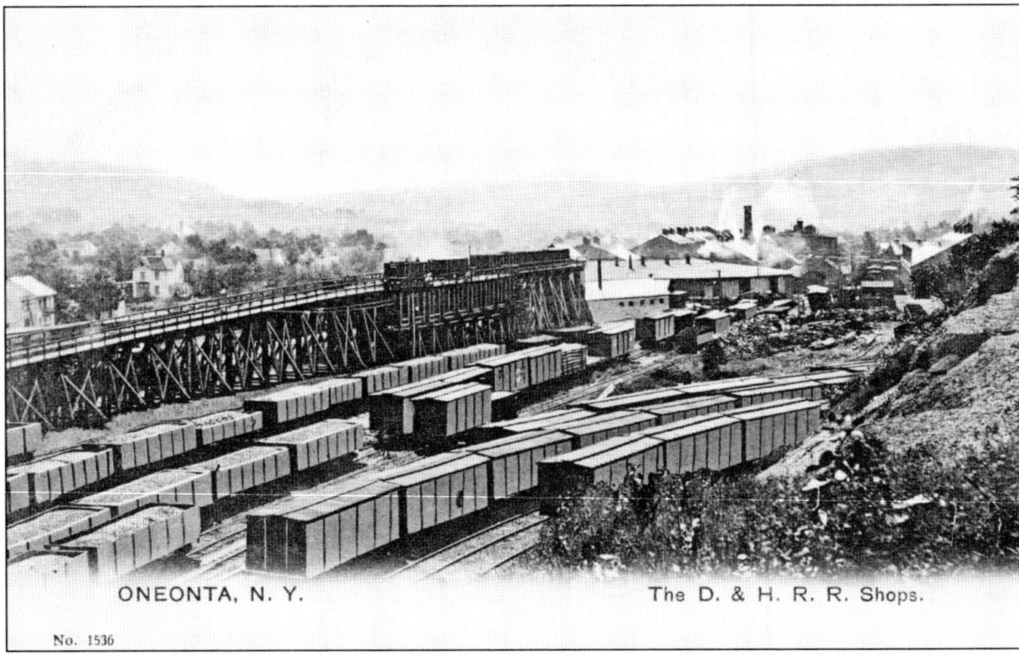

D&H SHOPS IN 1900. The Oneonta rail yard was a bustling hub of activity. The trestle to the left was for loading coal into cars in the coal pocket area. It was not unusual to have more than 400 tons of coal in the cars and chute. In 1946, a fire in the coal pocket destroyed the area. The D&H replaced the old wooden chute with an electric coal plant. Smokestacks from the roundhouse are visible in the distance.

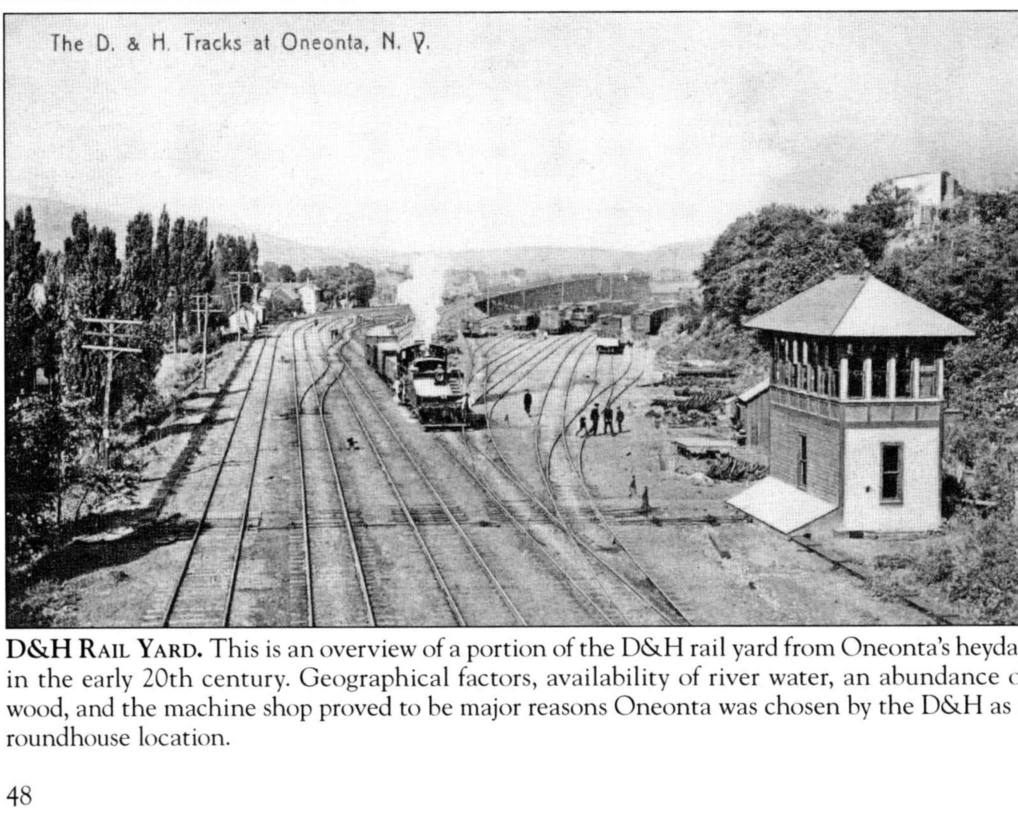

D&H RAIL YARD. This is an overview of a portion of the D&H rail yard from Oneonta's heyday in the early 20th century. Geographical factors, availability of river water, an abundance of wood, and the machine shop proved to be major reasons Oneonta was chosen by the D&H as a roundhouse location.

Four

More Stations

The Albany and Susquehanna Railroad was opened to Otego on January 23, 1866. Railroad commissioner Timothy Sheldon bonded the town for $70,000. In 1870, the railroad was leased by the Delaware and Hudson Canal Company for a 99-year term.

Union Station in Sidney was shared by two railroads: the Ontario and Western Railway and the Delaware and Hudson.

Most of the mail in 1909 was sent via the Delaware and Hudson. A pouch for the Albany depot post office was made up daily and forwarded when train No. 11 came by. Mail sent back on train No. 2 the following morning was for delivery between Worcester and Albany, and pieces addressed to the Binghamton area were returned on train No. 12.

There were about 40 stations on the 142 miles of track between Albany and Binghamton listed on the original Albany and Susquehanna timetable. Some stations outlived their usefulness and were torn down. Others were converted into storage buildings, business offices, and restaurants.

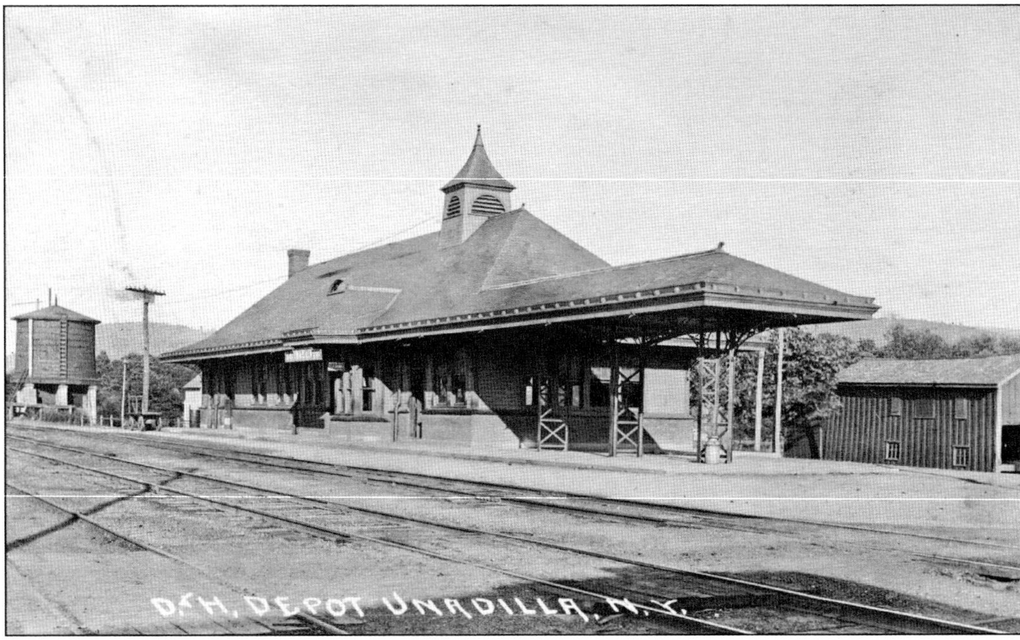

UNADILLA STATION. This is the second station built in Unadilla, which was erected in 1904–1905. Now vacant, the building is used for storage. The first Unadilla station, built in 1866, was torn down in 1903. Notice the cupola and water tower.

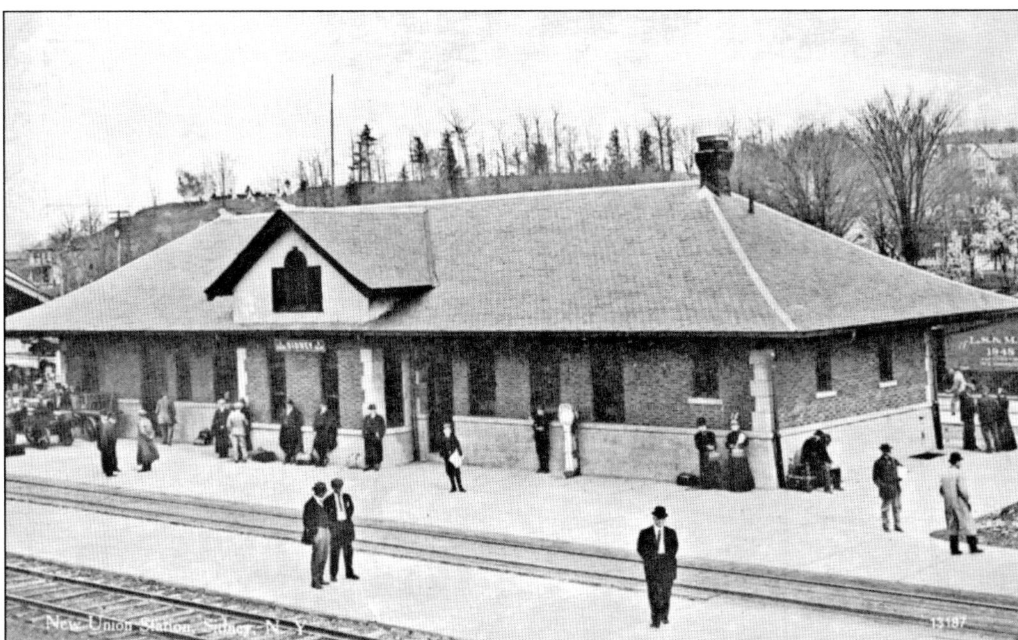

UNION STATION. The Ontario and Western Railway shared Union Station in Sidney with the Delaware and Hudson Railway. The main line of the D&H passed on the north side of the depot, and the O&W tracks were on the south side of the station. The new Union Station was built in 1913 in Sidney. The station and freight buildings are now gone.

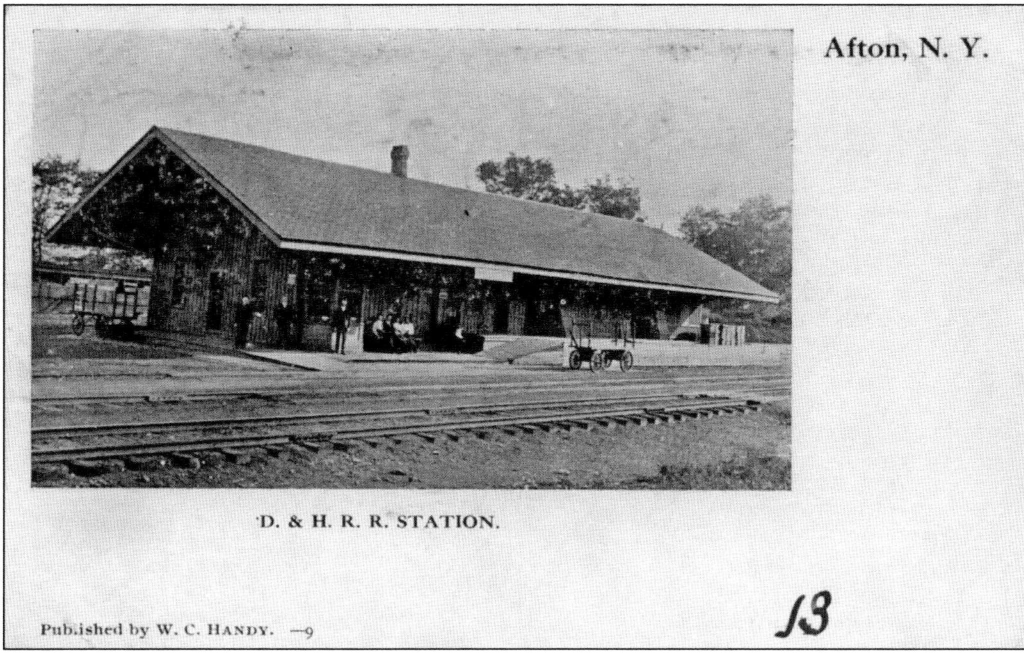

D&H STATION, AFTON. Afton was formed from Bainbridge on November 18, 1857. The station served the Albany and Susquehanna and the D&H. It is 114 miles from Albany. According to reports, this station is now a restaurant.

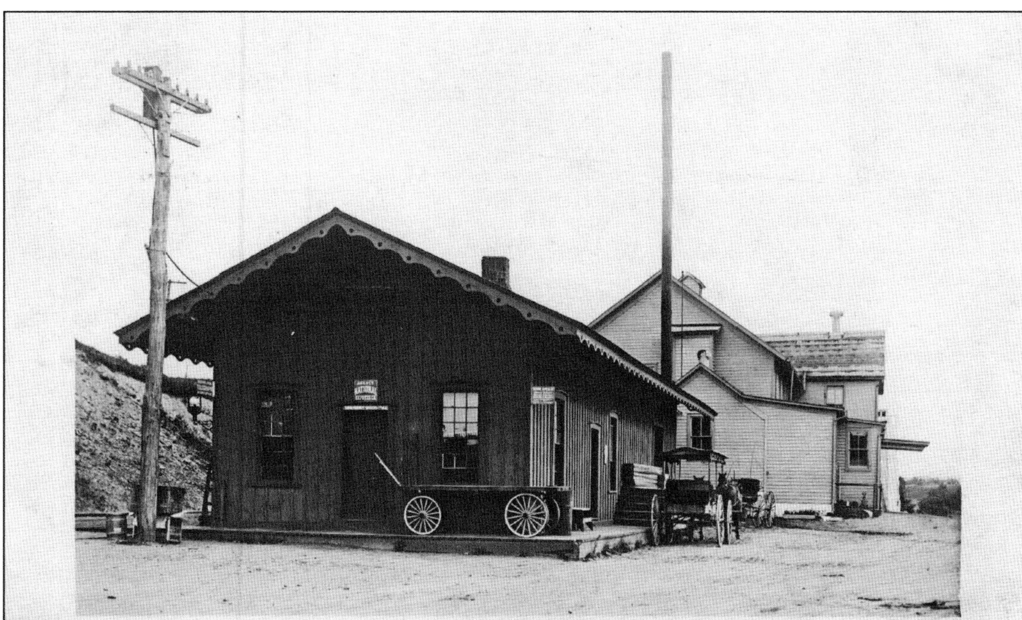

HARPURSVILLE STATION. The D&H station in Harpursville, in Broome County, was located next to Borden's creamery, making it convenient for shipping milk to city markets.

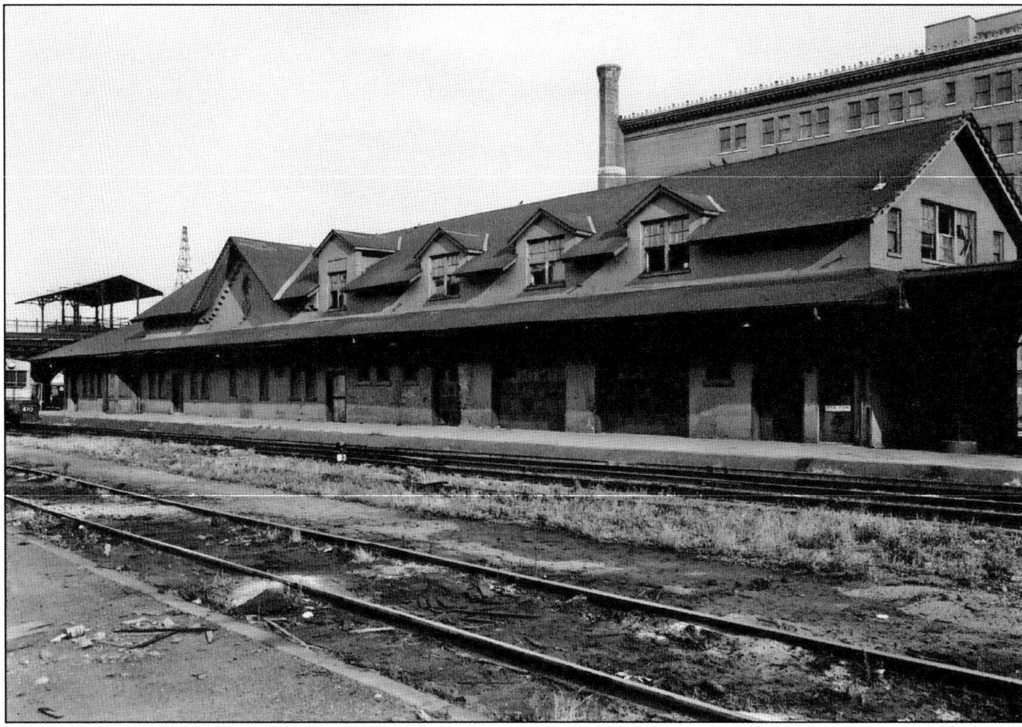

D&H AND ERIE-LACKAWANNA, BINGHAMTON. The D&H and Erie-Lackawanna shared a station in Binghamton, which is 142 miles from Albany.

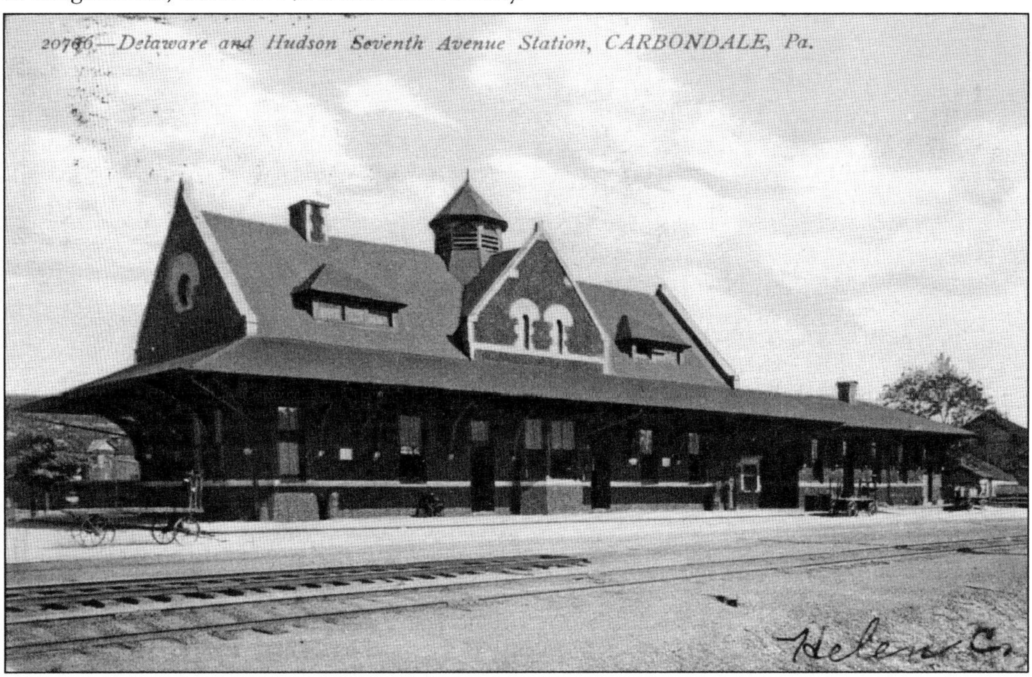

CARBONDALE, PENNSYLVANIA. The D&H had trackage rights over Erie rails from the D&H station in Carbondale, Pennsylvania, to Jefferson Junction near the New York state line. The D&H also had an agreement worked out with the Erie Railroad to use its station.

Five

D&H Locomotives

Locomotives have come a long way since the *Stourbridge Lion*, a jaunty little engine with a lion painted on the front. These little engines proved to be failures when it came to hauling coal over the Moosic Mountains in Pennsylvania.

When Lenore F. Loree became president of the Delaware and Hudson in 1907, he became known as a steam-power developer. American Locomotive Company in Schenectady turned out many experimental locomotives during Loree's tenure, which ended when he retired in 1938 at age 80. "Mother Hubbard" was the nickname for the G class 4-4-0 "camelback" locomotives used throughout the system. The first and last digits refer to the wheels under the front end and cab, while the middle numbers relate to driving wheels.

In the 1940s, the D&H introduced the Challenger, a locomotive with massive power and sleek beauty. In the mid-1940s, the Delaware and Hudson began to convert to diesel power. These diesel locomotives continue to run on the Delaware and Hudson rail lines, making history for the Bridge Line as they roll.

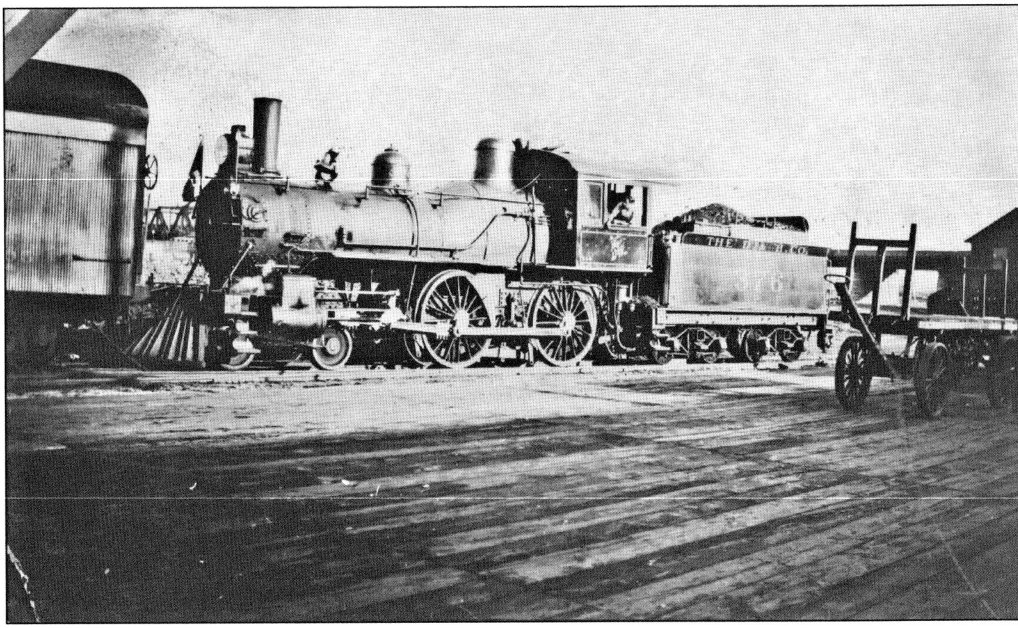

Delaware and Hudson No. 376. This photograph of Delaware and Hudson locomotive No. 376, a 4-4-0, was taken in Albany on July 21, 1914.

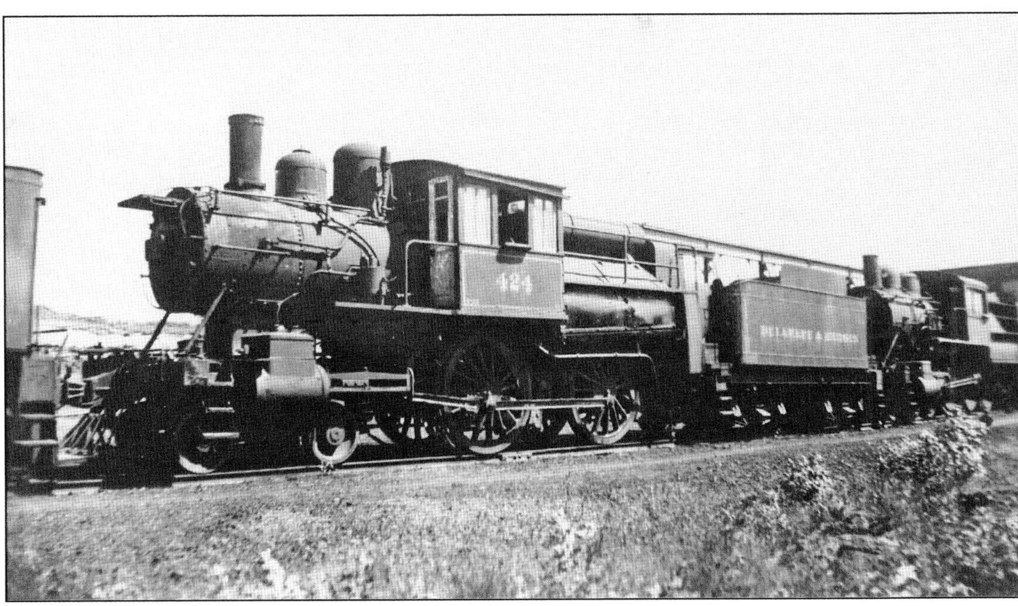

Delaware and Hudson No. 424. D&H locomotive No. 424 was photographed here in Colonie on June 26, 1936. This early D&H engine, built in 1866 for the Albany and Susquehanna, is a G-3 class 4-4-0 double cab camelback with 69-inch driving wheels and 18-inch-by-24-inch cylinders.

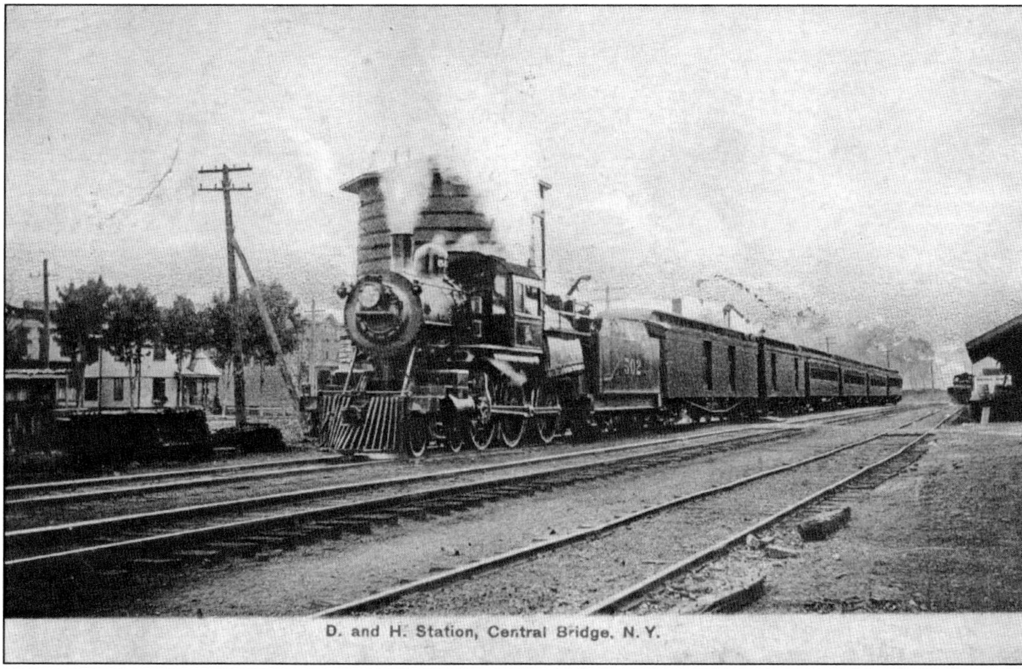

PASSENGER TRAIN. Passenger train No. 502 is stopping at the Central Bridge station in June 1910. Four passenger cars and two baggage cars make up this train headed for Albany.

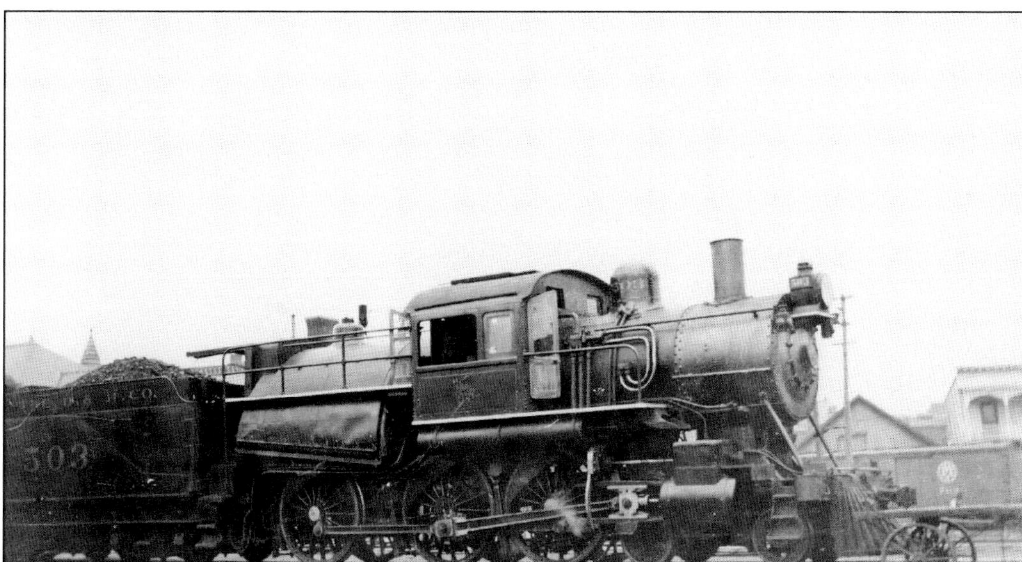

D&H ENGINE NO. 503. D&H engine No. 503, a type 4-6-0 that was built by Alco in Schenectady in 1903, is pictured here in Oneonta in July 1910.

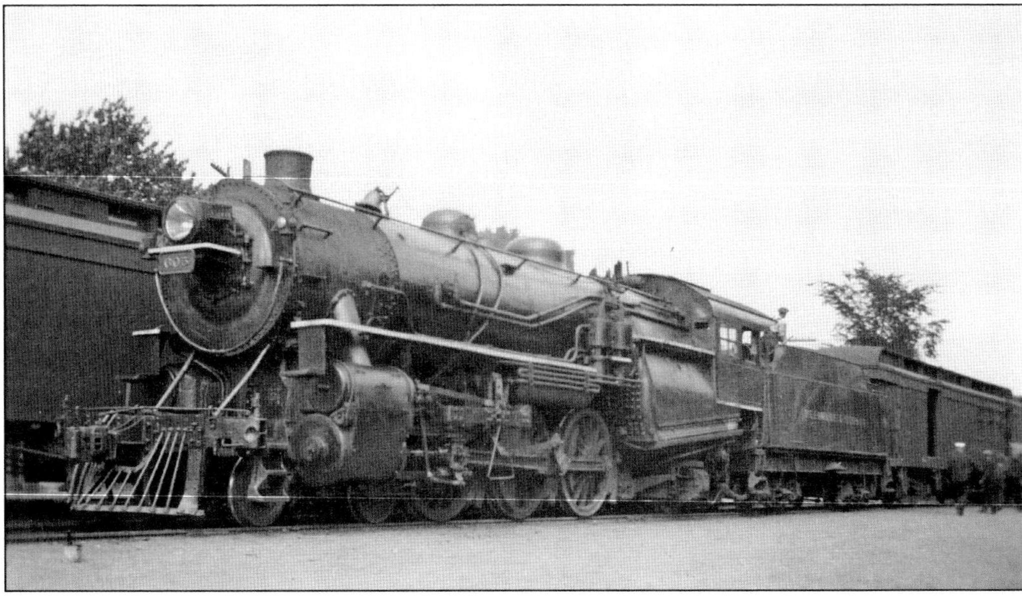

LOCOMOTIVE NO. 605. Alco in Schenectady was the builder of this 1914 D&H locomotive No. 605. The train was photographed at Rouses Point.

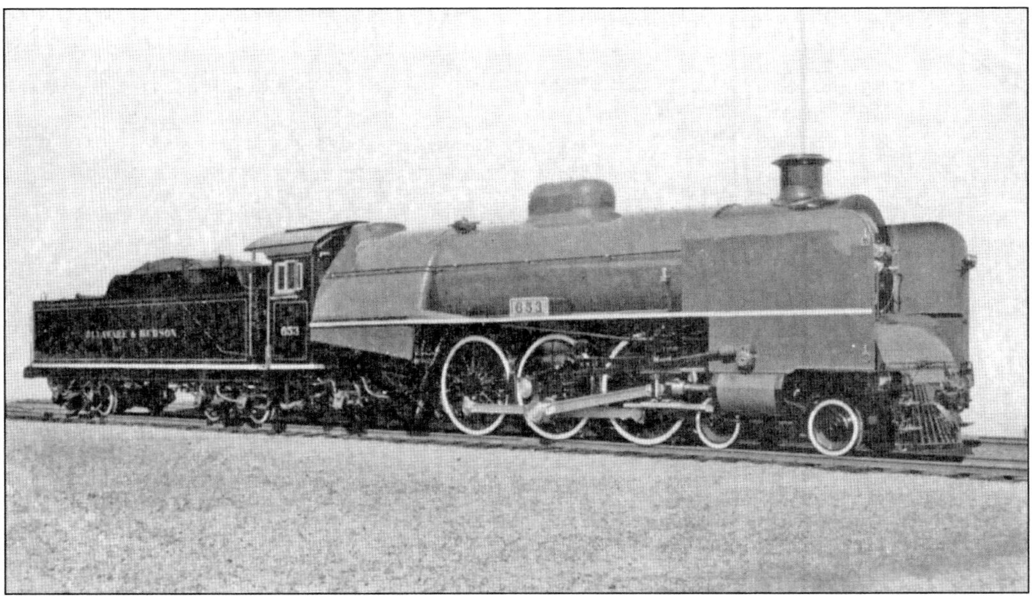

CENTURY OF PROGRESS EXPOSITION. D&H 4-6-2 steam engine No. 653 and coal tender took part in the Century of Progress Exposition in Chicago in 1934. The locomotive features a clean, pipeless boiler jacket, giving it a British appearance. Its highlights include white-striped wheel rims and polished main rods and side rods.

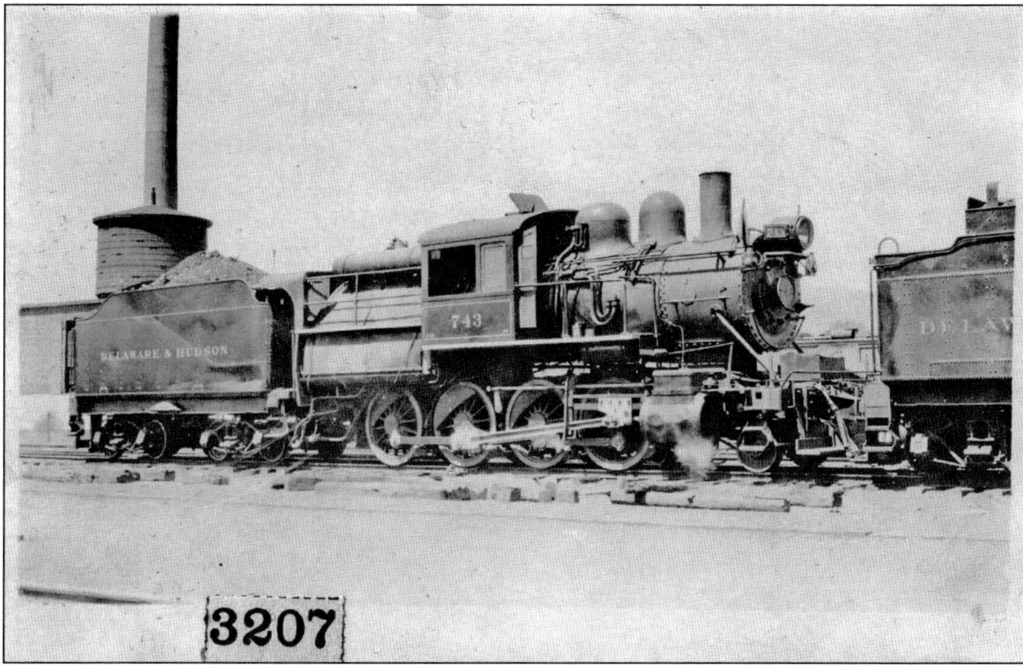

D&H Locomotive No. 743. Dickson in Scranton, Pennsylvania, built locomotive No. 743. This engine is shown in Carbondale, Pennsylvania, on June 22, 1924. Before being rebuilt, the engine was No. 331 and in class E-2a.

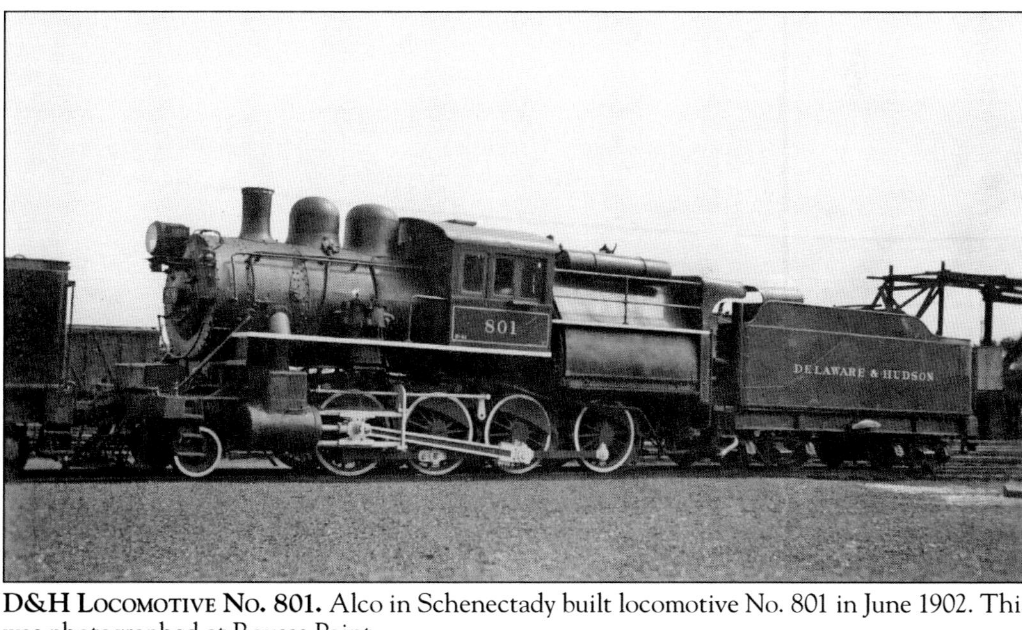

D&H Locomotive No. 801. Alco in Schenectady built locomotive No. 801 in June 1902. This was photographed at Rouses Point.

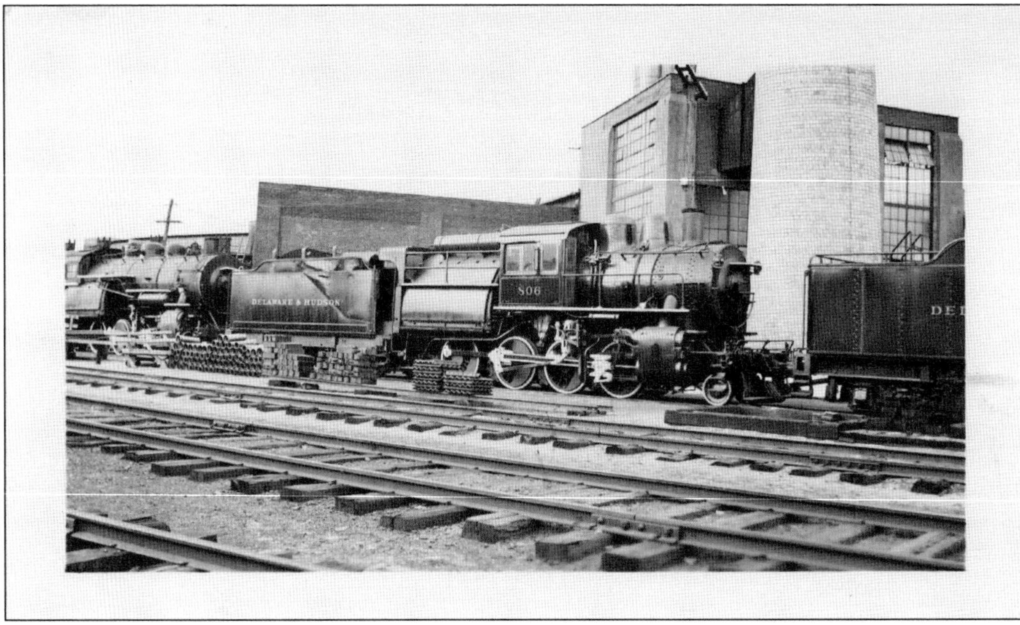

D&H Locomotive No. 806. D&H locomotive No. 806 is photographed here in Oneonta in September 1936. Other engines await service behind the roundhouse.

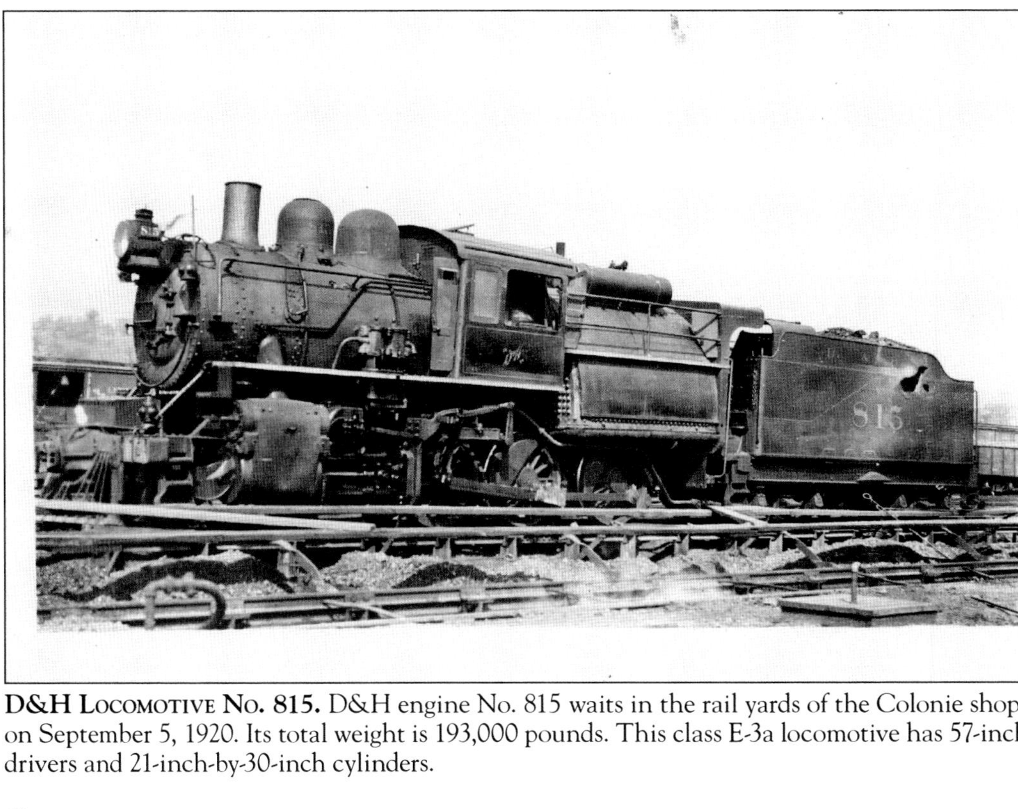

D&H Locomotive No. 815. D&H engine No. 815 waits in the rail yards of the Colonie shops on September 5, 1920. Its total weight is 193,000 pounds. This class E-3a locomotive has 57-inch drivers and 21-inch-by-30-inch cylinders.

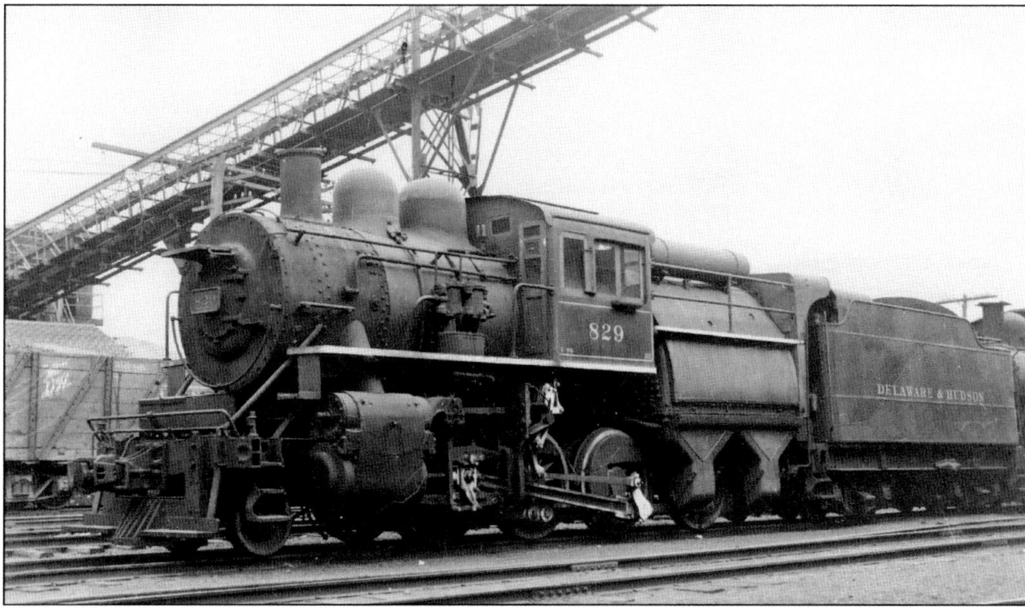

ENGINE NO. 829. Alco in Schenectady built Delaware and Hudson engine No. 829 in 1904. This photograph was taken in Oneonta on September 20, 1936. It is an E-3a class 2-8-0 formerly known as No. 208.

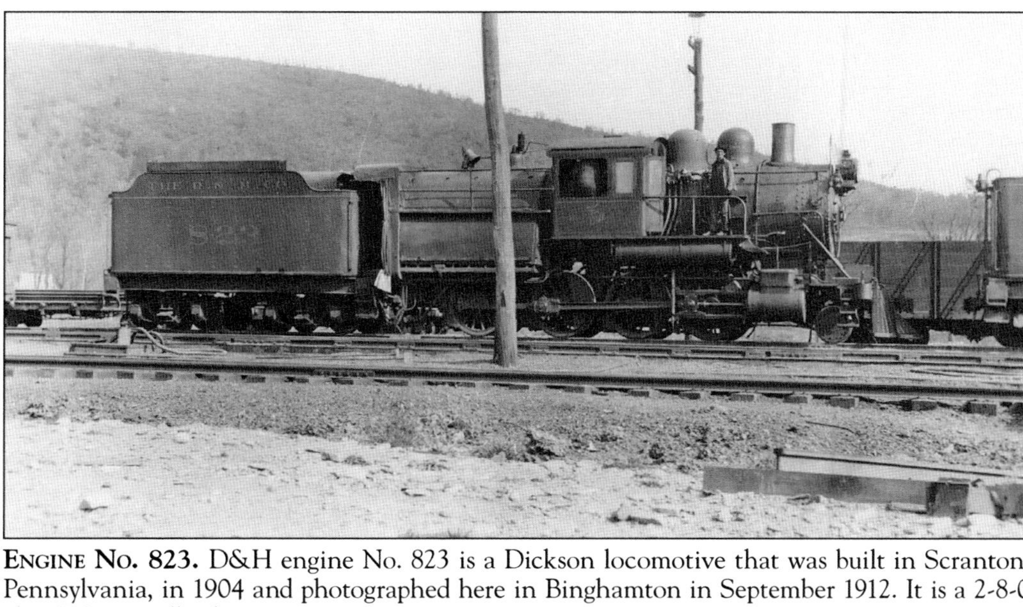

ENGINE NO. 823. D&H engine No. 823 is a Dickson locomotive that was built in Scranton, Pennsylvania, in 1904 and photographed here in Binghamton in September 1912. It is a 2-8-0 class E-3a camelback.

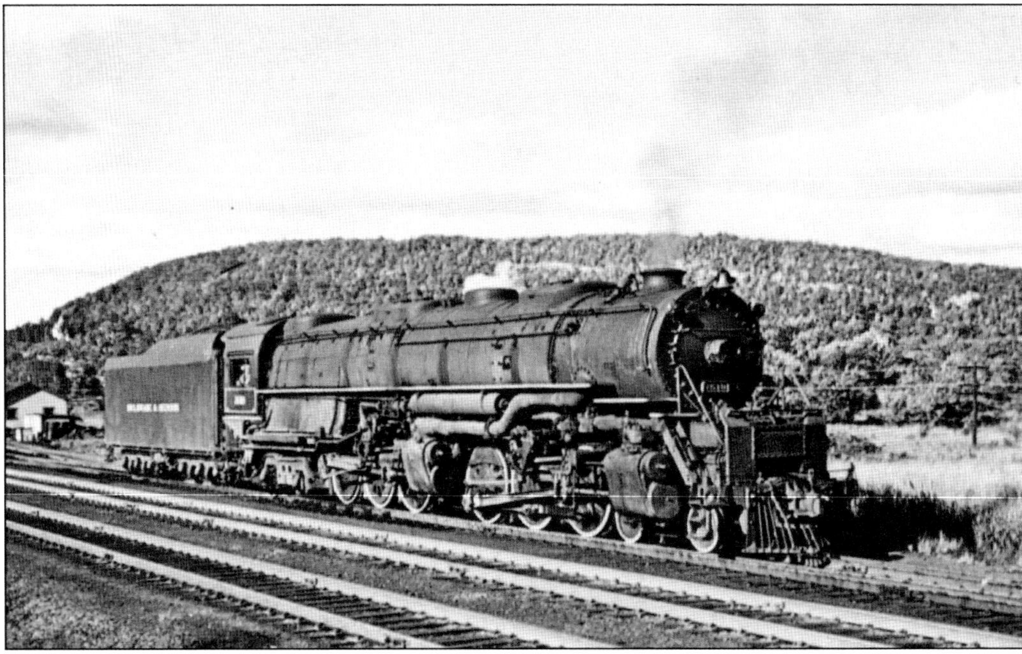

Delaware and Hudson Challenger. The No. 1519, class J 4-6-6-4, Challenger is photographed here in Whitehall. The Challenger type supplied high horsepower, high speed, and in the 1940s provided a new concept for the future of the D&H. The back of the picture, which was taken August 17, 1952, reads, "These 1500s were turned here for the run south as they were too large to continue traveling north."

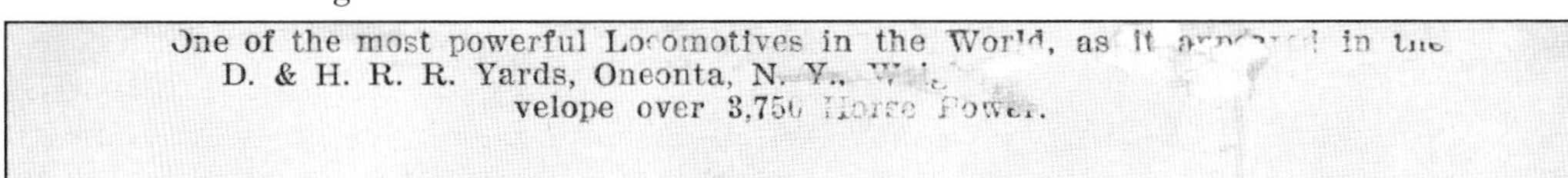

D&H Locomotive No. 1601. The D&H's H class 0-8-8-0 was one of the most powerful steam locomotives at the time it was put into service. It is shown arriving in the rail yards of Oneonta. Alco in Schenectady built D&H locomotive No. 1601.

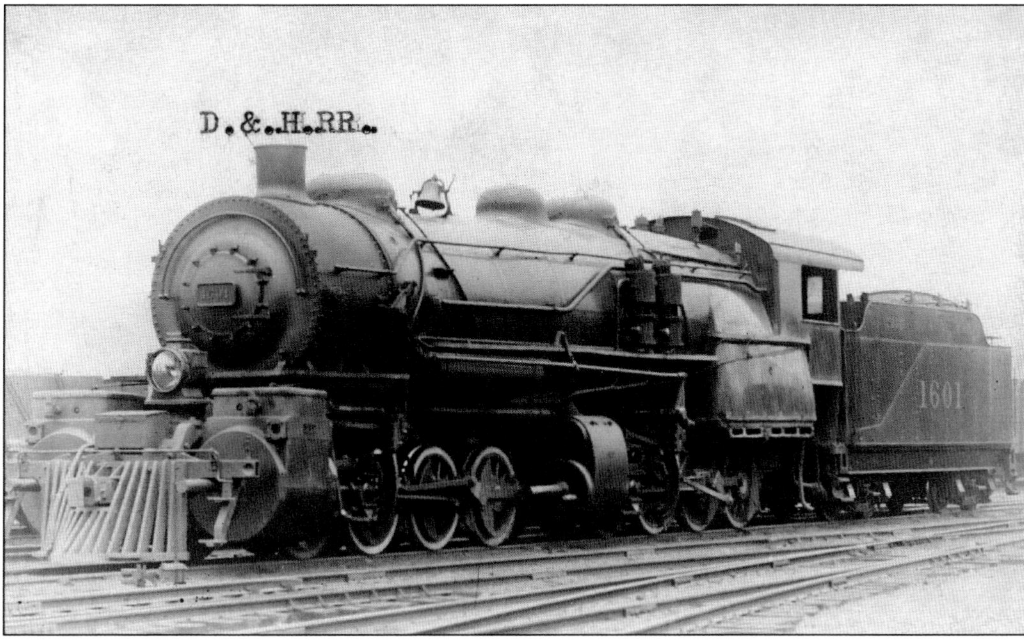

LOCOMOTIVE NO. 1601 CLOSE-UP. The No. 1601 D&H locomotive was rebuilt in 1930 with a new boiler pressure of 245 psi, 57-inch drivers, and a total engine weight of 469,400 pounds.

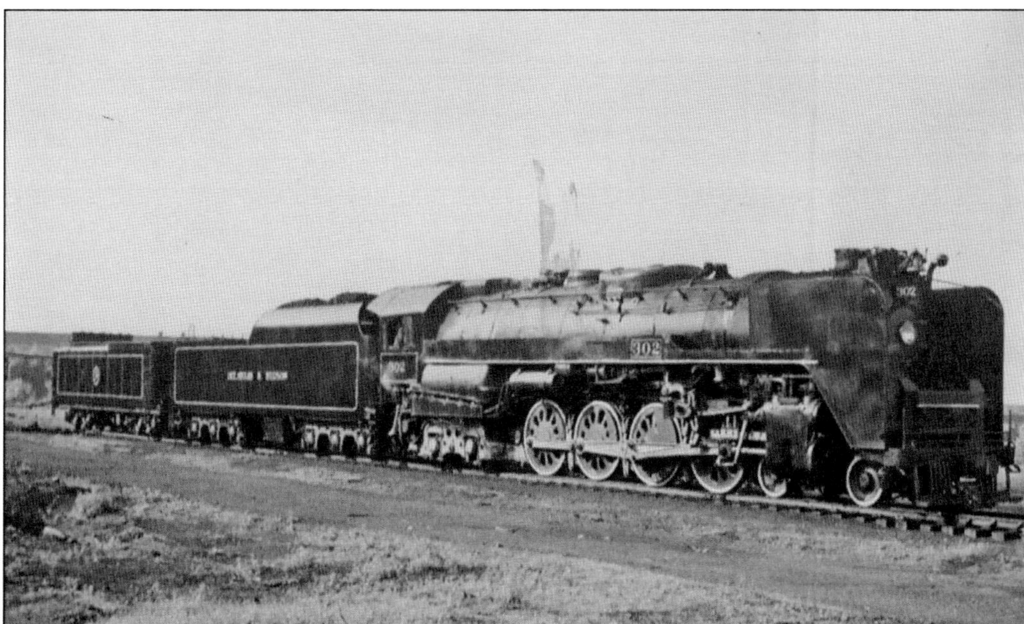

SESQUICENTENNIAL, 1823–1973. The Delaware and Hudson Company altered the appearance of an ex-Reading locomotive No. 2102 to resemble one of its own for participation in the railroad's 150th anniversary. (Courtesy Jim Shaughnessy.)

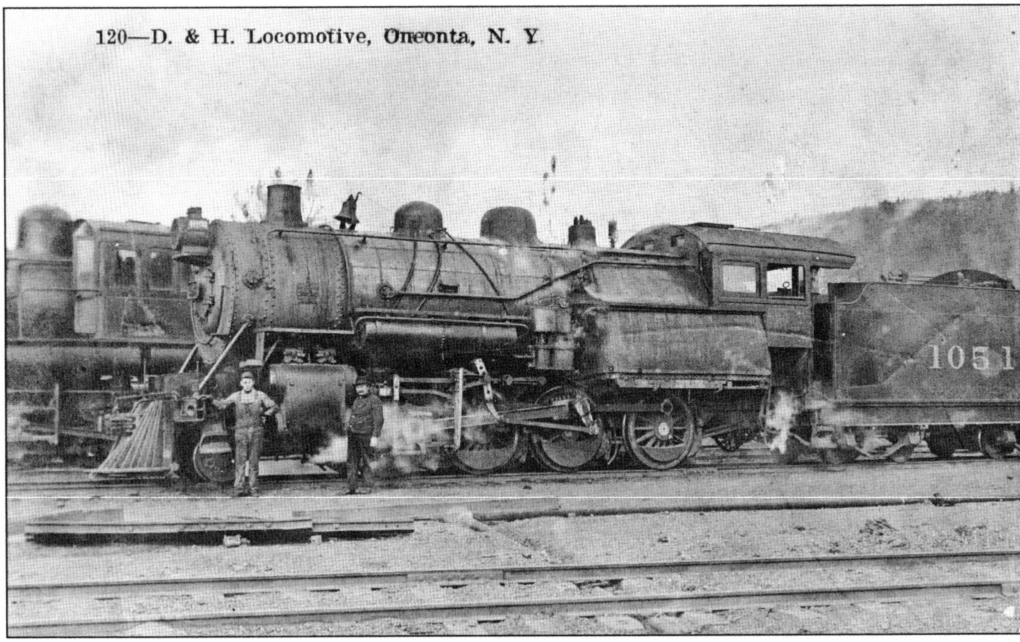

Locomotive No. 1051. D&H engine No. 1051, built by Alco in Schenectady in 1908, is in the Oneonta rail yards. The engineer and fireman stand in front of the engine.

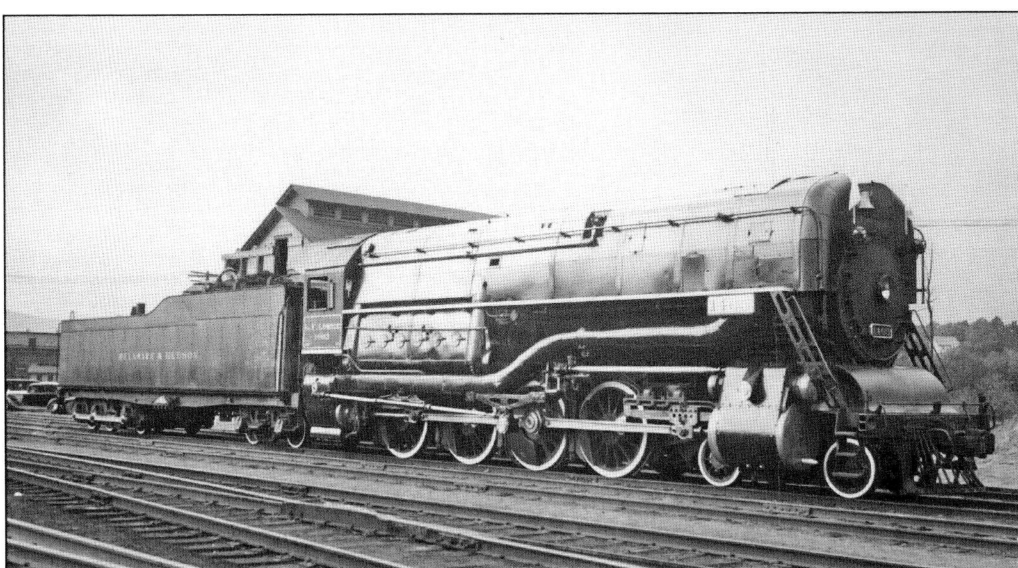

L. F. Loree No. 1403. The eighth president of the D&H from 1907 to 1938 was L. F. Loree. Known for his ingenuity and development of powerful locomotives to haul freight and passenger cars over the hilly sections on the D&H rails, the No. 1403 was the fourth of the experimental high-pressure locomotives named in his honor. Built in 1933 by Alco, this unit is pictured in the Oneonta rail yard on September 20, 1936. It is an E-7 with a wheel type of 4-8-0.

Six

Wrecks and Derailments

Railroads have a far better safety record in modern times than they did in the early years. On July 15, 1941, the Delaware and Hudson suffered one of its most costly wrecks. The accident took place about 2.5 miles east of Richmondville at 6:00 a.m. The 1510 Challenger-type engine exploded, hurling three men 300 feet to their death. Low water had exposed the crown sheet of the 9-foot-by-12-foot firebox in the steam locomotive, instantly turning water to steam in the big boiler and causing the explosion.

In 1921, the D&H owned a wrecking crane with a 160-ton capacity, which was purchased at a cost of $44,418.98. The crane and flatcar were accompanied with a riding car fashioned from an old coach containing a kitchen, sleeping quarters, and office.

In February 1945, Challenger No. 1517 turned over in the Central Bridge area, spilling 15,000 gallons of water and 20 tons of coal. It was necessary to build a 250-ton-capacity crane to pick up the locomotive. In the meantime, the engine was left near the tracks for three months awaiting the new crane.

The area's worst wreck and fire took place in Emmons on February 12, 1974, when a northbound freight train derailed, causing propane tanks to explode. More than 40 firemen and others were injured at the scene.

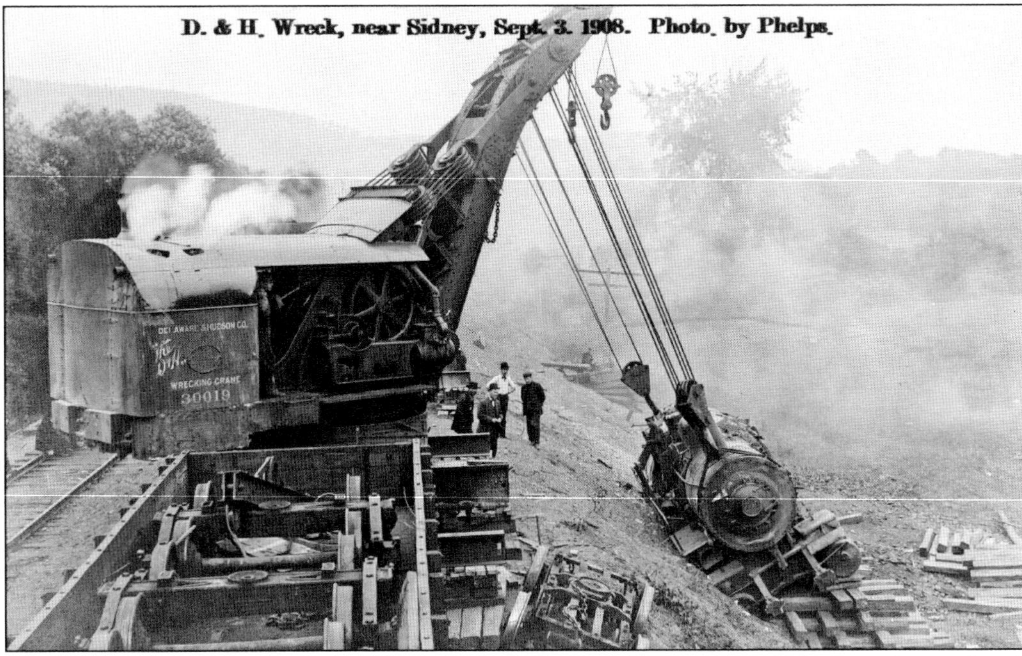

D&H Wreck. The D&H Railway brought large locomotive cranes to Sidney on September 3, 1908, to clean up the destruction caused when engineer Dimmick failed to slow down from a speed of 50 miles per hour at a temporary crossover due to repairs. The accident happened to Mother Hubbard No. 500.

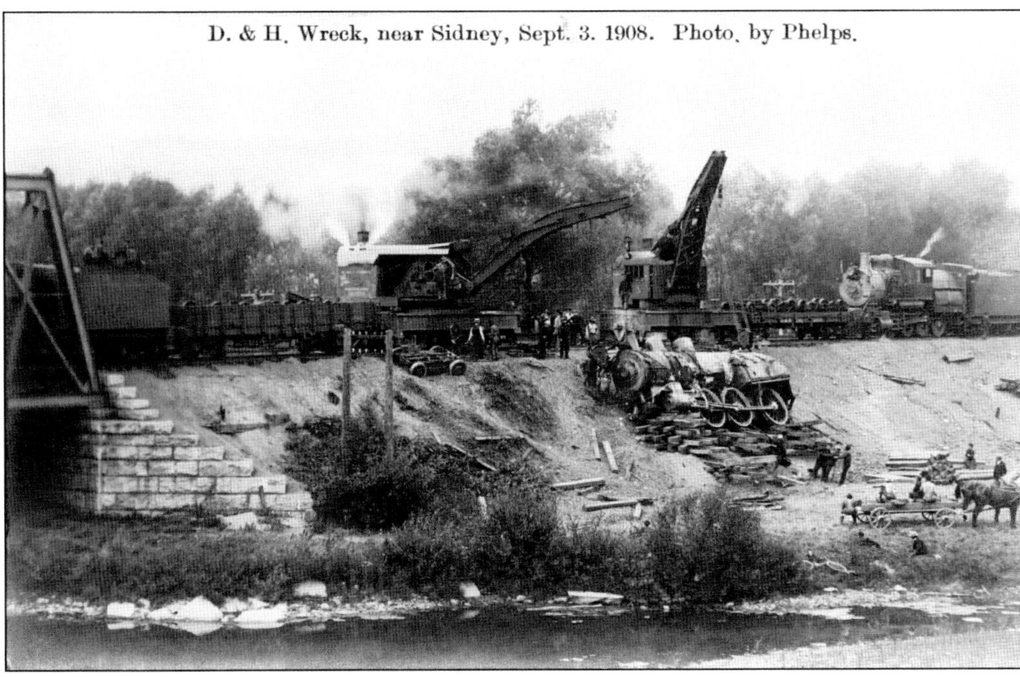

D&H Cranes. Two large cranes drag the derailed engine up the side of a hill near Sidney. Engineer Dimmick, after applying the brakes, jumped from the locomotive when it was going about 35 miles per hour. The wrecking cranes were from Oneonta and Binghamton.

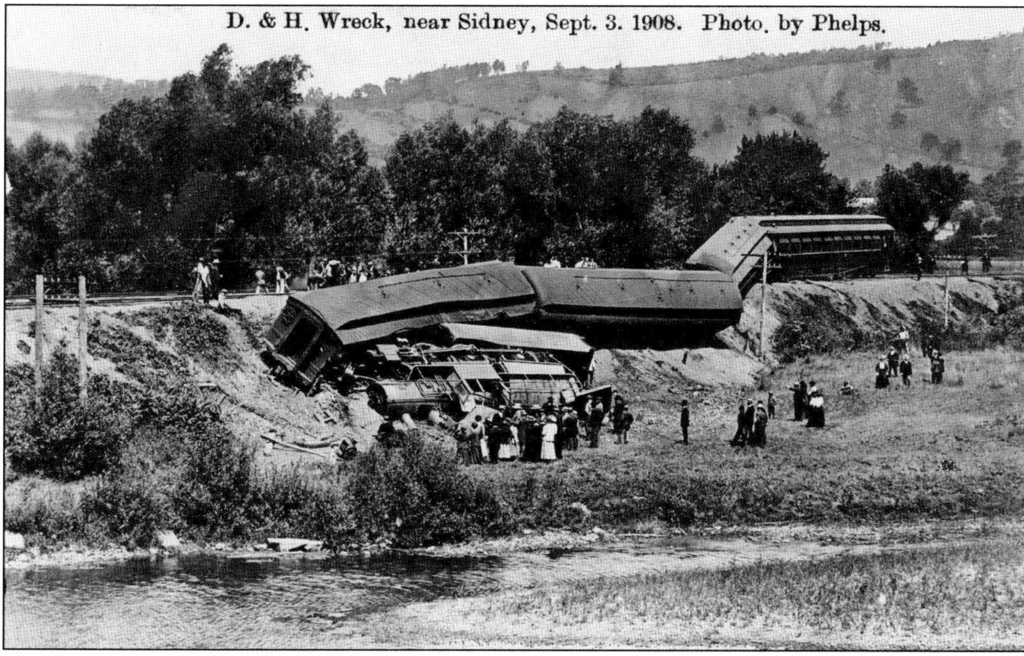

PASSENGERS BRUISED. The last coach of the derailed train did not leave the tracks at all. Passengers in the smoking car were bruised as they were thrown about. The message on the back of this photograph reads, "How would you like to have been riding on this train?" A number of people are shown viewing the damages of the wreck that took place September 3, 1908.

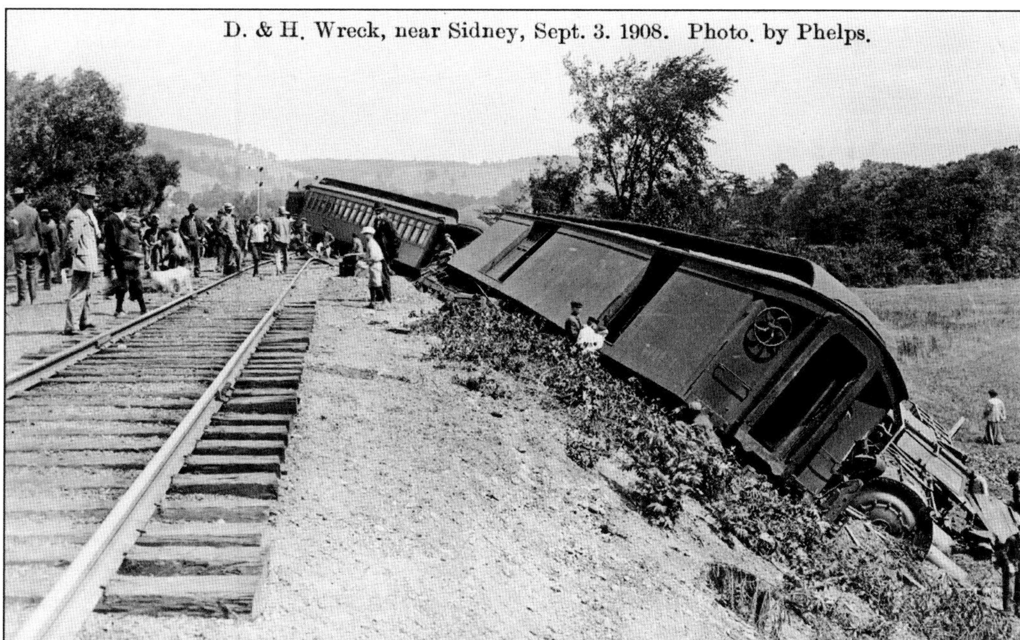

VIEWING THE WRECK. The late C. H. Phelps, a photographer from Sidney, captured all these shots of the Delaware and Hudson wreck in 1908. Folks turned out to view the cleanup operations, which took several days.

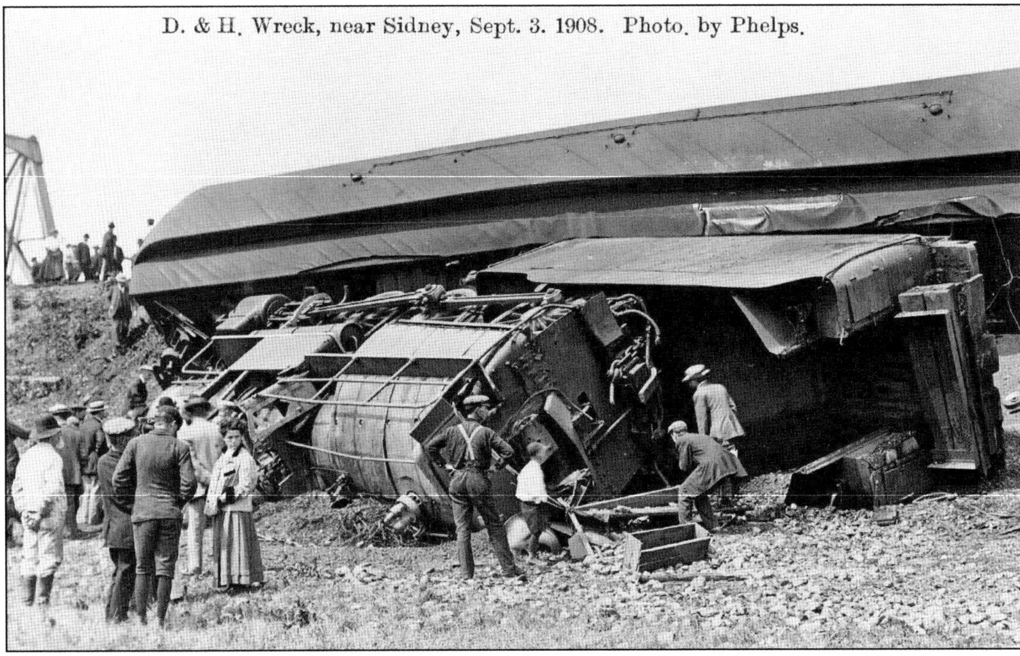

Poor Mother Hubbard. Men and women stand around at the 1908 derailment scene to view the overturned engine No. 500. The crash happened about 11:00 a.m. on September 3, 1908.

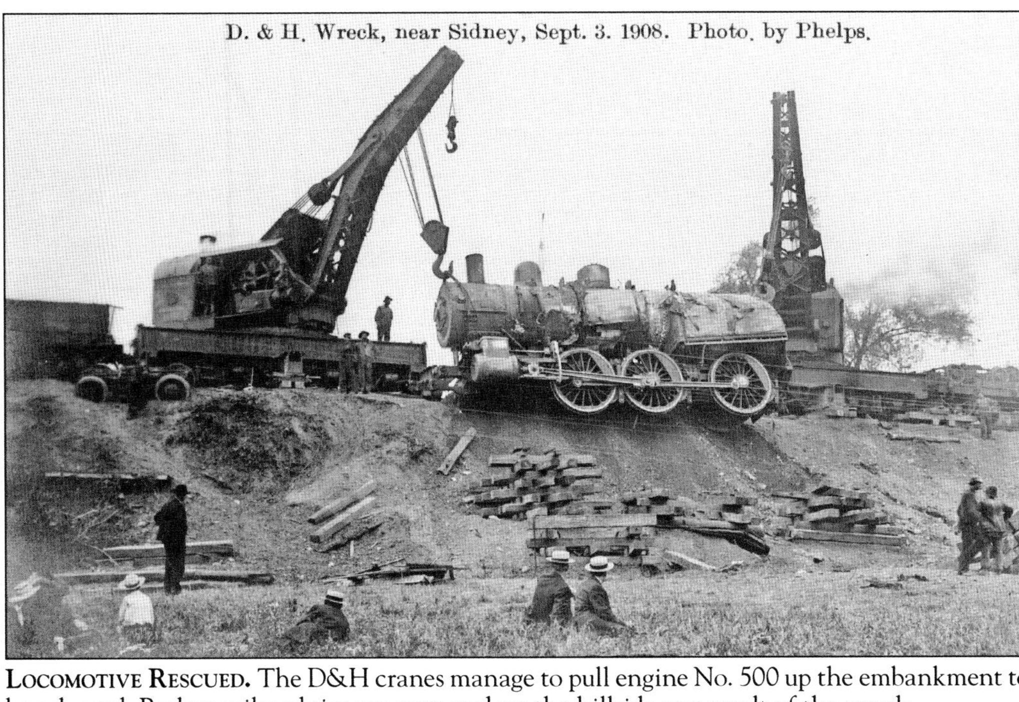

Locomotive Rescued. The D&H cranes manage to pull engine No. 500 up the embankment to be salvaged. Broken railroad ties are scattered on the hillside as a result of the wreck.

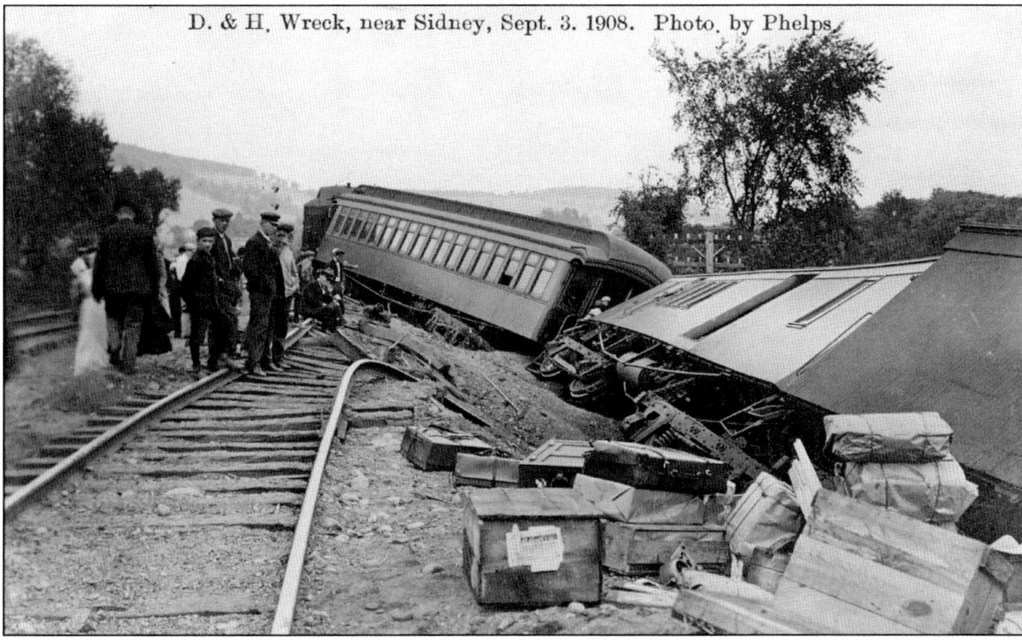

Derailment Scene. Many packages are strewn across the derailment scene after a September 3, 1908, D&H wreck. A baggage car and coach are off the rails. The baggage man, W. G. Everett of Binghamton, was pinned beneath a pile of baggage when the car finally tipped sideways. He was not seriously injured according to a report in the *Binghamton Press*.

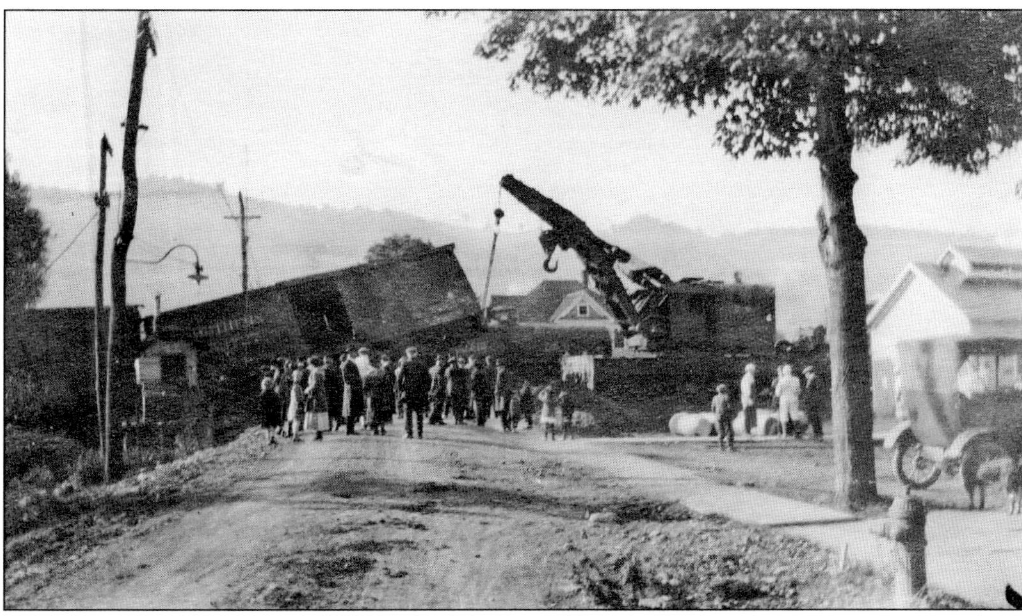

Worcester Crossing. An accident took place at Worcester's railroad crossing sometime in the 1920s. One of the boxcars was transporting a load of canned sardines that spilled out during the derailment. It is alleged that many people in town enjoyed sardine sandwiches for days afterward. The D&H crane cleared the wreckage under the watchful eye of these spectators.

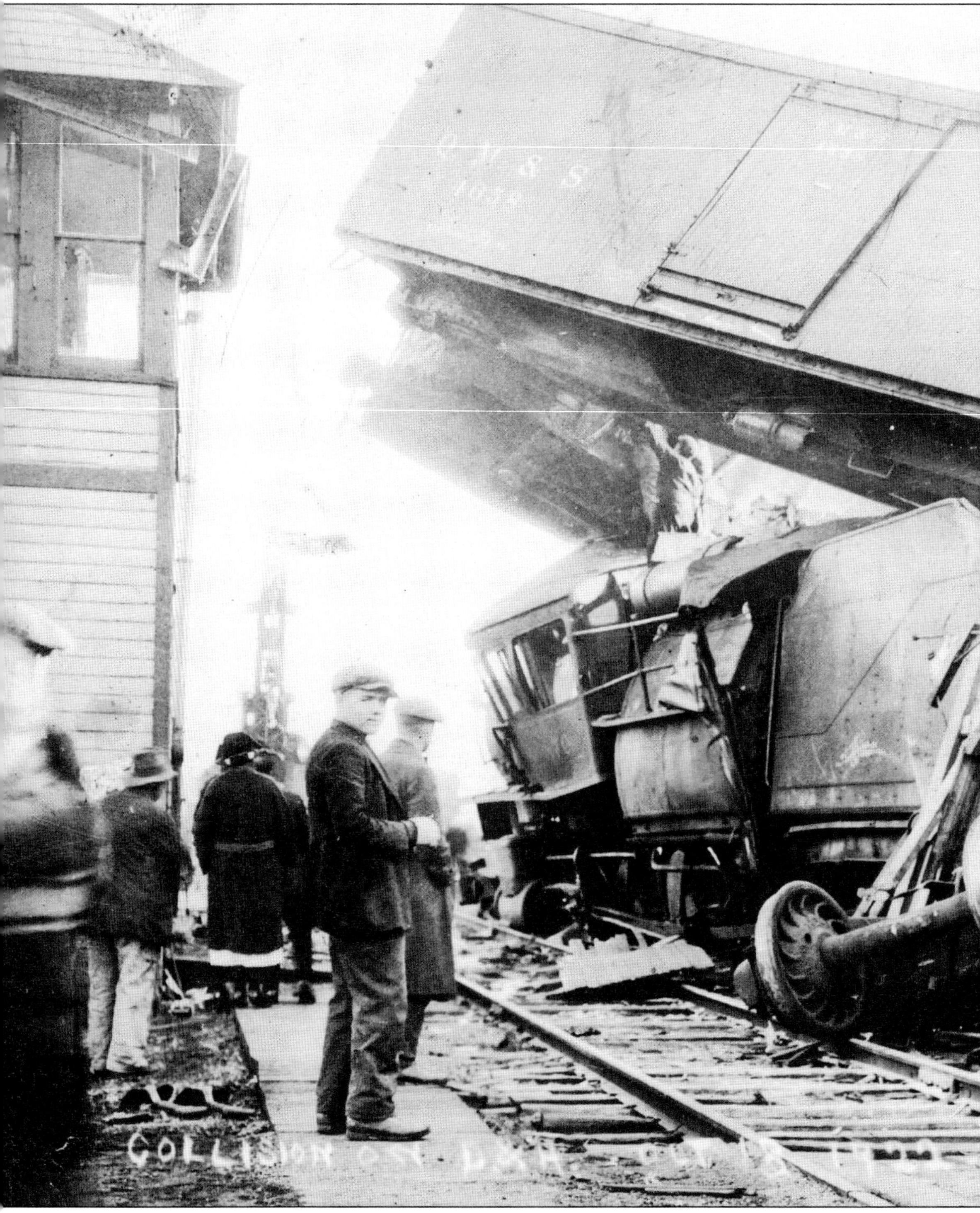

Engineer Dies in Crash. Engineer William P. Toal of Binghamton was killed in the early morning hours of October 18, 1922, when the Delaware and Hudson train hit the side of an Ontario and Western freight that had halted in the Sidney rail yards and was just leaving the switch area.

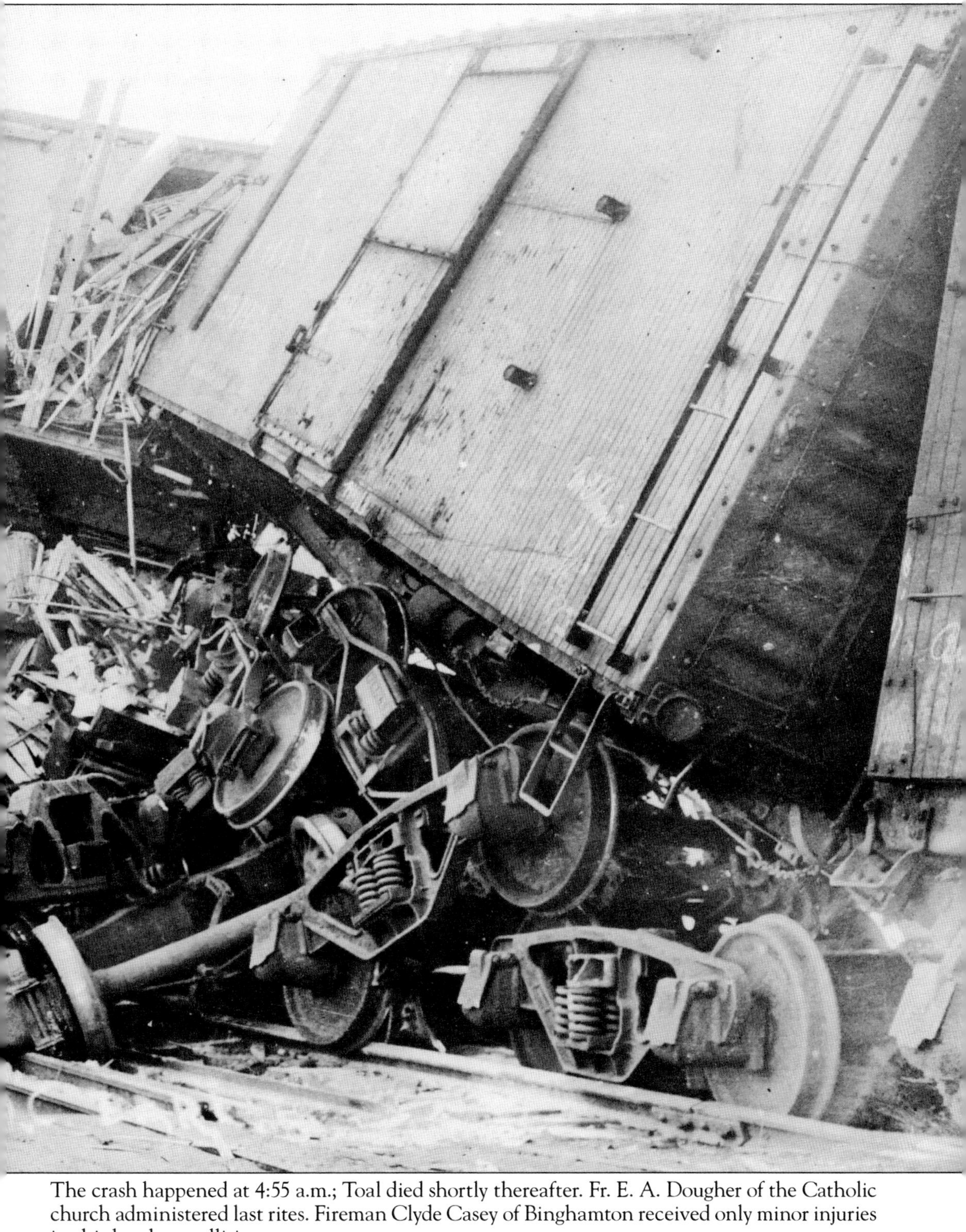

The crash happened at 4:55 a.m.; Toal died shortly thereafter. Fr. E. A. Dougher of the Catholic church administered last rites. Fireman Clyde Casey of Binghamton received only minor injuries in this head-on collision.

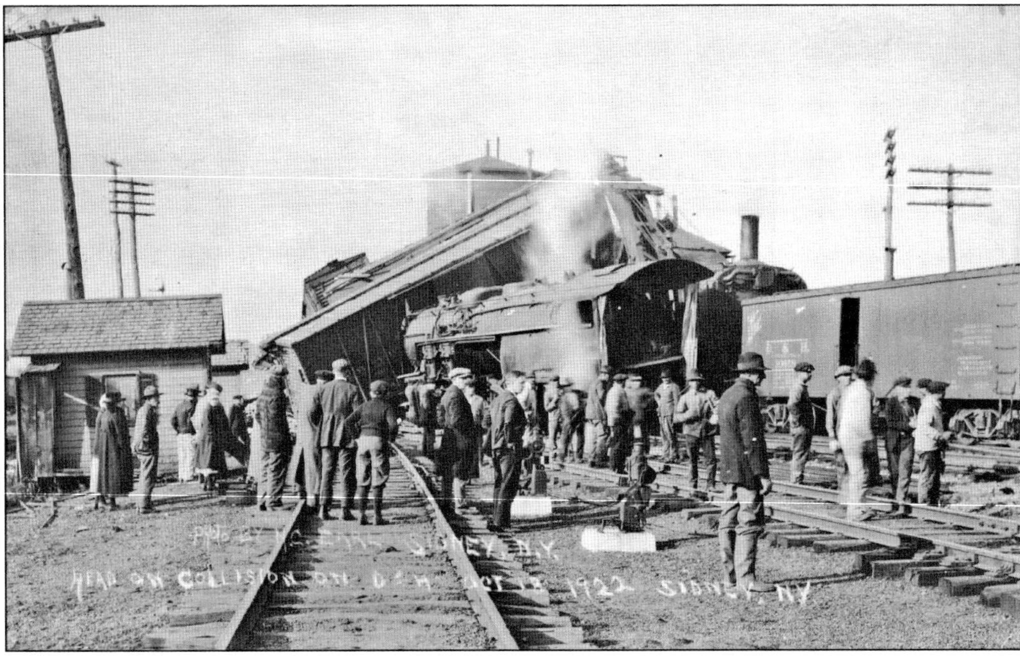

Sidney Crash. Spectators mill around the crash scene in the Sidney area on October 18, 1922, of a Delaware and Hudson train and a freight owned by Ontario and Western Railroad. The Sidney station is seen in the background.

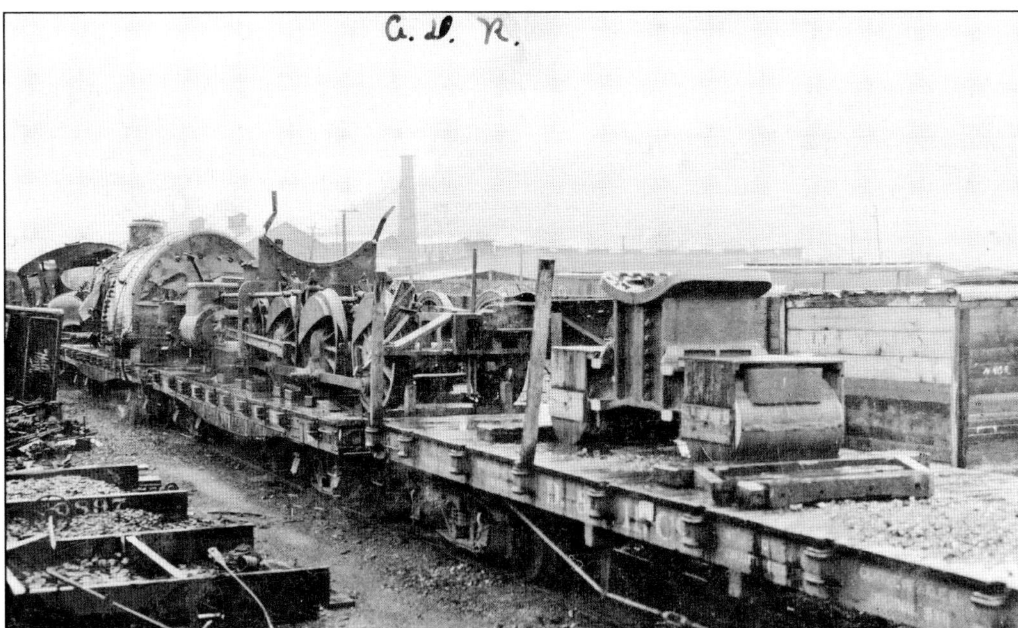

Crash Debris. Debris following a crash on the D&H was loaded onto a flatbed car for return to the Oneonta yards. The message on the reverse side of the card states, "April 21, 1908, I tied up in Oneonta this morning. Was pluged [sic] on Richmondville Hill for four hours or we would have made Binghamton. Probably will not be on that run again right away." The writing seems to hint that Mr. A. D. R. was an engineer on the D&H and held up because of an accident.

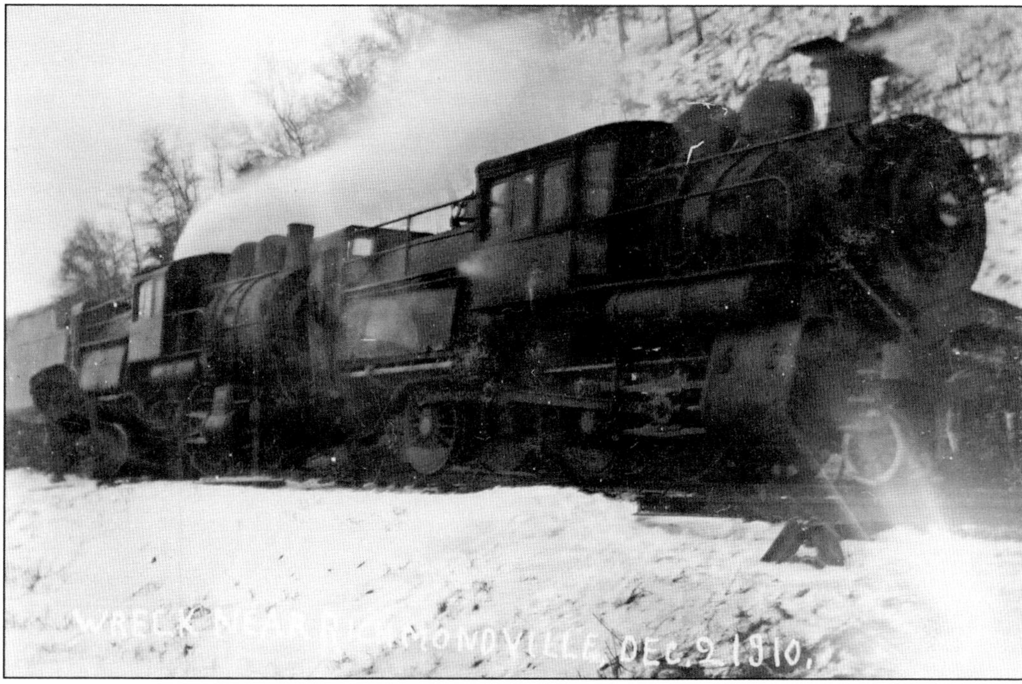

WRECK NEAR RICHMONDVILLE. A D&H train is stopped because of a wreck on Richmondville Hill that took place on December 2, 1910. The Richmondville Hill area was always a concern for the Delaware and Hudson because of the 1.31-percent grade from East Worcester on up the rails to Richmondville.

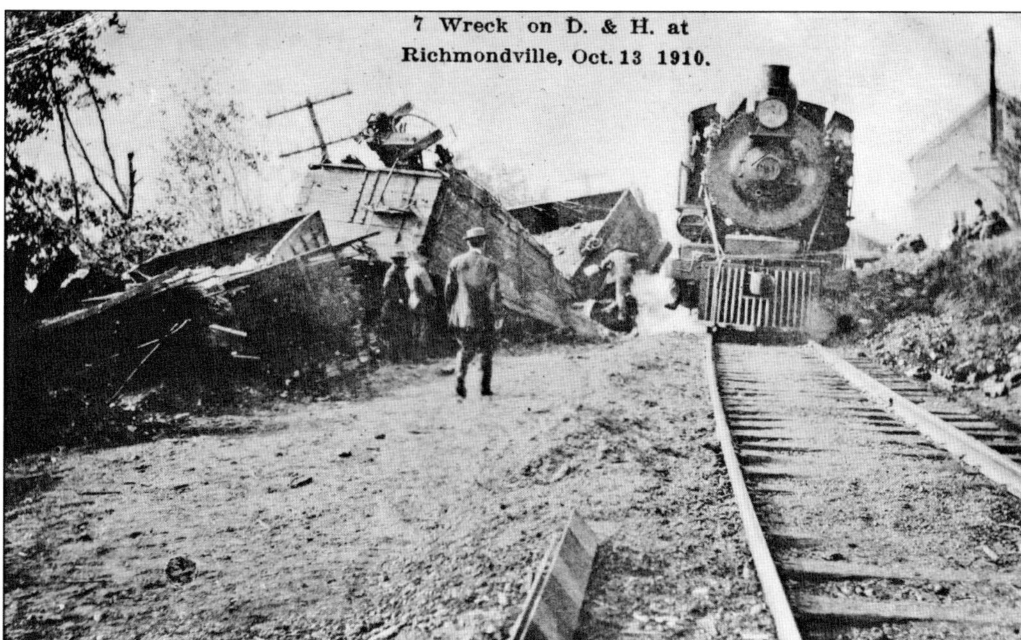

WRECK AT RICHMONDVILLE. An extra northbound freight train wrecked around 10:00 p.m. on Friday, October 13, 1910, on a sharp curve an eighth of a mile east of the Richmondville depot. Involved in the wreck were 19 cars of soft coal and two freight cars.

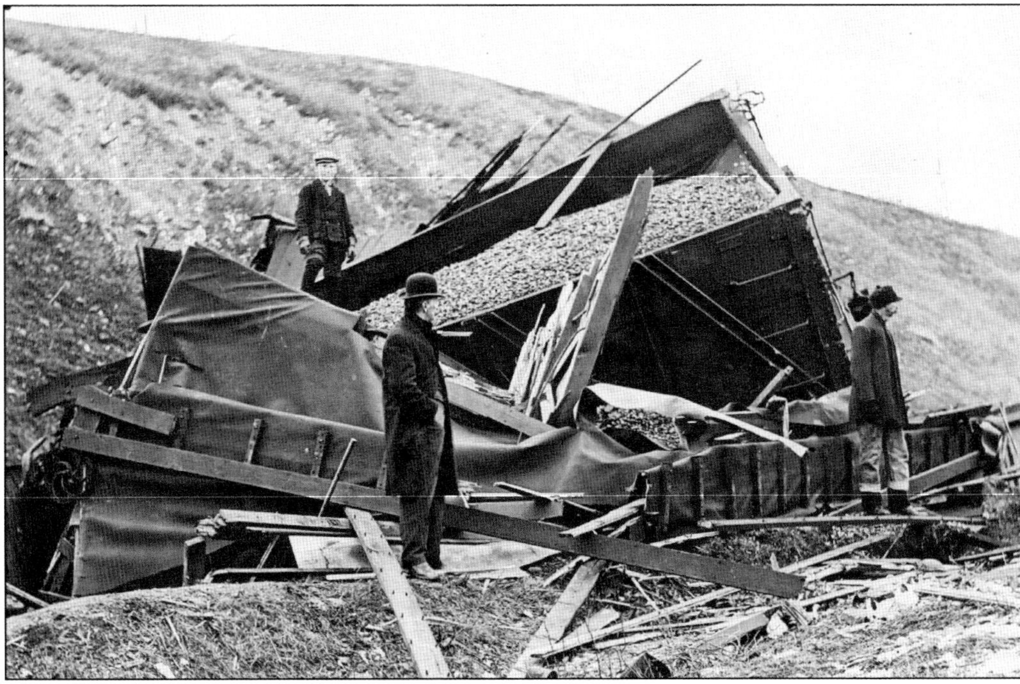

Coal Cars in Wreck. A pileup of some of the cars carrying soft coal is shown in this photograph taken on October 13, 1910. The exact cause of the accident would probably never be known according to a *Worcester Times* article on October 21, 1910.

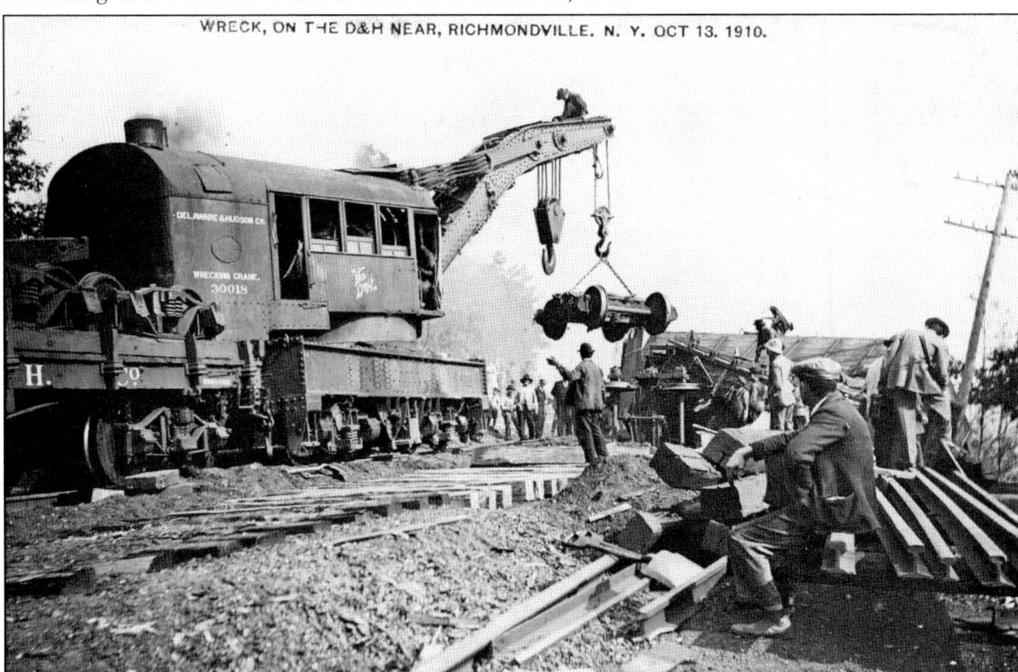

D&H Crane Cleaning Up. The Delaware and Hudson sent in its large "big hook" crane for cleanup after the wreck near Richmondville on October 13, 1910. The crane lifts wheels up in the air from one of the coal cars.

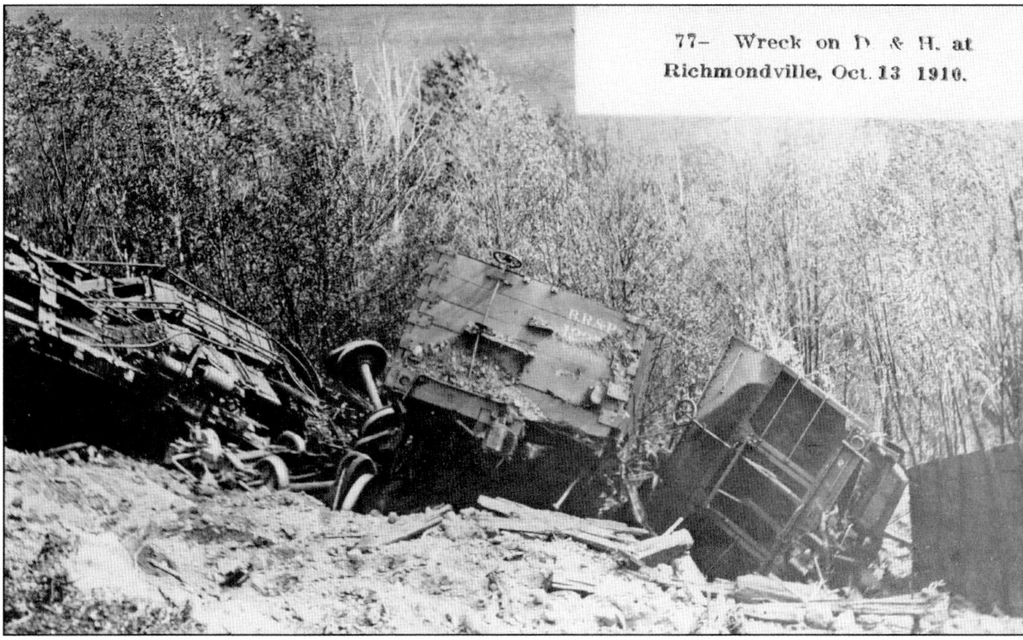

Coal Cars Down Embankment. This is the final resting place of some of the 19 coal cars involved in the October 13, 1910, wreck. A write-up in the October 21, 1910, issue of the *Worcester Times* stated that most of the cars tumbled down a 250-foot embankment. Only the caboose remained on the track. Hyndsville photographer H. B. Calkins captured many of the accident scenes on film.

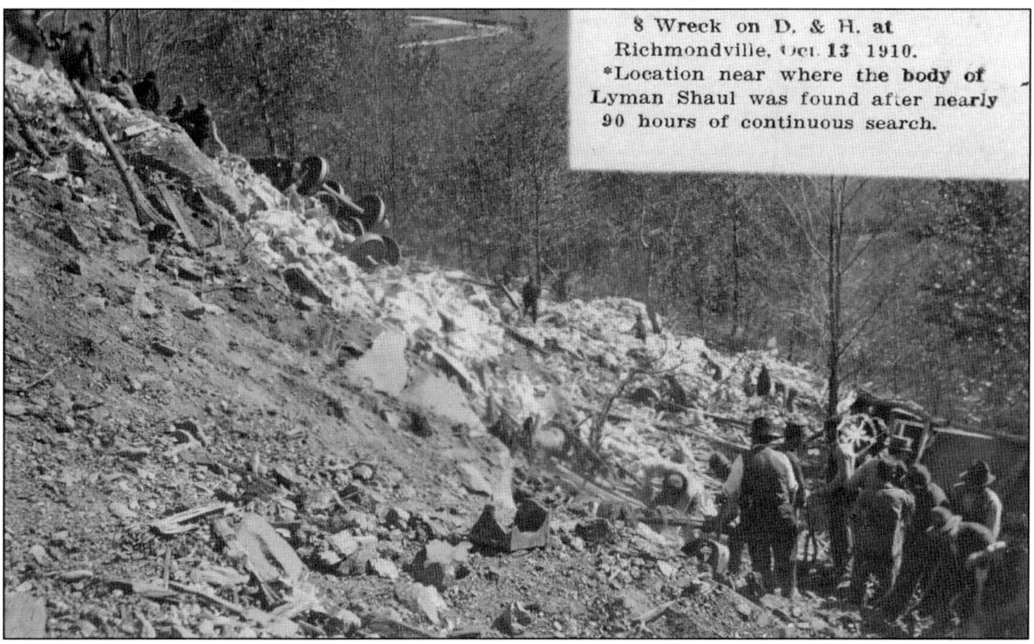

Body Found. After nearly 90 hours of searching, the body of engineer Lyman Shaul was found under a heap of dirt beneath a steel coal car 250 feet down the bank. Fireman Joseph Hickey, also killed, was found buried under a heap of coal near the track between the engine and tender. Both men were killed on October 13, 1910, as the result of an accident on Richmondville Hill. Shaul, from Binghamton, left behind a wife, and Hickey was unmarried.

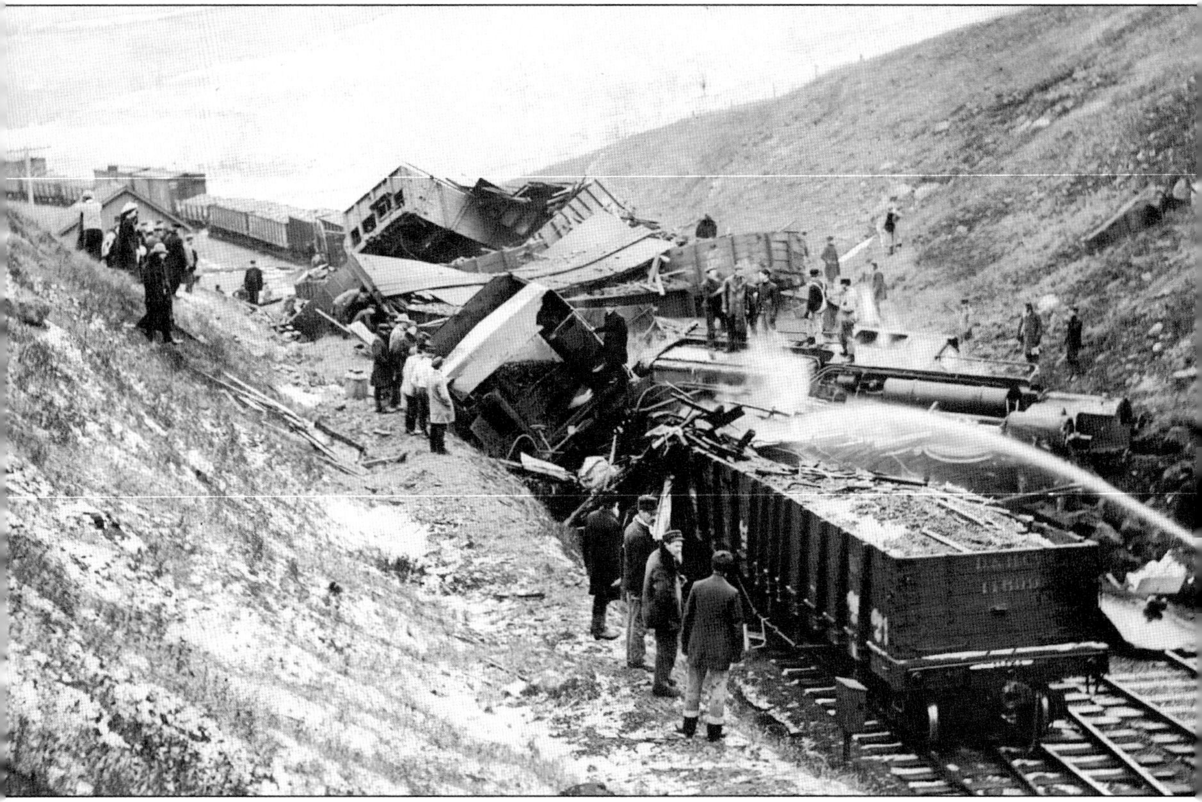

Onlookers at the Scene. Two brakemen, E. D. Lapan and John Perry, were on a coal car that went flying down the bank when the crash occurred. Although badly bruised, both escaped with their lives. Conductor Gallivan, the other crew member, was in the caboose and not hurt. All the men were from Binghamton. Onlookers are shown at the crash scene of the D&H wreck on October 13, 1910, near Richmondville.

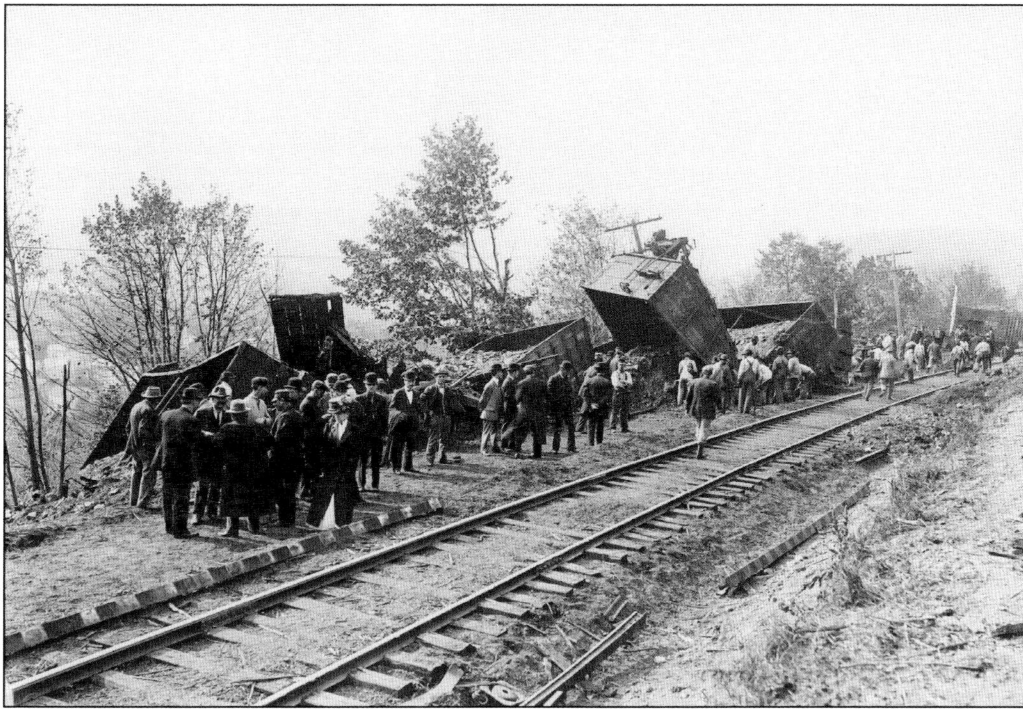

SPECTATORS VIEW WRECK. The D&H wreck on Richmondville Hill on October 13, 1910, was viewed by many spectators. This photograph, which was taken by Reightmeyer, shows the bystanders wanting to view the accident scene and overturned coal cars.

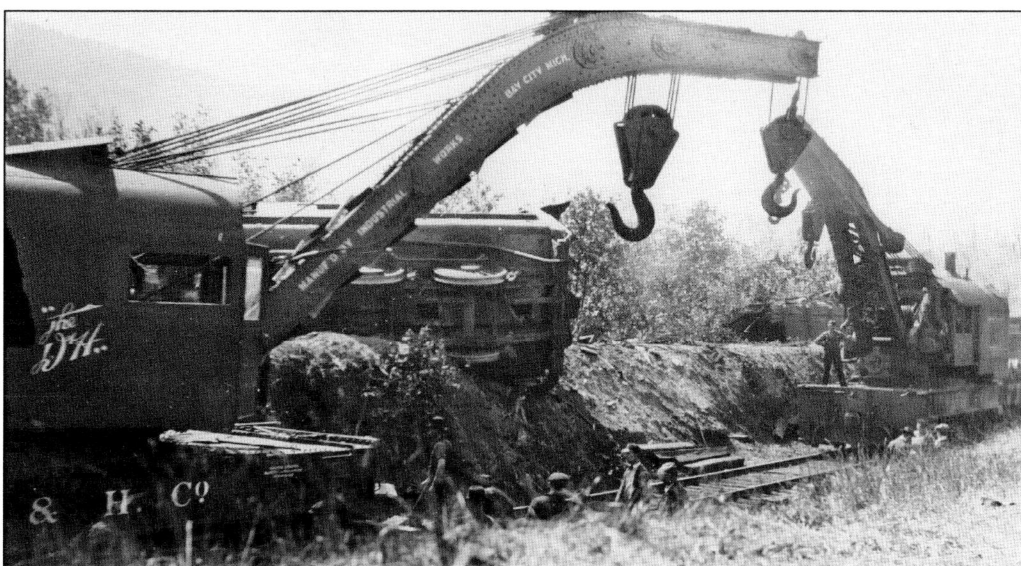

CENTRAL BRIDGE WRECK. Oneonta wreckers and cranes are at the scene of an accident on the Delaware and Hudson tracks in Central Bridge on September 28, 1913. The accident took place at 7:15 a.m. Sunday on the northbound track at a sharp curve about a half mile south of the Central Bridge station. A northbound freight had stopped for water, with proper flag protection and signals set at "danger." Another freight train crashed into the end of the standing train.

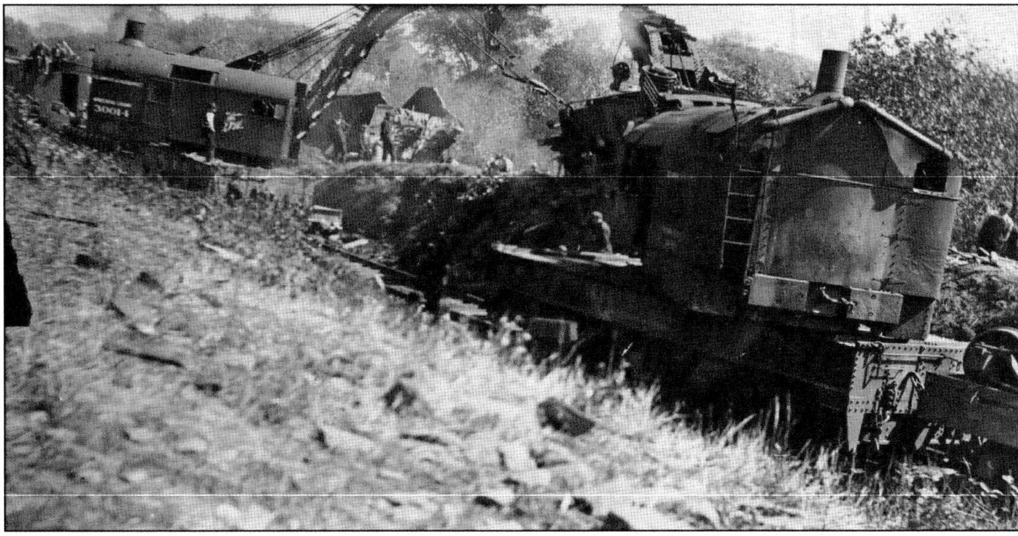

Caboose Smashed. The caboose of the northbound train involved in the D&H wreck on September 28, 1913, at Central Bridge was smashed into kindling wood. Engineer George Spencer of Oneonta was in charge of the lead engine, which overturned and was forced up over the wreckage on top of a 12-foot embankment. The cause of the accident, according to the *Cobleskill Index*, was due to the failure of the air brakes on the second engine.

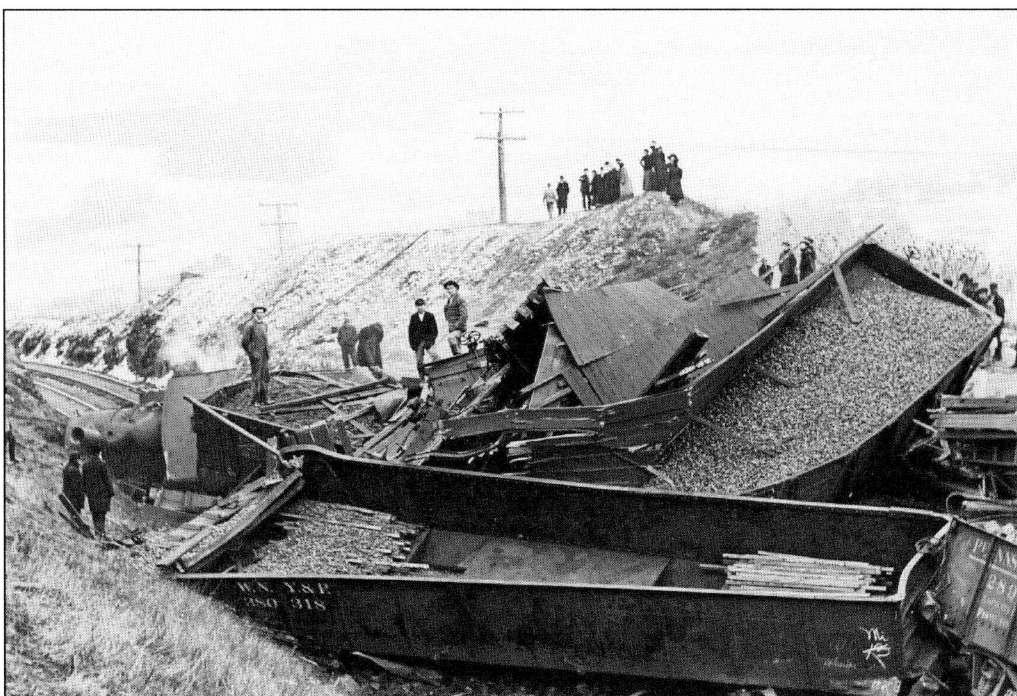

Death of a Fireman. A wreck on the D&H, about 1 mile south of Richmondville, caused the early morning death of fireman Thomas Berger. A fast-moving northbound freight train crashed into another freight train moving slowly in the same direction. The wreck took place on Friday, January 29, 1909. The dead fireman was found beneath an overturned coal car at about 1:00 a.m. Saturday.

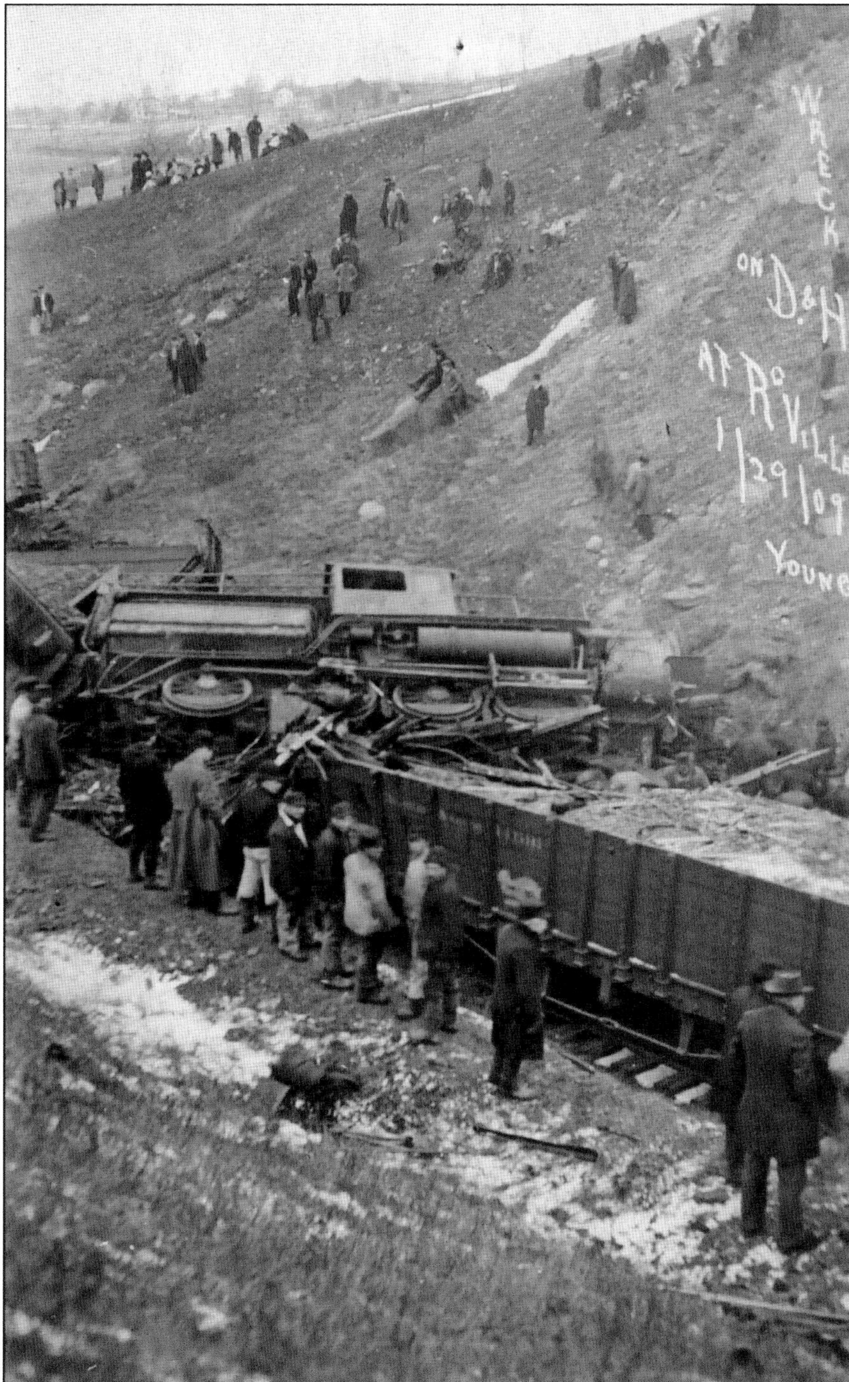

Richmondville Hill. Many wrecks on the Delaware and Hudson line happened in the Dante area of Richmondville Hill, which was named after former D&H employee H. T. Dante of Cobleskill. This accident took place on January 29, 1909. Spectators stand along the ridge to view the wreckage. Both tracks were blocked for 24 hours. The men in the caboose jumped off the train in time to save their lives when they saw danger.

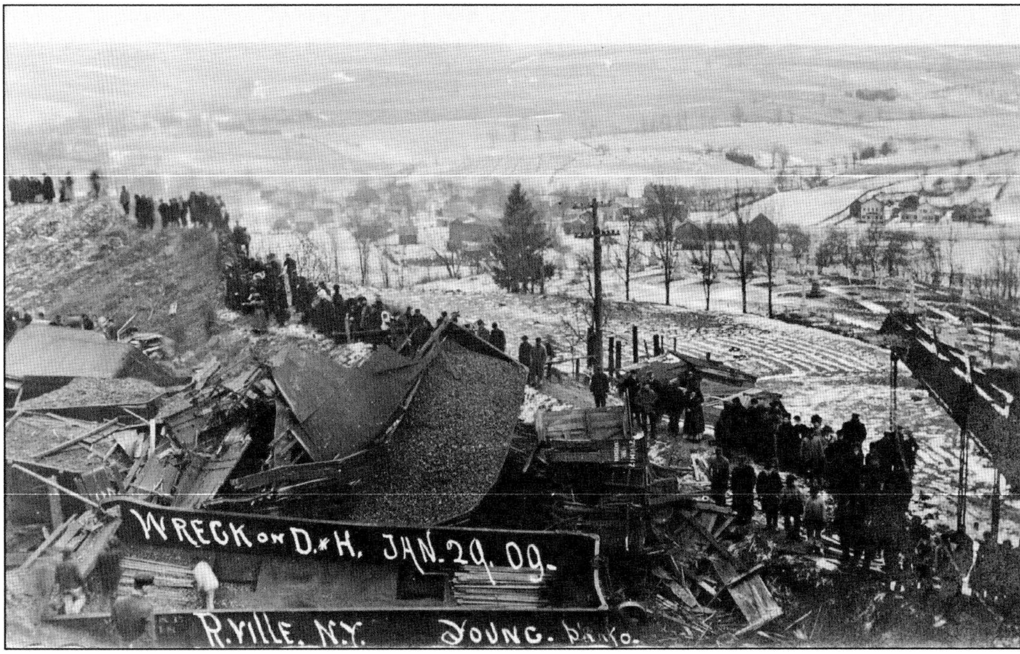

SPECTATORS AT THE SCENE. Pictured is the wreckage of a Delaware and Hudson engine and cars near Richmondville on January 29, 1909. A row of spectators stretches across the hillside the entire length of the picture.

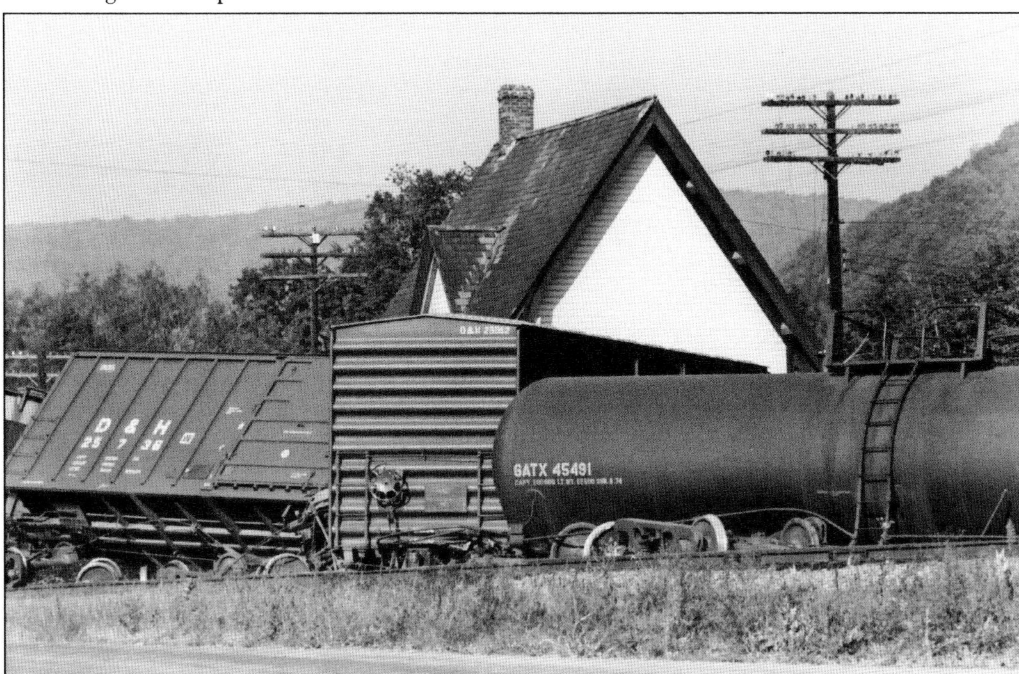

DERAILMENT AT WORCESTER. On Sunday, September 13, 1981, a derailment took place involving eight freight cars on a northbound train. Several cars went off the track and crashed into the station, knocking a corner off the building. The accident's resounding impact surprised nearby residents.

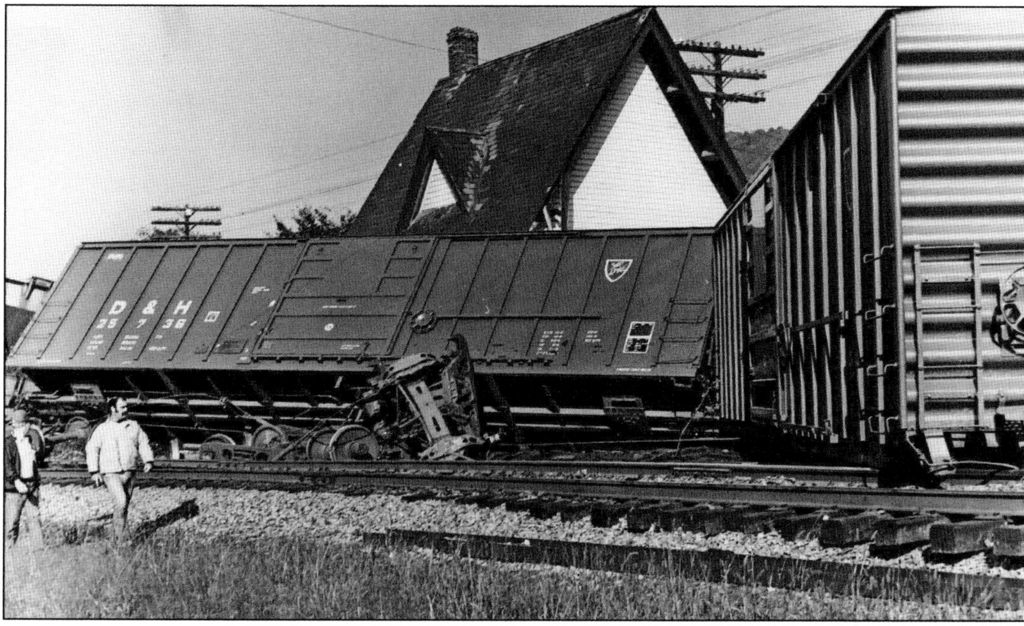

Freight Cars Involved. Worcester station was hit by a number of freight cars during the September 13, 1981, derailment. The cleanup crew, Hulcher Emergency Service from Gettysburg, Pennsylvania, had rail traffic moving by Monday morning. Of the 96 cars on the train, one contained feed, one had groceries, and the others were empty. The train was traveling from Oneonta to Albany.

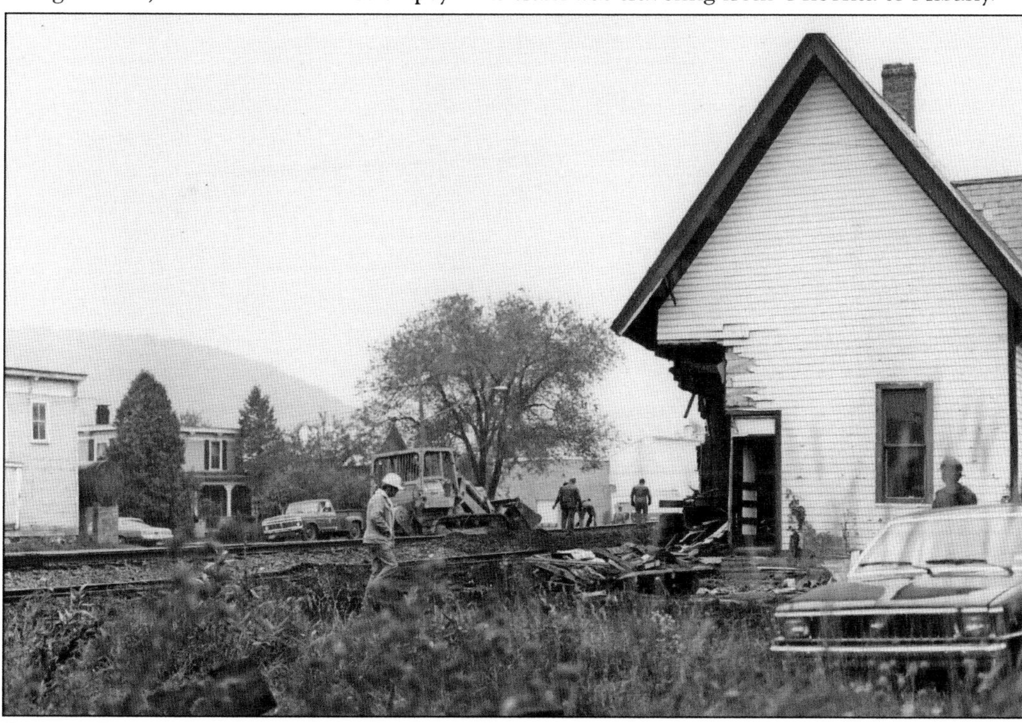

Station Damaged. Worcester's Delaware and Hudson station was hit broadside in the September 13, 1981, derailment. The front corner was completely taken out when hit by the freight cars. After that, the D&H had the building boarded up.

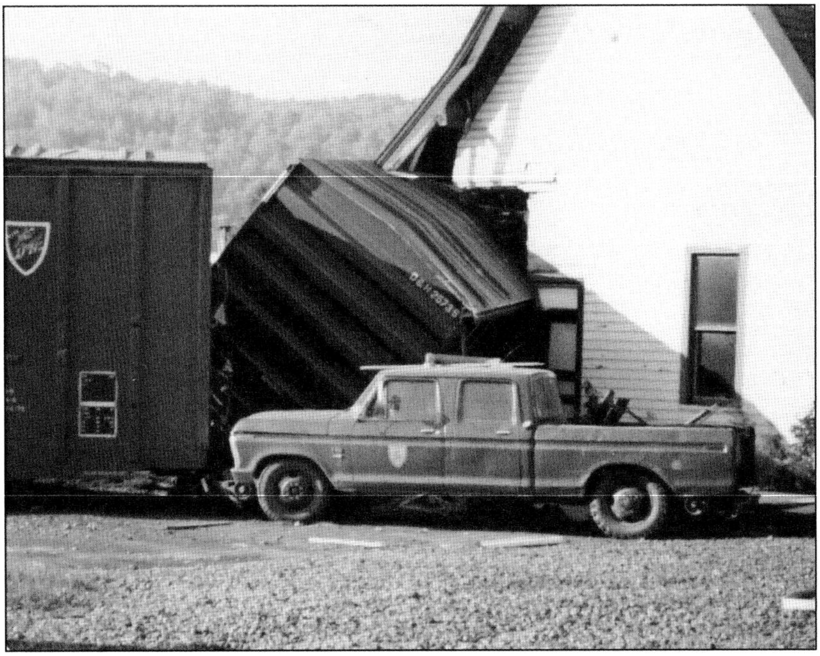

STATION SITE OF DERAILMENT. The scene of the derailment on September 13, 1981, brought out Delaware and Hudson management to check on the situation. A D&H vehicle is shown in the foreground. No cause was given for the accident.

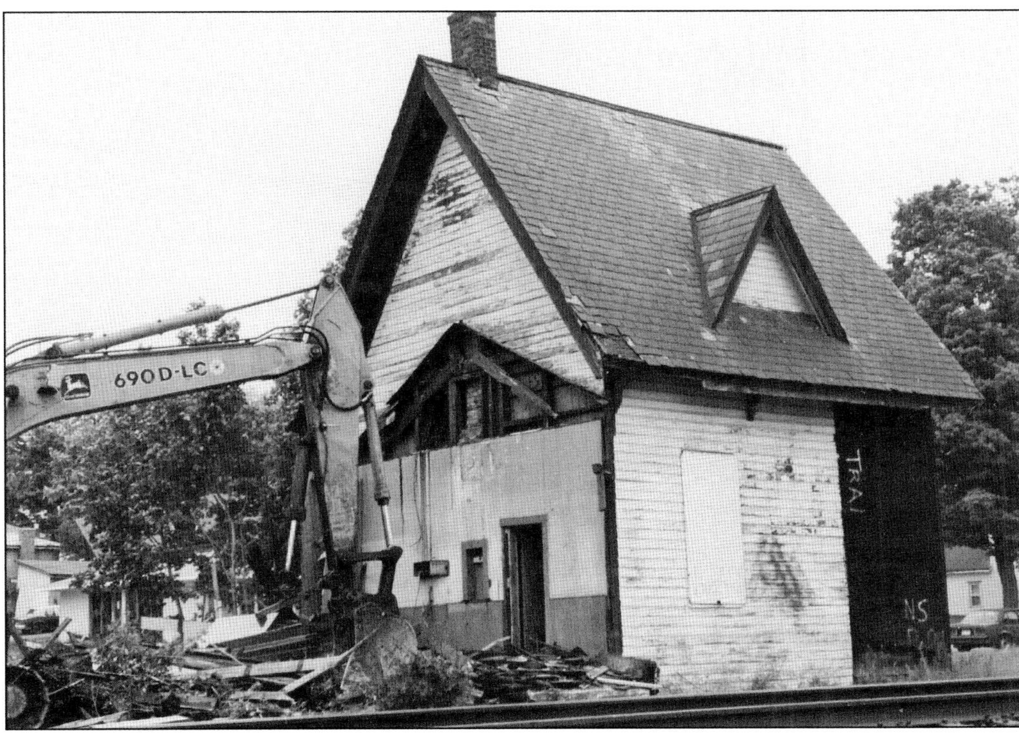

STATION DEMOLISHED. In the spring of 1999, Canadian Pacific sent in a crew and equipment to raze what remained of the little Worcester station, which was built in 1879. Slate from the roof, siding, fixtures, and doors were hauled away in dumpsters. The station closed after the last passenger train stopped there on January 24, 1963.

Seven

D&H Employees

Dedicated men of vision, steady nerves, and brawn are descriptions of the workers of the Albany and Susquehanna and Delaware and Hudson Company of yesteryear. Railroading was often a dangerous occupation. The old link and pin system of coupling cars was responsible for many employees losing their fingers.

Employees earned 25¢ per hour in 1923, and in 1942 wages increased to $1.10 per hour. During World War I, several women worked as agents or telegraphers. Elizabeth Miller of East Worcester devoted 30 years of continuous service to the D&H Railway. She began her career on September 1, 1907, with the midnight to 8:00 a.m. shift, retiring in 1937 as the only remaining woman telegrapher in the service of the company.

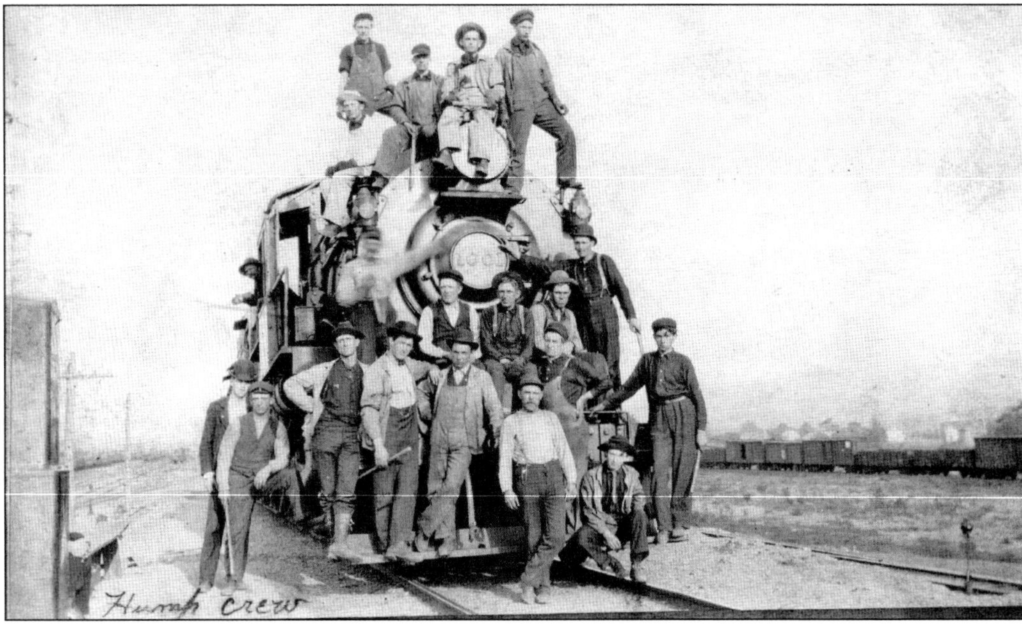

THE HUMP CREW. "Humping" cars involves pushing a string of cars from a receiving yard track over a hump at the entrance of a "classification" yard into a different track to make up varied trains. In the days of steam locomotives, it would take many men, such as the engine crew, to "pull the pins" at the top of the hill and someone at each switch to direct cars into the proper tracks.

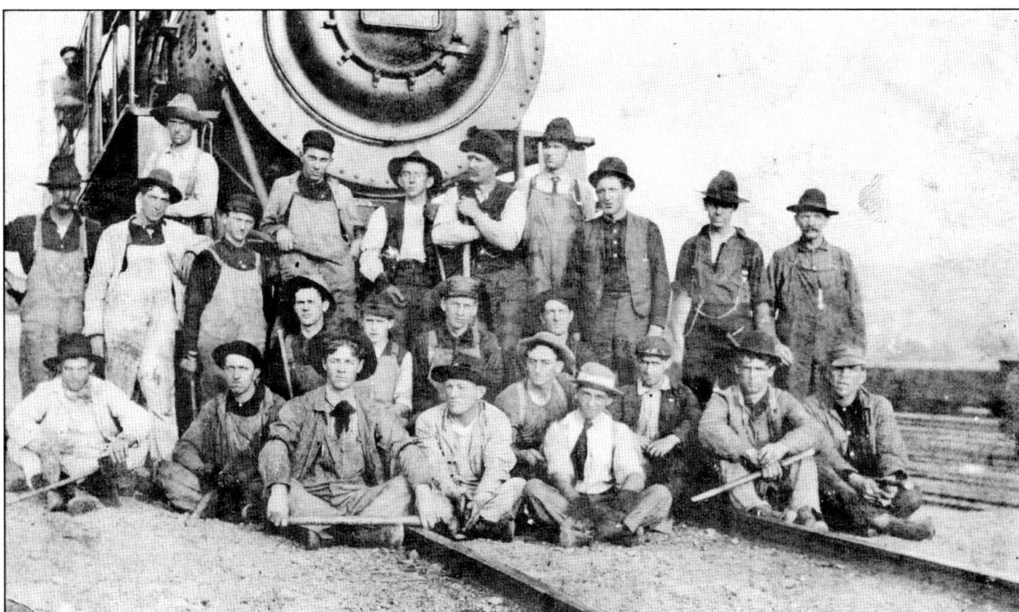

D&H YARD. Another group of men employed by the D&H rail yard in Oneonta was the "hump" crew. Today some of the humps are automated—switches get thrown from a control tower and only one man on the ground is the "pin puller." The sticks held by the men were placed behind wheels of a car so it would not roll back.

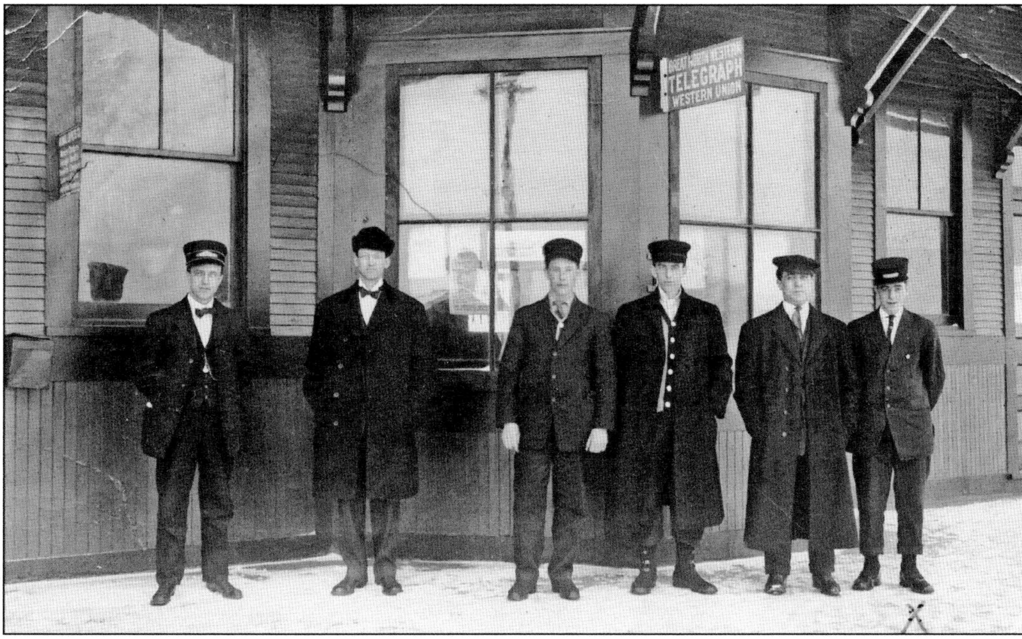

TELEGRAPHERS AND STATION AGENTS. Uniformed telegraphers and station agents line up for a photograph. This card, which was mailed to a Vermont address, is signed, "Regards to all, your son Thomas." The man on the far right, by the X, must be Thomas Bowes.

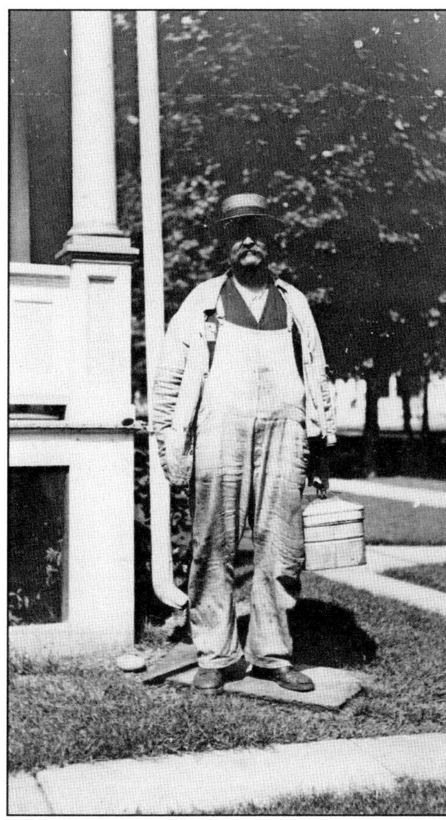

CONDUCTOR A. D. CUCK. Cuck, of Oneonta, poses with his dinner pail before going to work at the Delaware and Hudson station to catch a train.

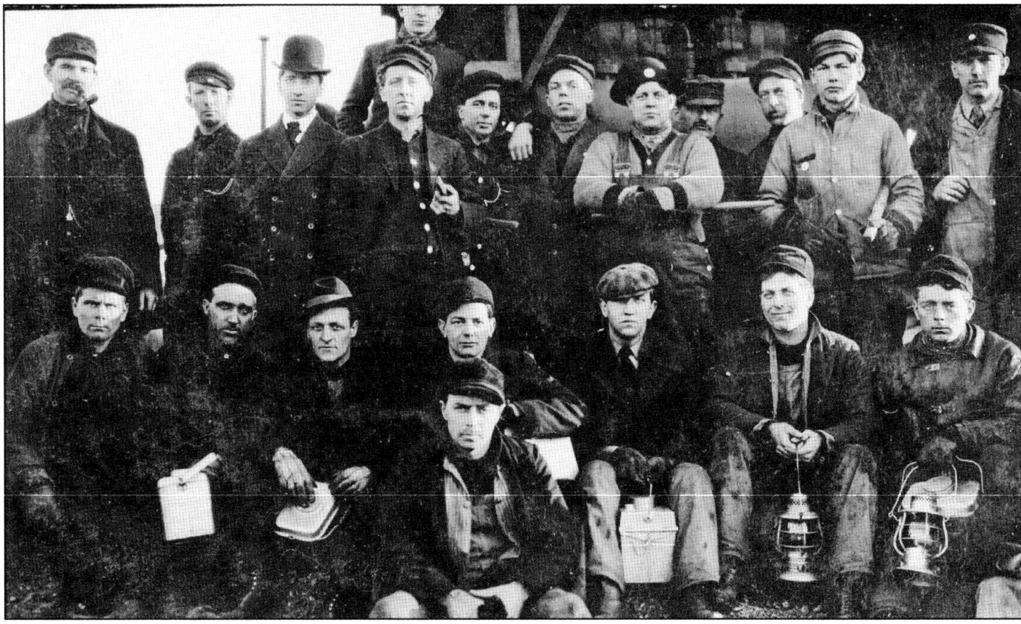

D&H Employees. A group of D&H employees gathers at the Oneonta yard for a picture. The gathering includes engineers, conductors, brakemen, "hump" crew, and signalmen with lanterns.

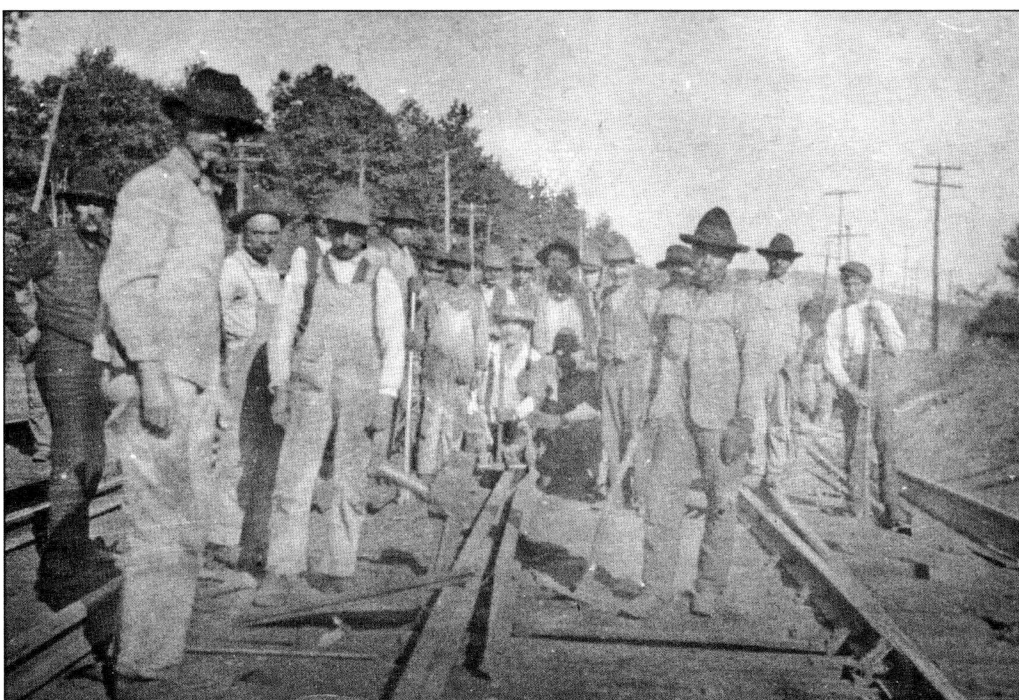

Railroad Gang. This is an early shot of men working on the railroad laying iron rails and ties. This was hard, physical work, and many strong men were needed when the railroad came through from Albany to Binghamton.

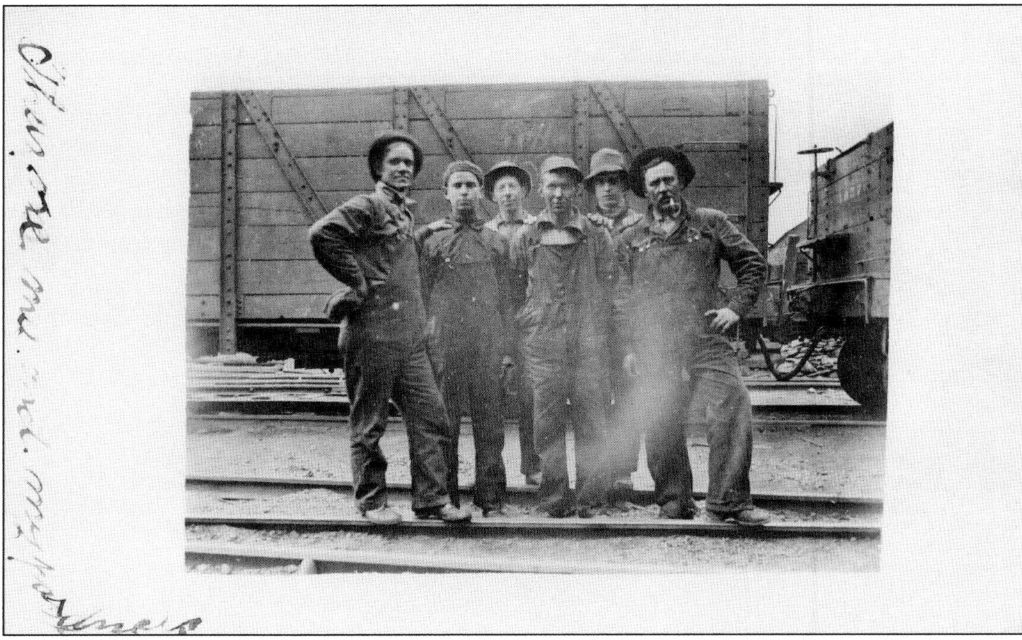

D&H Workers. Another group of workers is shown on a card mailed from Quaker Street on October 18, 1911. The message on the front of the card reads, "This was me and my partners."

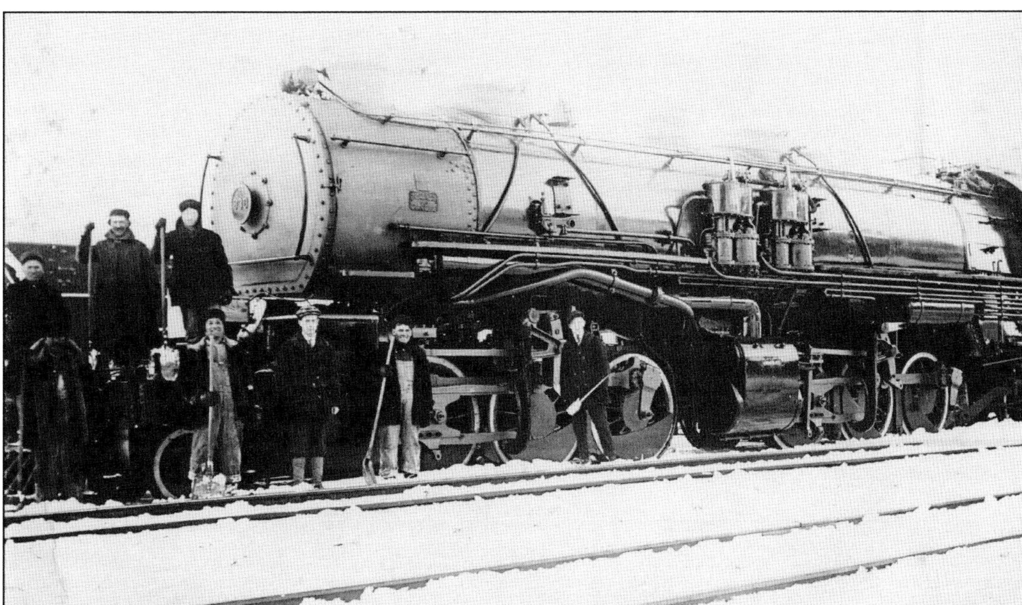

Engine Crew. The engine crew prepares to shovel snow off the locomotive as it waits at the Worcester station.

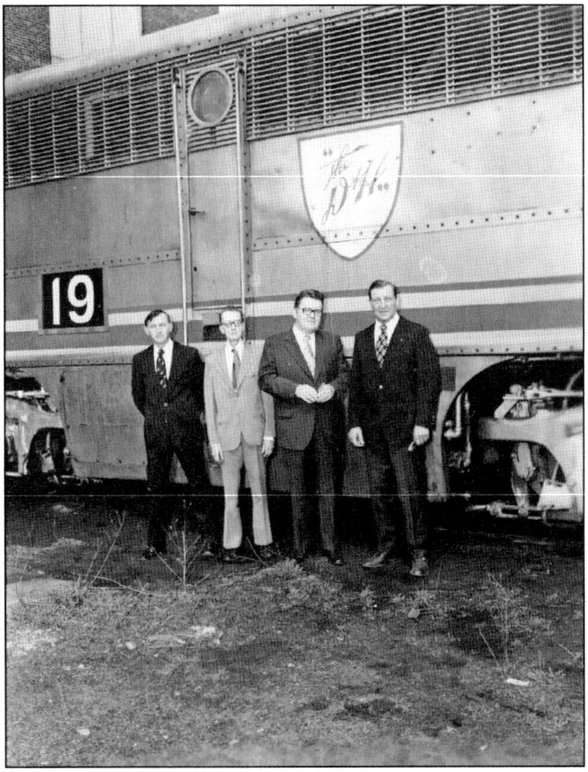

Management Team. A D&H Company management team stands in front of a new locomotive in the Albany area.

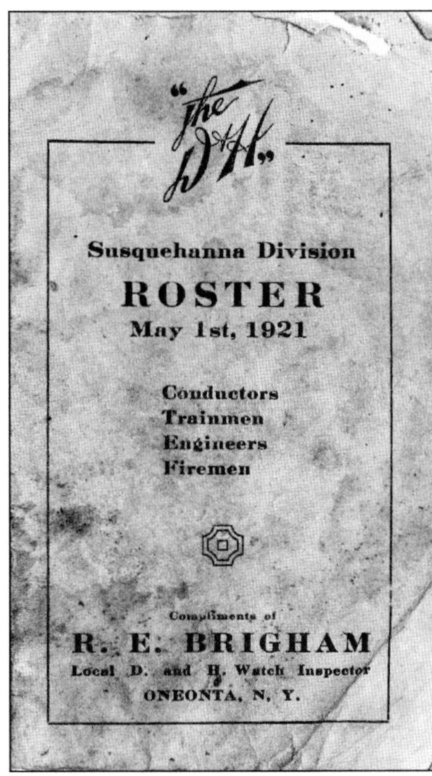

D&H Roster. This little booklet by the Susquehanna Division of the D&H is dated May 1, 1921. It gives a list of all the conductors, trainmen, engineers, and firemen in that division. This was a complimentary book given out by R.E. Brigham, a local D&H watch inspector.

Eight

Trains

Manifest freight trains filled with anthracite coal filled the coffers of the Delaware and Hudson during the early 20th century. A steady parade of coal trains kept the tracks humming.

Trains also provided mail service, transportation for circuses, farm produce delivery, and a means for delivering tankers of milk to city markets. Shipments of milk ended when bulk tanks were added to farms for tractor-trailer pickup.

The 1993 *Kaatskill Life* story by Peter L. Finch states, "Everytime a freight train rolls by, over 100 tractor trailers are riding rails instead of congesting highways, stressing and weakening bridges, and costing taxpayers billions of dollars in road repairs." The author maintains that railroads are more environmentally friendly, using far less fuel, creating less pollution, and disturbing smaller areas of land compared to interstate highways. They also ship bulk products much more economically.

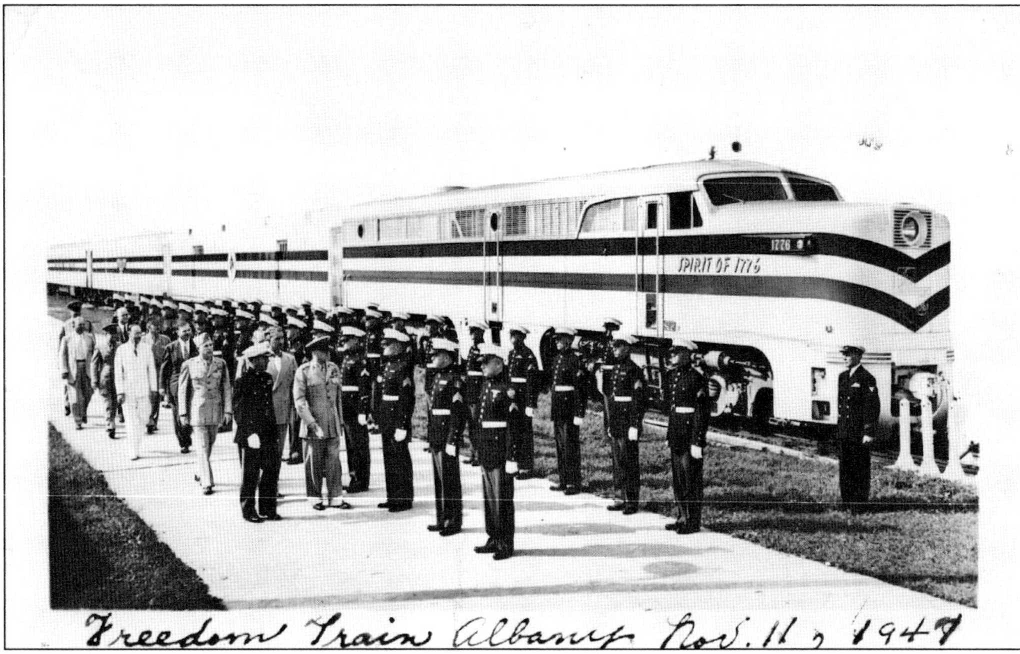

"Freedom Train." A group of Marines was assigned to accompany the "Freedom Train" to Albany on November 11, 1947. The *Spirit of 1776* hauled a precious cargo—the U.S. Constitution, the Declaration of Independence, the Bill of Rights, the Gettysburg Address, and other important historic documents. The train spent several days in the area to allow schoolchildren to view the traveling history exhibit.

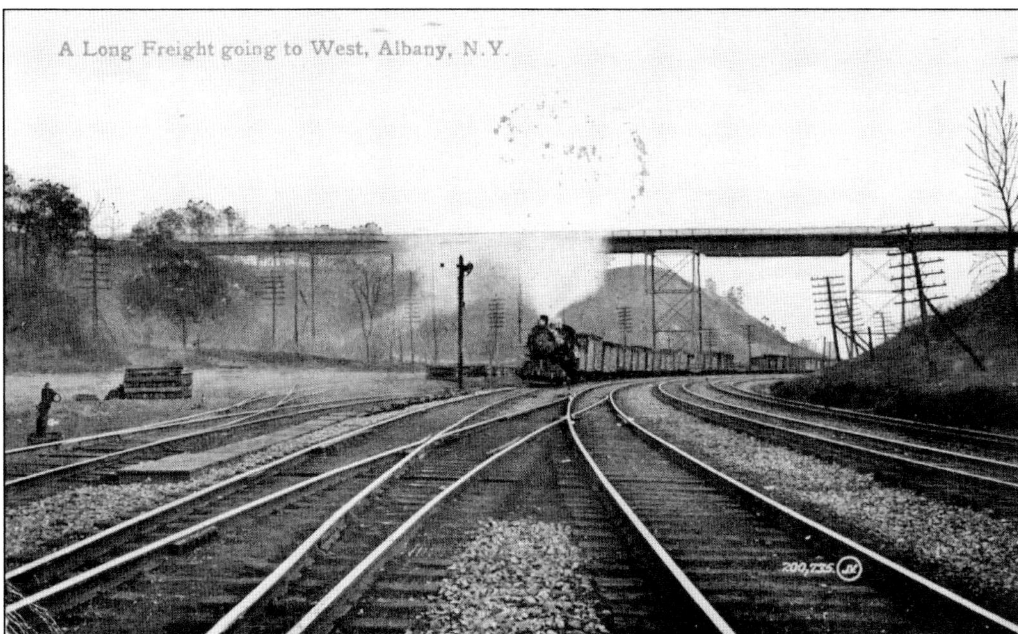

Westward Bound. This is possibly a New York Central freight train traveling west on its way to the West Albany yard in 1909.

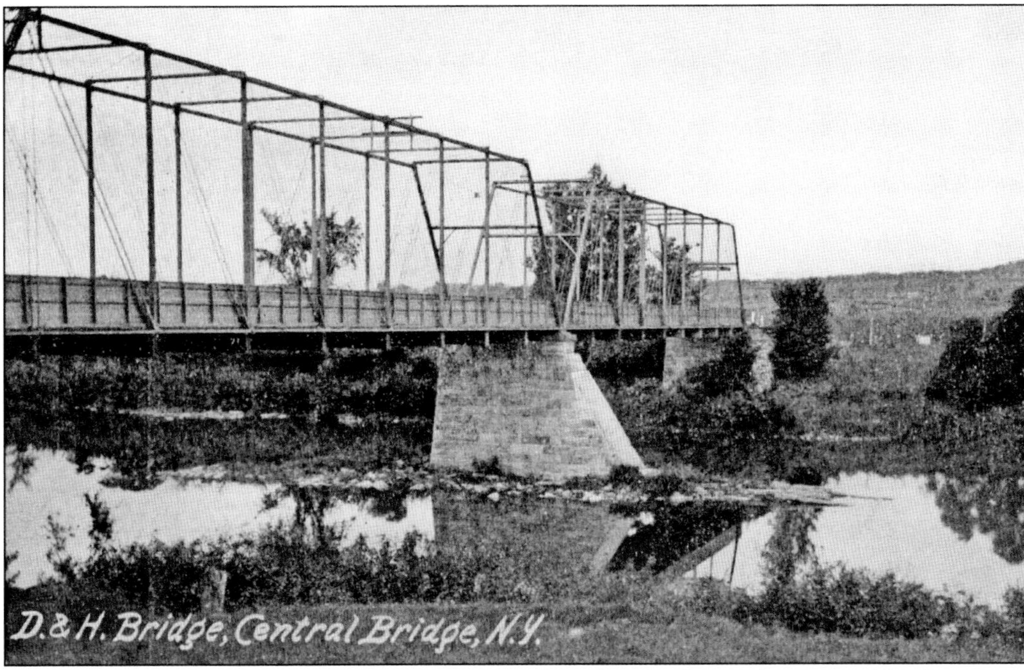

D&H Bridge. This is a view of the Delaware and Hudson bridge in the Central Bridge area.

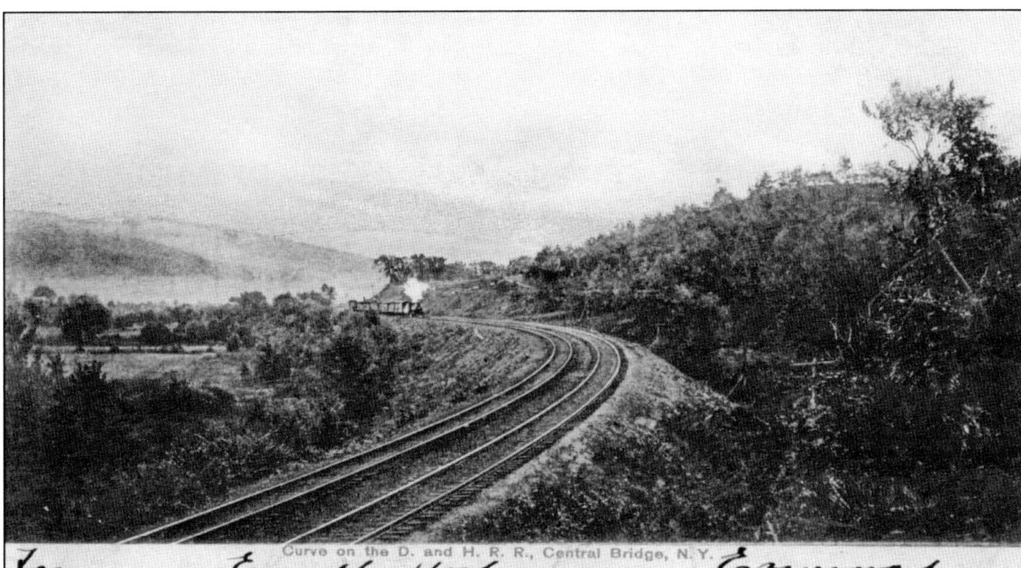

Sharp Curve. Smoke billows from a freight train as it negotiates a sharp curve near the Central Bridge area in 1907.

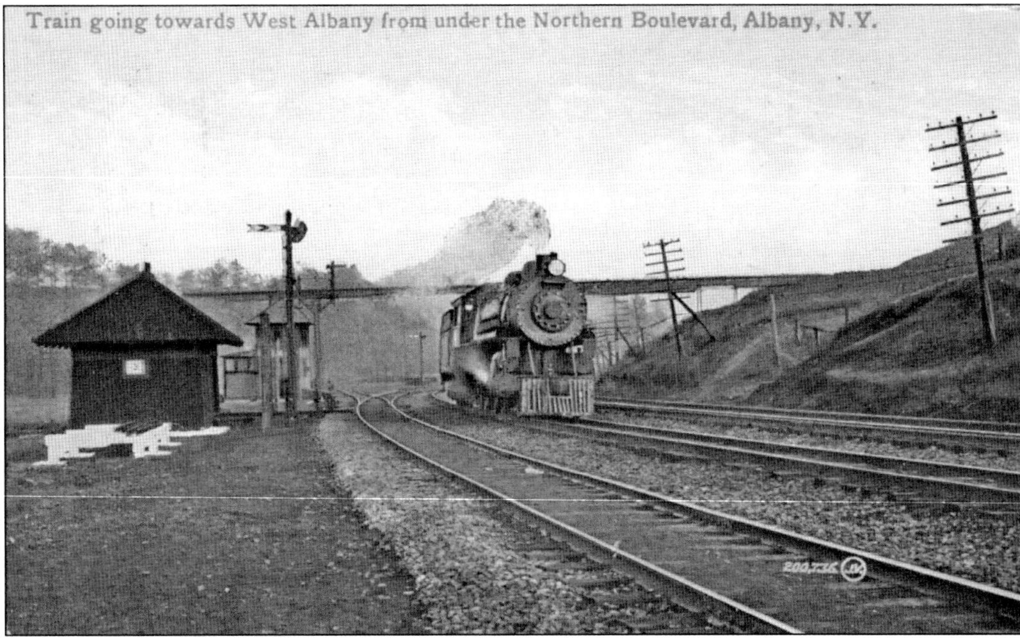

TRAIN GOING WEST. This is possibly a New York Central train heading toward West Albany from the Northern Boulevard area.

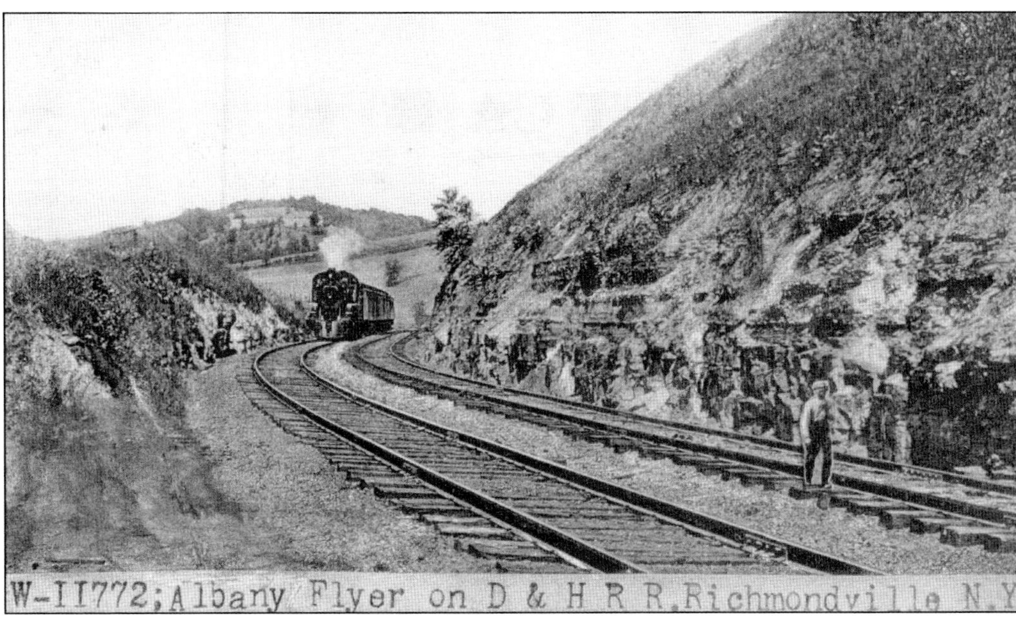

ALBANY FLYER. The *Albany Flyer* travels on tracks near Richmondville Hill. Flyers offered reliable, satisfactory service to the area.

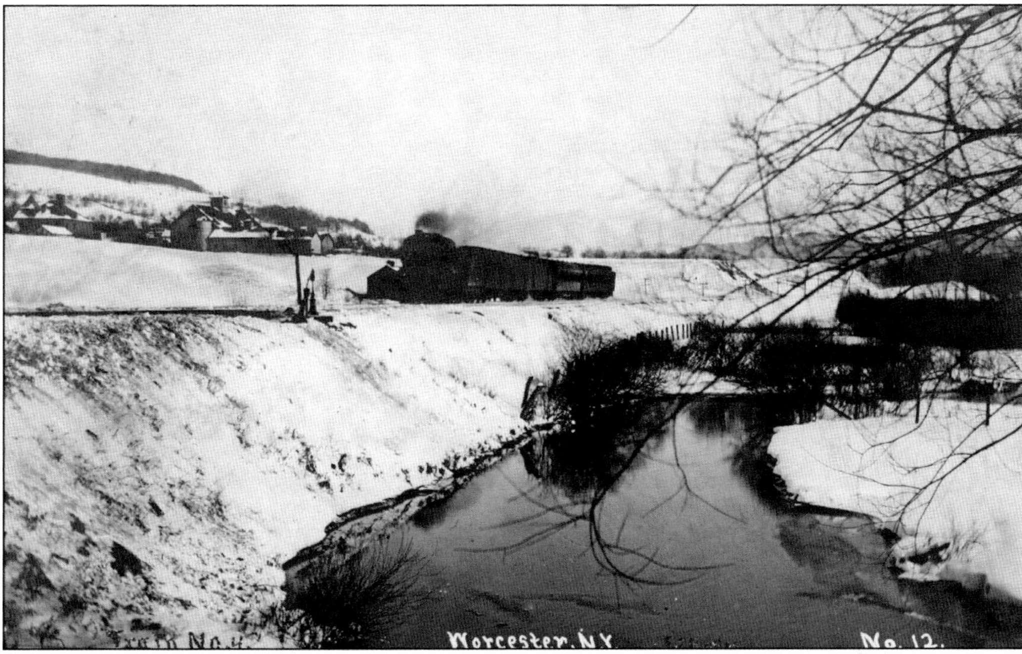

PASSENGER TRAIN. A D&H passenger train from Albany heads into Worcester and its station in 1903. On January 24, 1963, the final passenger train traveled through Worcester and other towns and villages on the line.

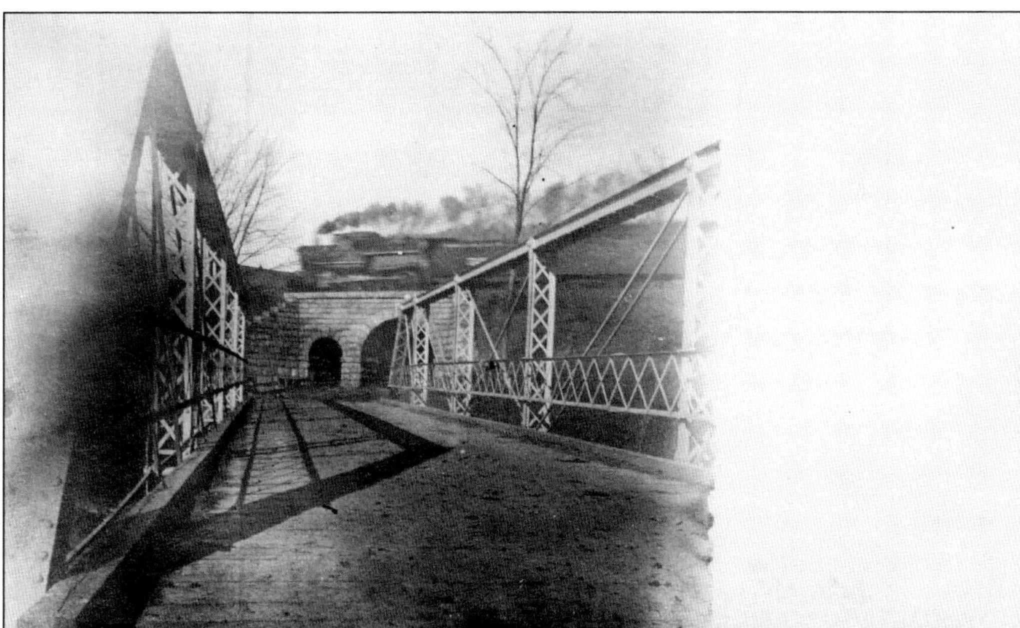

OLD GRISTMILL BRIDGE. A steam locomotive heads toward Oneonta near the old gristmill bridge not far from Maryland. This postcard shows the south side of the bridge leading to stone archways and Route 7 on the other side of the railroad.

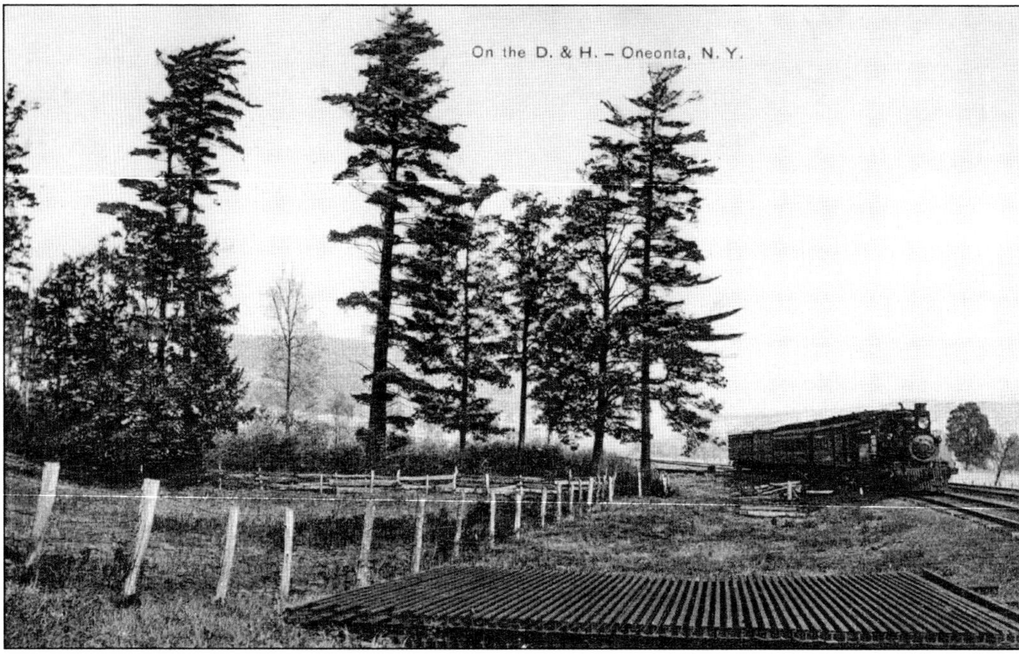

D&H Train. This passenger train is traveling near Oneonta in 1911 on its way back to Albany.

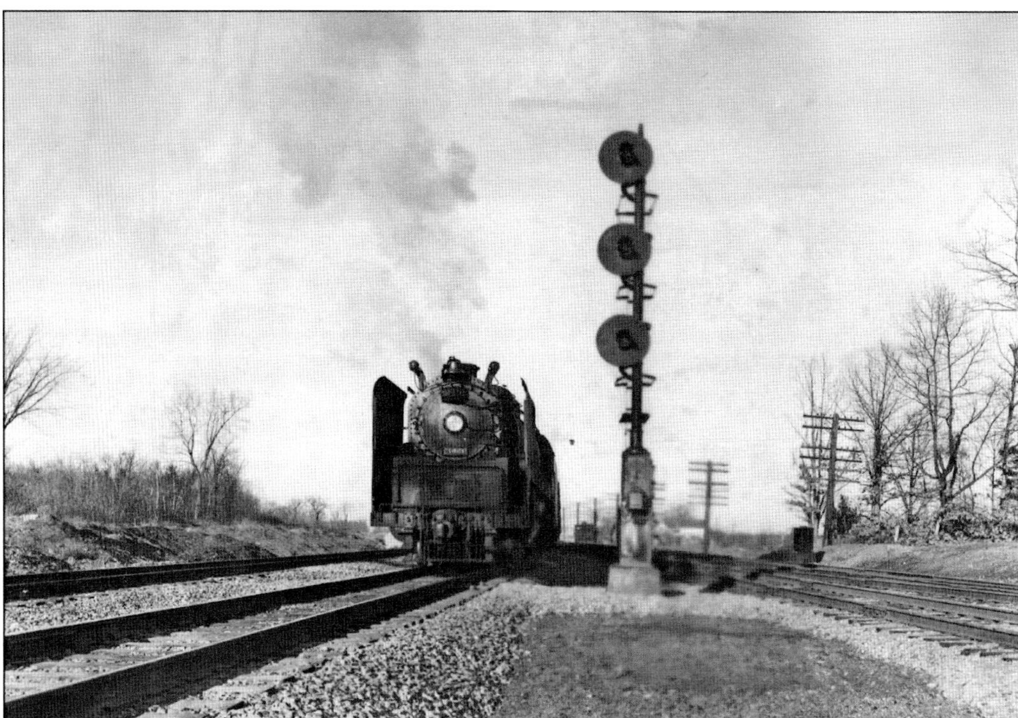

Signal Lights Ahead. A D&H train approaches the railroad's signal lights. In the early days of railroading, signals were often set by hand; today everything is automatic.

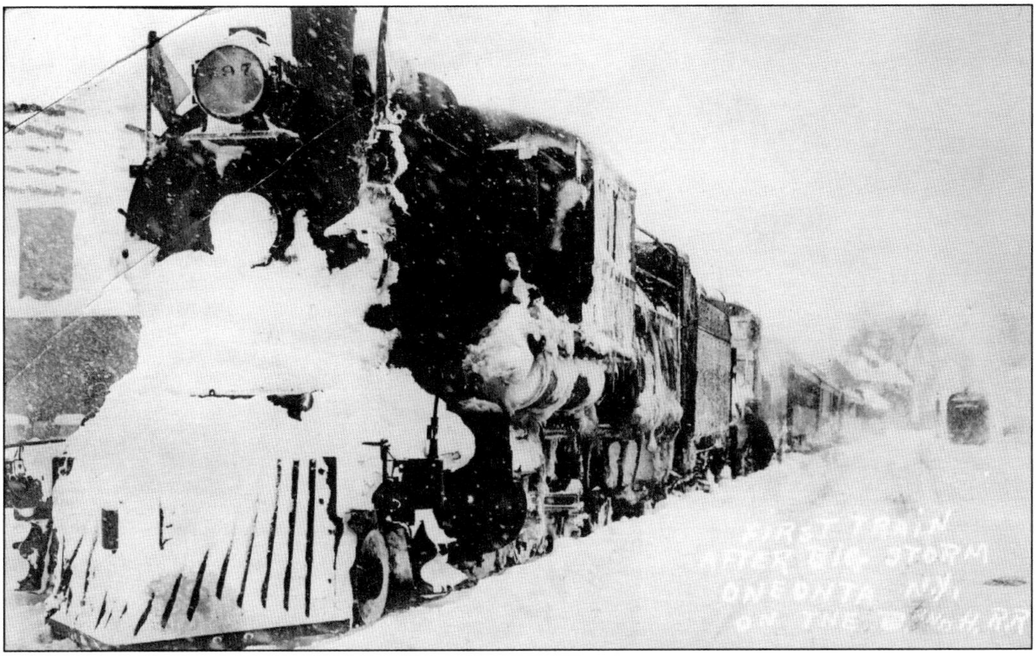

WINTER ON THE D&H. The message on the reverse side of this card reads, "This is one of the passenger trains on the D&H snowed in. The snow is about three feet deep." The card was mailed from Oneonta in 1914.

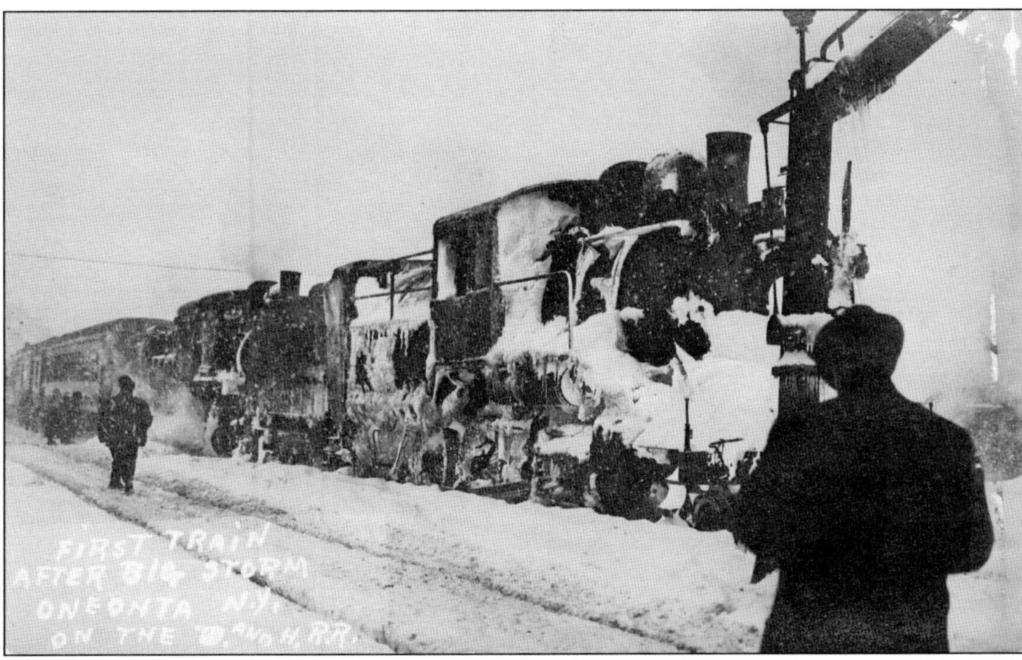

AFTER THE STORM. This is the first train that arrived in Oneonta after a big storm in 1914. The engine and cars are covered with snow and icicles.

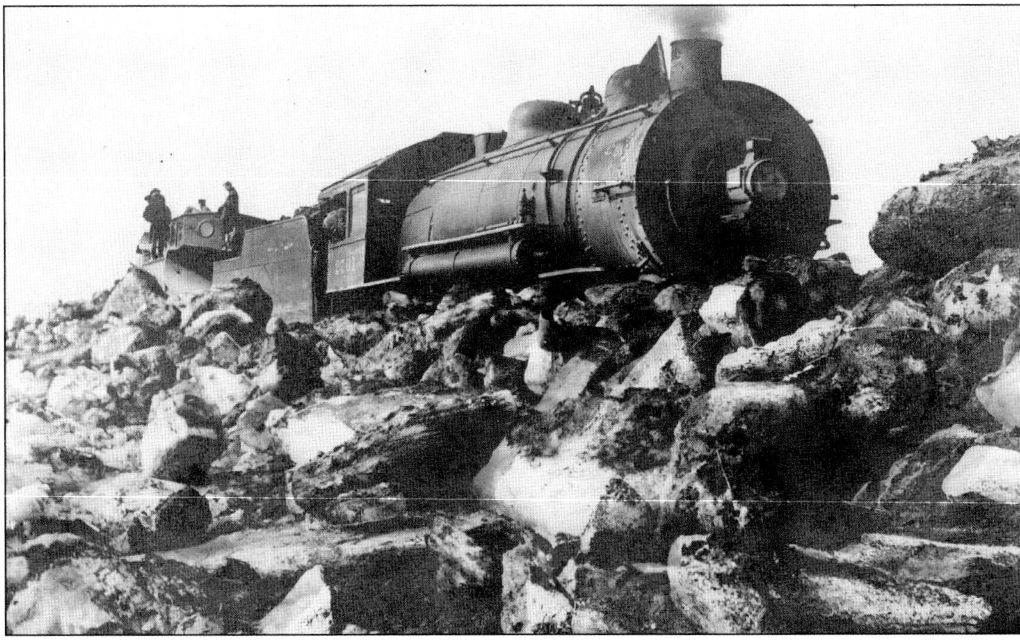

Storm Picture. This is another photograph of a D&H locomotive after the 1914 storm. The storm, which gathered off the coast of Georgia, went out to sea and doubled back and struck New Jersey and New York as a nor'easter in January 1914. Railroad traffic was altered temporarily.

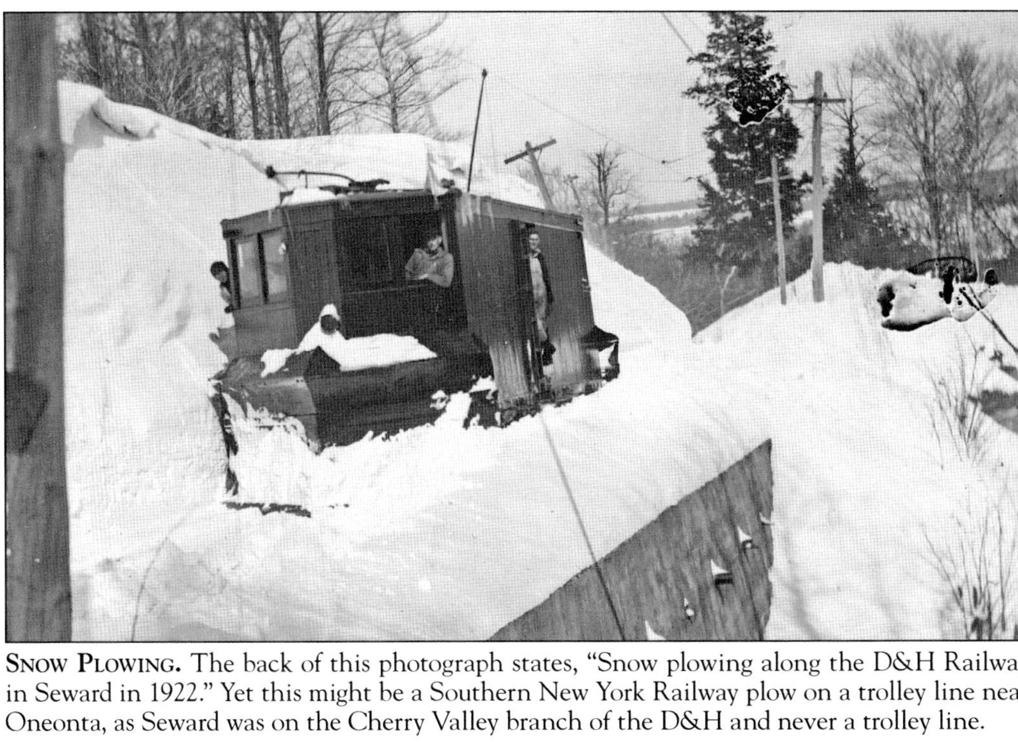

Snow Plowing. The back of this photograph states, "Snow plowing along the D&H Railway in Seward in 1922." Yet this might be a Southern New York Railway plow on a trolley line near Oneonta, as Seward was on the Cherry Valley branch of the D&H and never a trolley line.

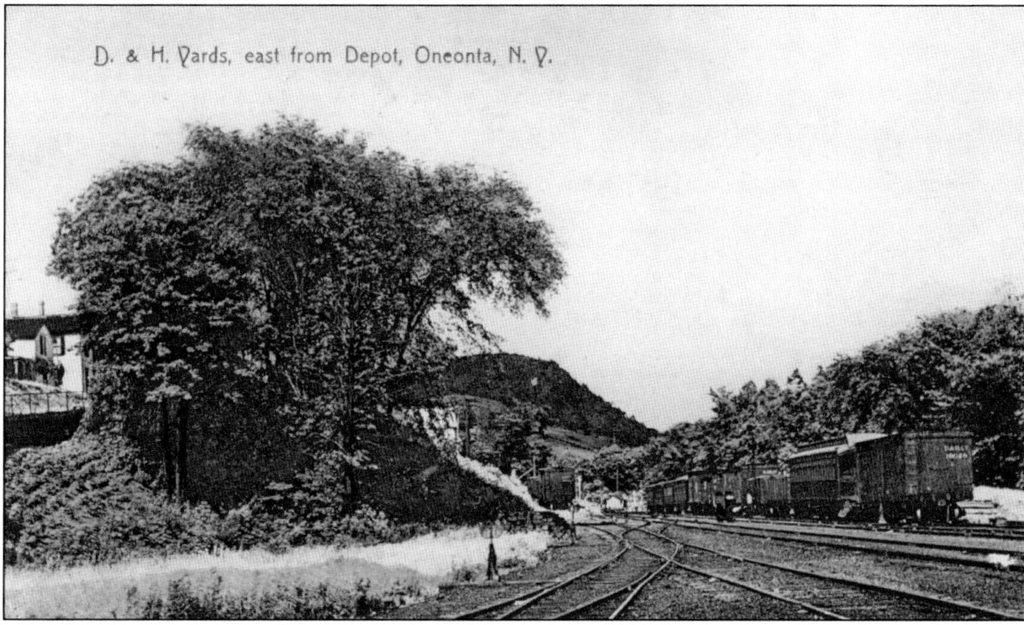

A VIEW OF THE YARDS. A freight train pulls into the D&H yards in Oneonta in 1907; this was east of the station.

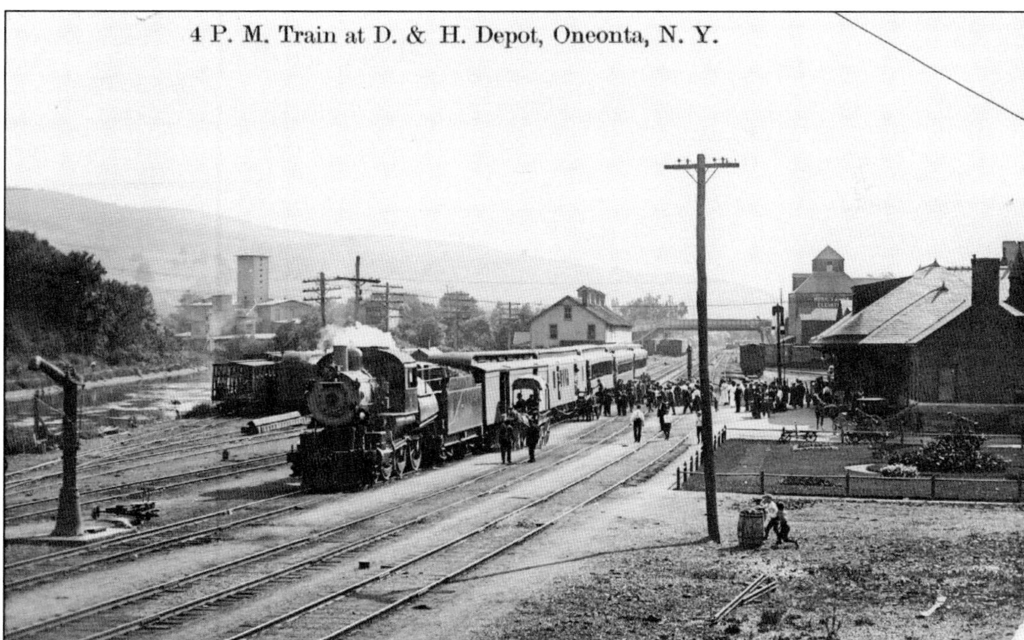

4:00 P.M. TRAIN. A 4:00 p.m. passenger train pulls into Oneonta station. At least five or six passenger trains traveled back and forth from Albany to Binghamton in the heyday of the D&H in the early 20th century.

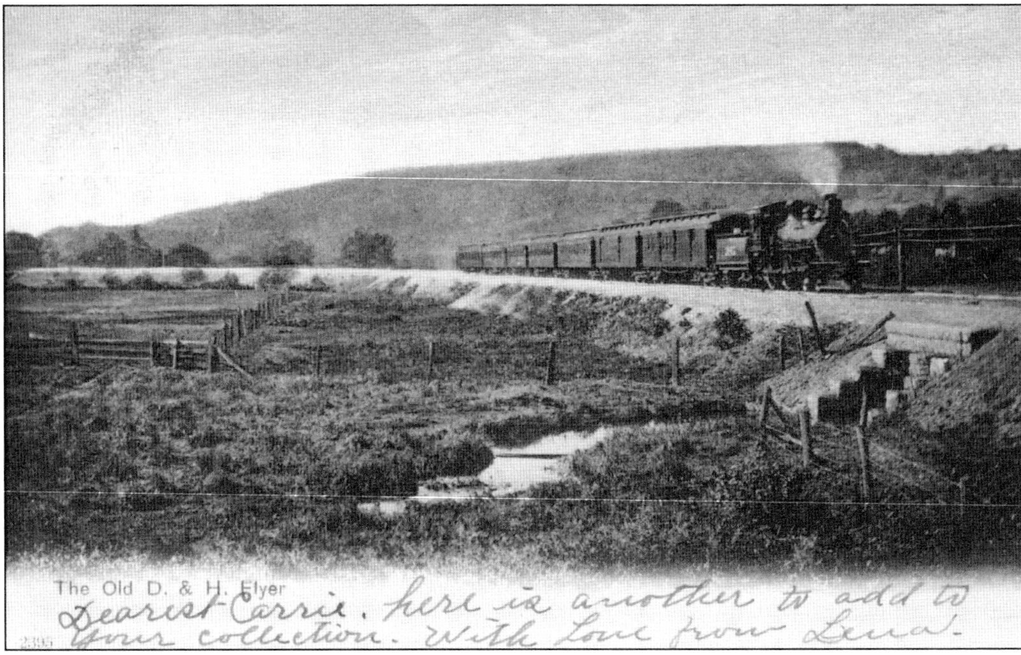

The Old Flyer. This 1906 postcard features a photograph of the old D&H Flyer, one of the daily passenger trains from Albany to Binghamton.

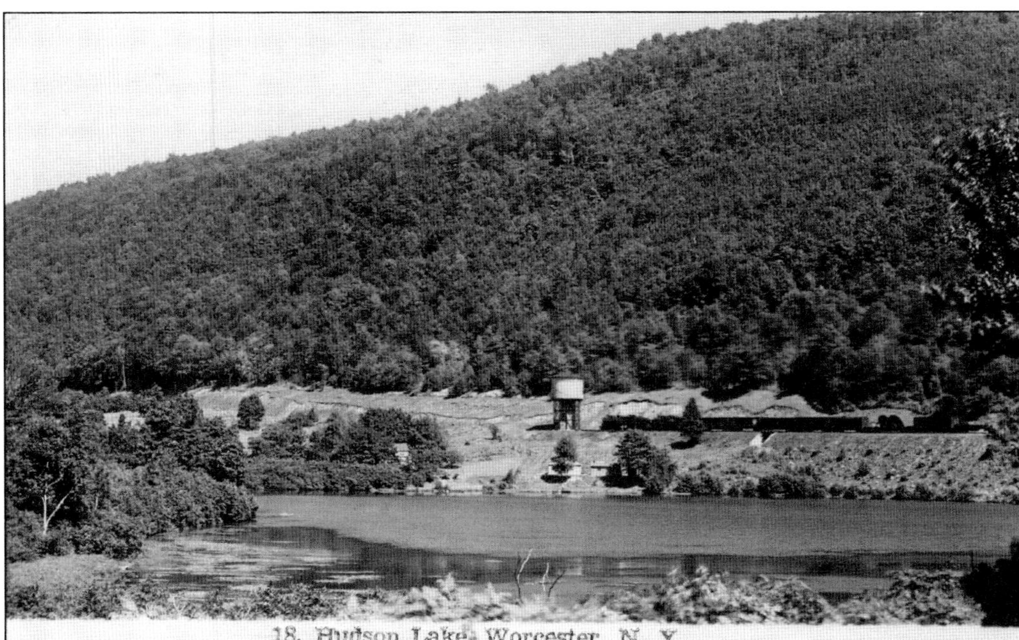

Hudson Lake. A D&H freight train travels the upper tracks, now no longer there, between East Worcester and Worcester. The water tower (near the train) received water from Hudson Lake. At one time, beavers built a dam in the area, making it difficult to keep water in the tower.

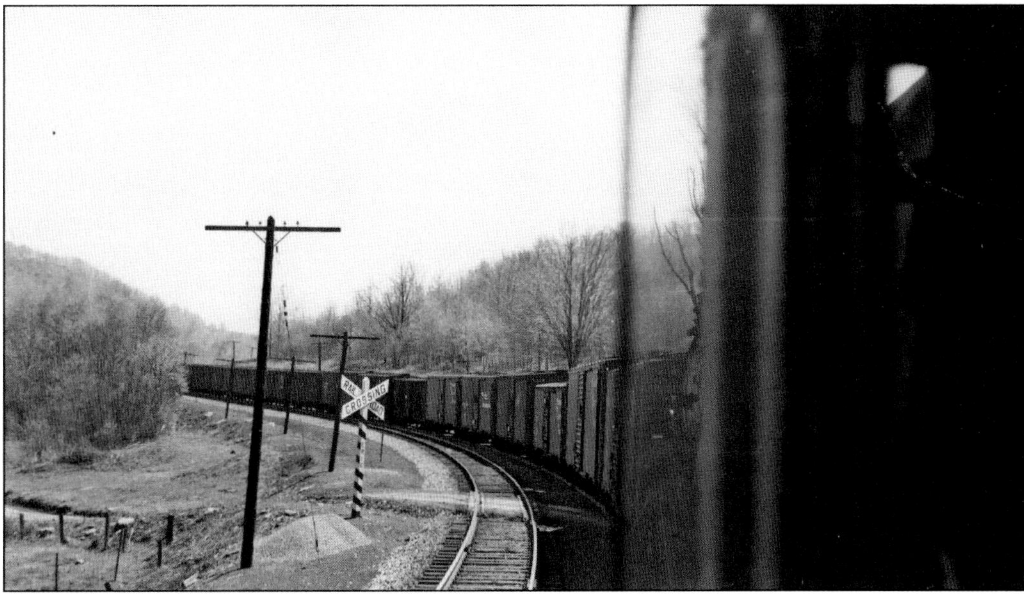

Up the Grade. Delaware and Hudson train No. 3 is shown ascending the grade at Richmondville Hill. The photograph was taken from a pusher that was necessary for the engine and freight cars to negotiate the hill. Note the railroad crossing sign in the middle of the photograph.

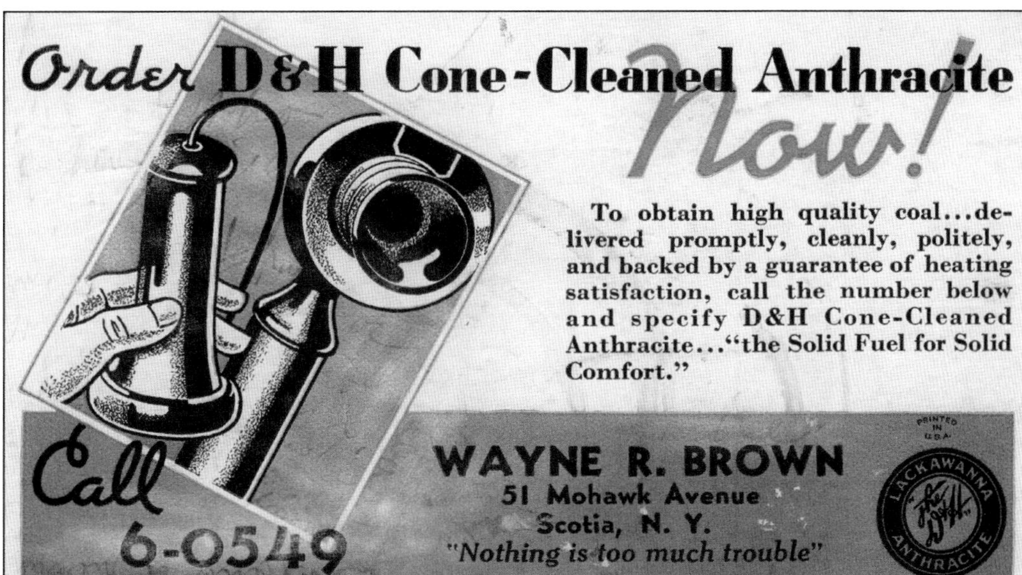

Old-Time Blotter. An old-time blotter reminds the reader that D&H had lots of cone-cleaned anthracite for sale. Paper items advertising the D&H are highly collectible.

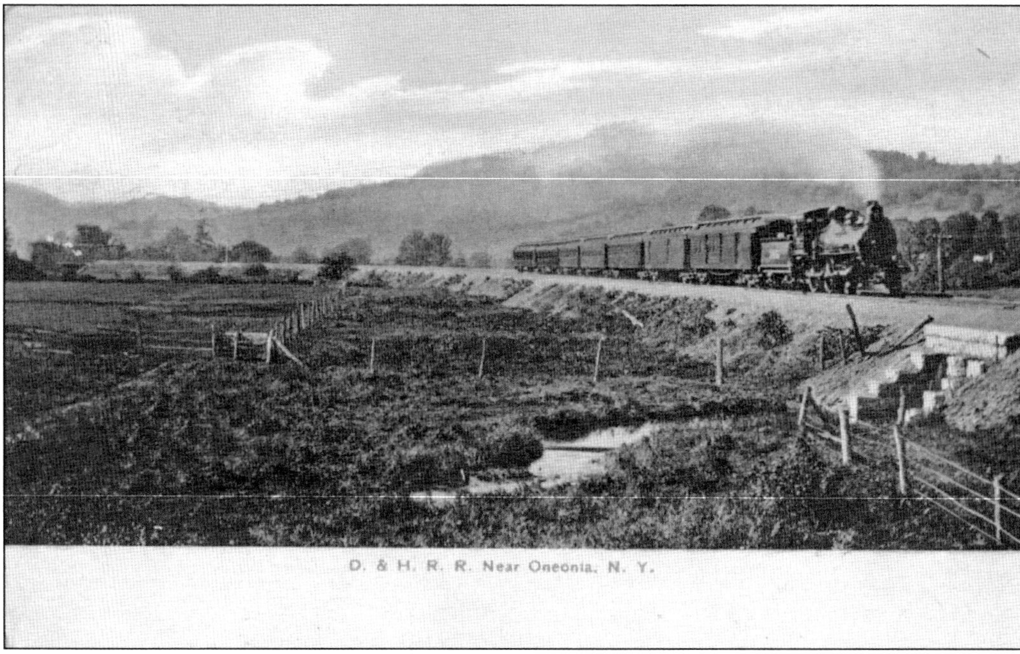

STEAM LOCOMOTIVE. A Delaware and Hudson steam locomotive puffs along toward Oneonta in this October 1910 postcard.

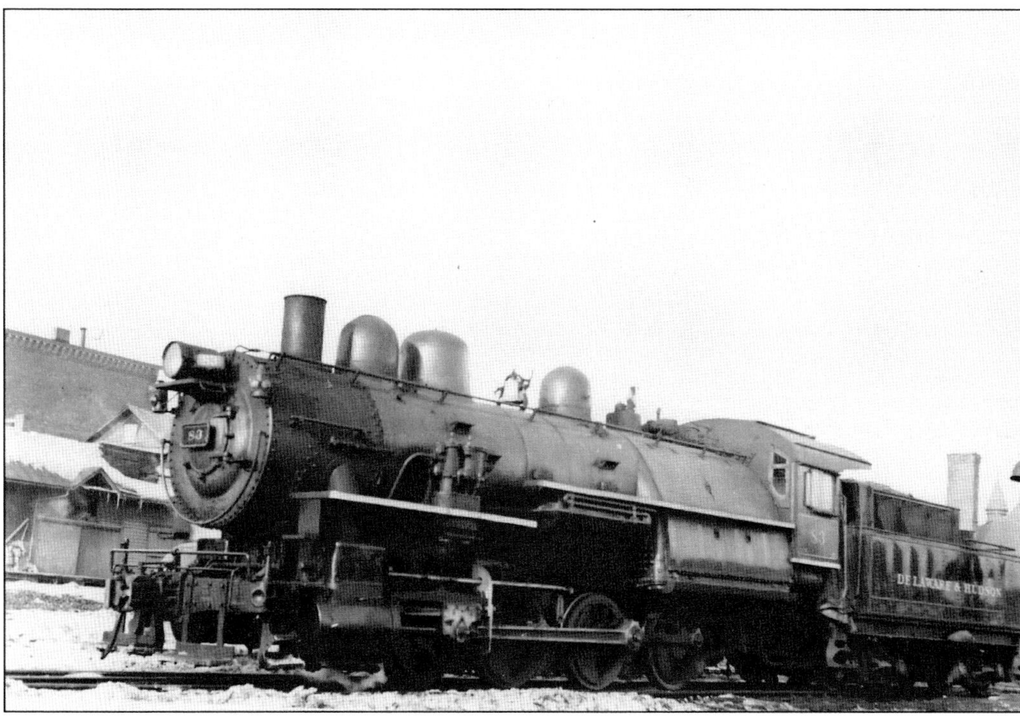

D&H LOCOMOTIVE. Delaware and Hudson locomotive class B-5 No. 83, originally built by Schenectady in 1899 as E-4 class 2-8-0, was rebuilt at Colonie Shops in April 1922. The photograph was taken in Oneonta on February 7, 1948.

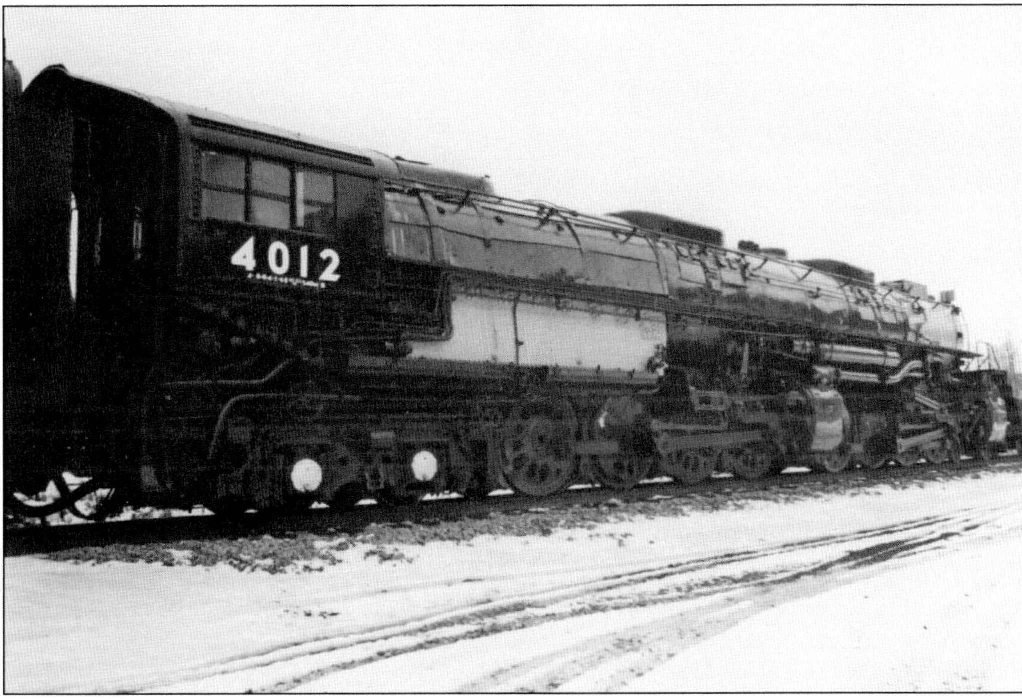

"BIG BOY." Built by American Locomotive Company in Schenectady in 1943, this 490-ton locomotive, nicknamed *Big Boy*, was hauled through Worcester in the 1980s on its way to Steamtown's new home in Scranton, Pennsylvania. The locomotive was the biggest in the world. The late Neil Holmes, a local plumber, worked on No. 4012 while employed at Alco in Schenectady.

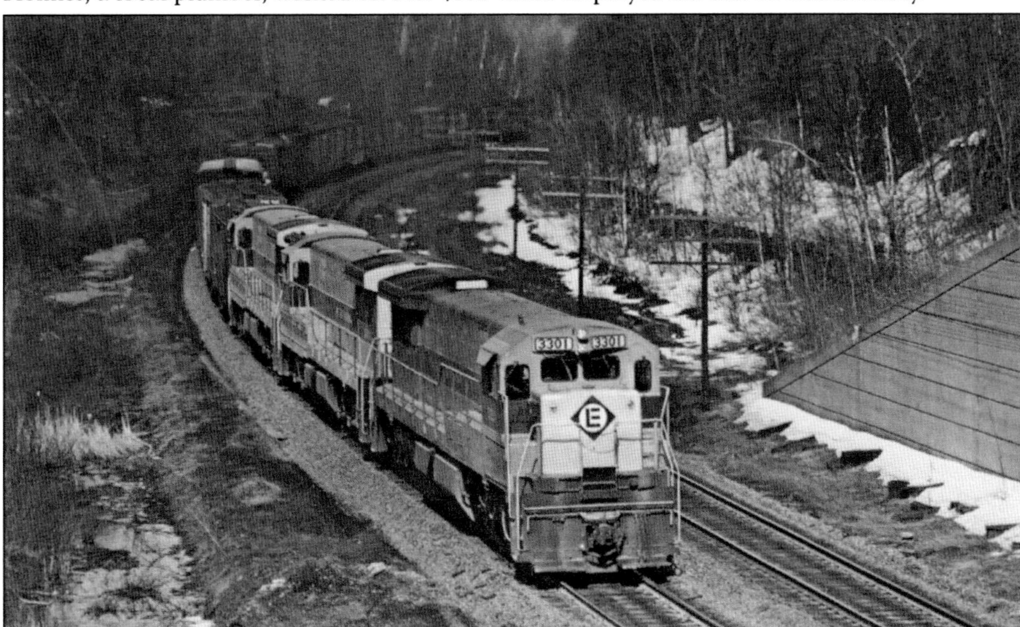

LOCOMOTIVE NO. 3301. Three Erie-Lackawanna locomotives, No. 3301, No. 3302, and No. 3303, are being used in pool service on the D&H rails. This photograph shows the diesels about to crest Richmondville Hill. (Courtesy of Jim Shaughnessy.)

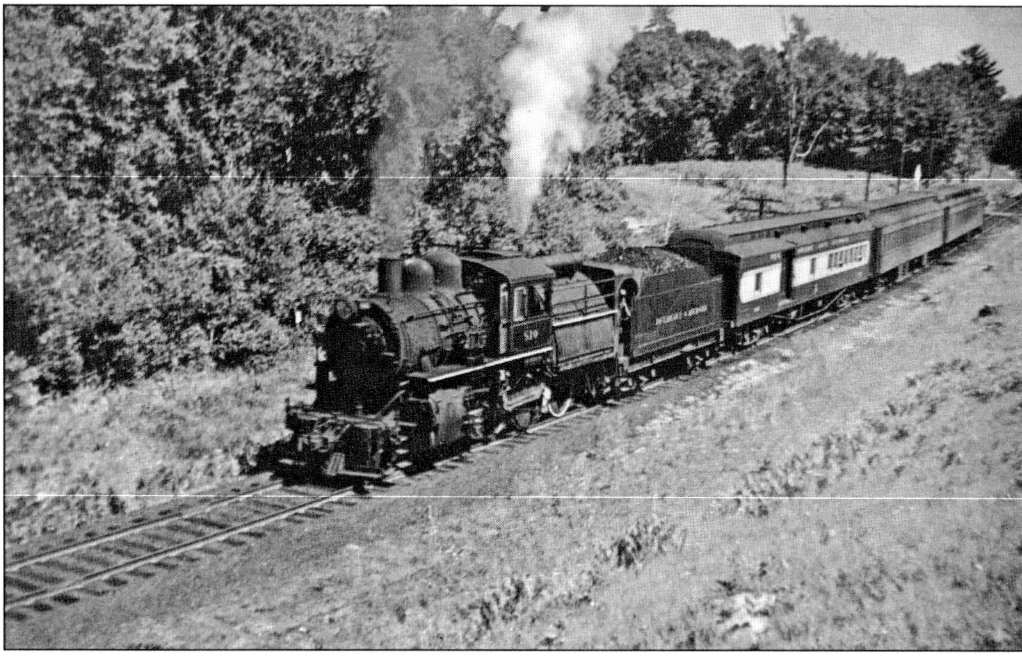

D&H 810. Camelback Consolidation 810, 2-8-0, built in the summer of 1904 in Schenectady, is pulling a passenger train on a scenic trip south of Lake George in the summer of 1946.

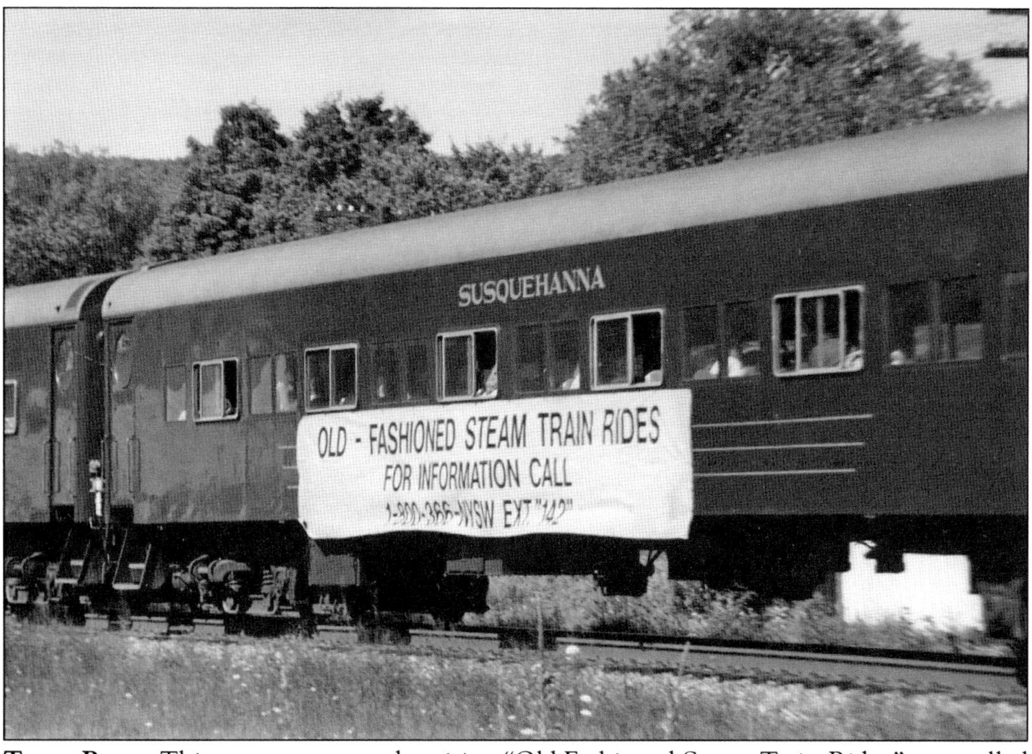

Train Rides. This passenger car, advertising "Old-Fashioned Steam Train Rides," was pulled by a locomotive traveling through Worcester on Delaware and Hudson tracks in the summer of 1992.

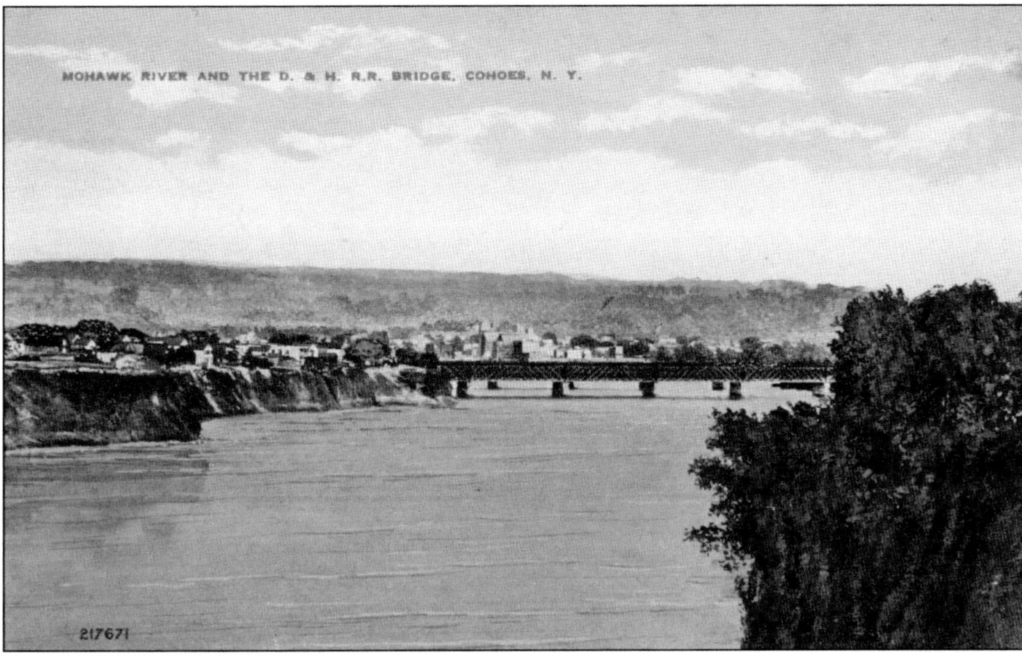

Mohawk River. This is a view of the Mohawk River and the Delaware and Hudson Railway bridge.

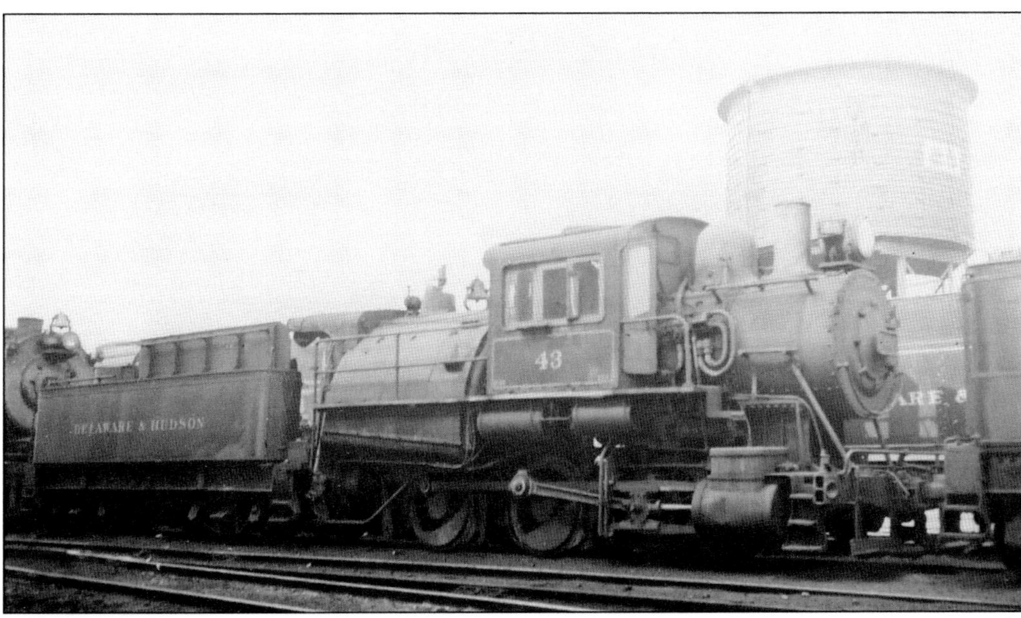

D&H Switcher No. 43. This Alco (Dickson-built) locomotive No. 43, representative of the B-4a class, stops at the Oneonta rail yard in July 1947. Note the water tower in the background. Harold Vollrath of Shreveport, Louisiana, took this photograph.

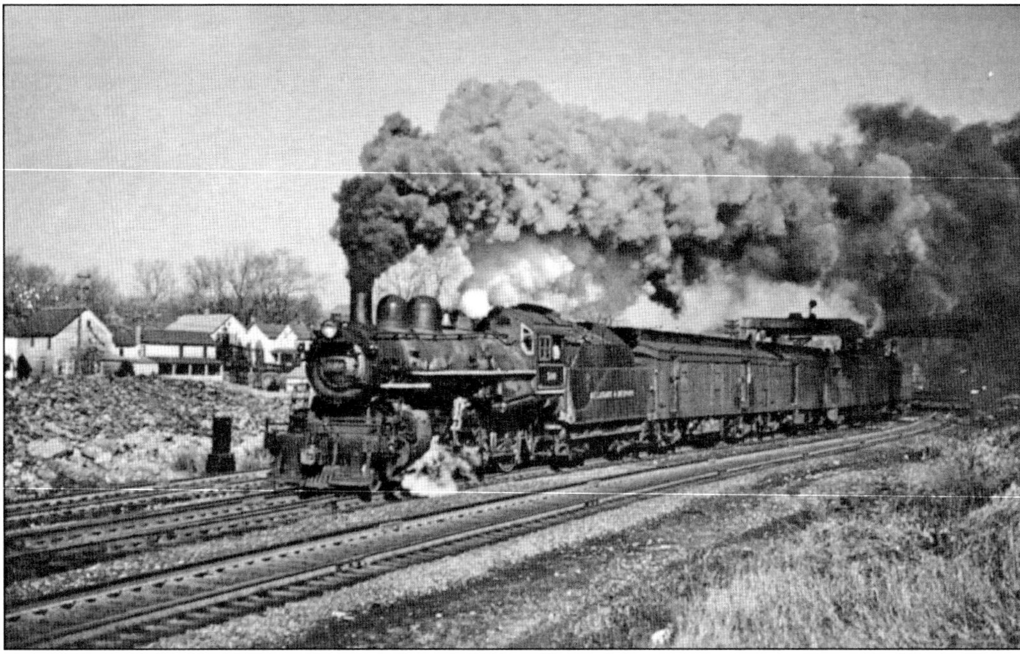

D&H No. 500. Ten-wheeler No. 500 travels through Carbondale, Pennsylvania, on the Delaware and Hudson Pennsylvania Division on November 9, 1951. Alco in Schenectady built this locomotive in 1903, styled as a camelback with a double cab and rebuilt in 1927. This is the locomotive seen earlier on pages 64–67 in the wreck at Sidney.

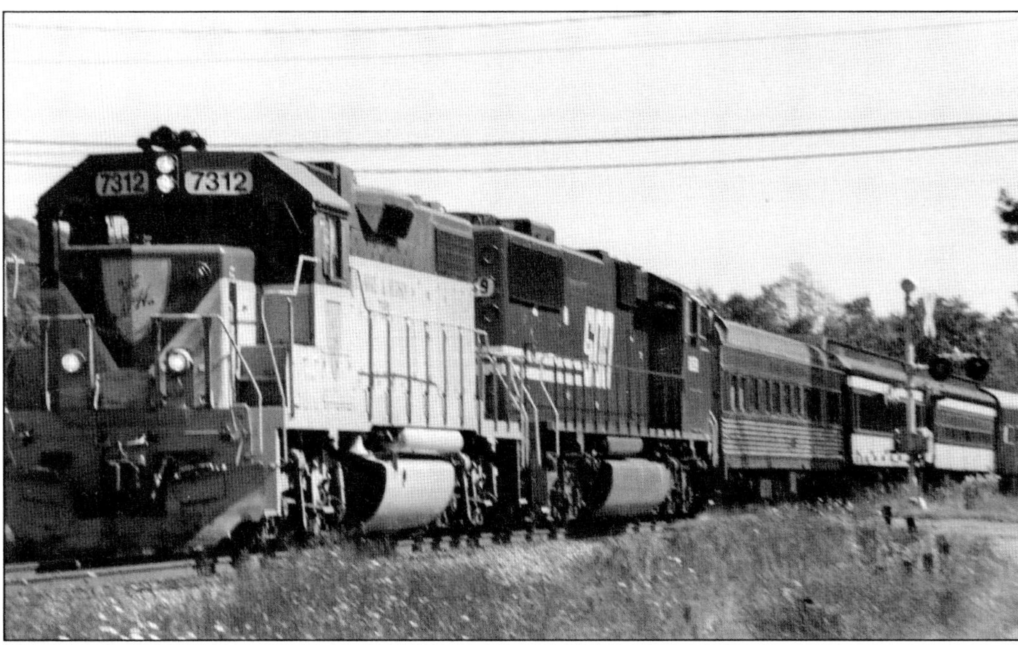

Diesel No. 7312. Delaware and Hudson GP38-2 No. 7312 travels through Worcester on its way to Albany with a passenger extra.

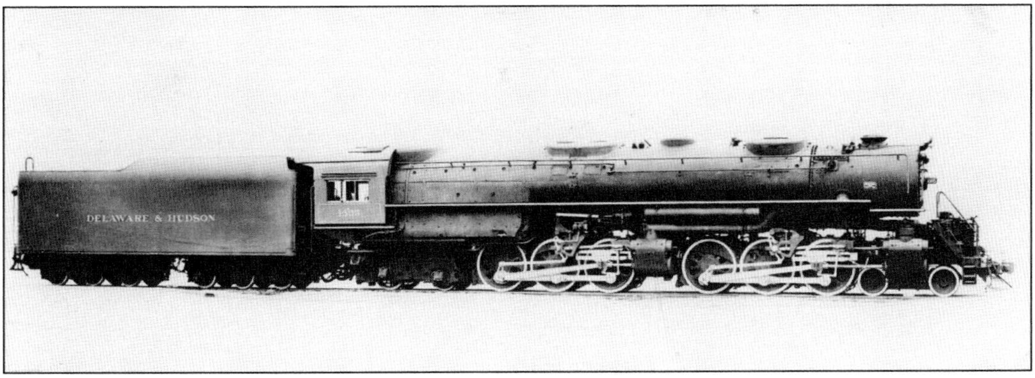

DELAWARE AND HUDSON NO. 1505. Delaware and Hudson's locomotive No. 1505 is a powerhouse of energy. This is the famous J class Challenger series.

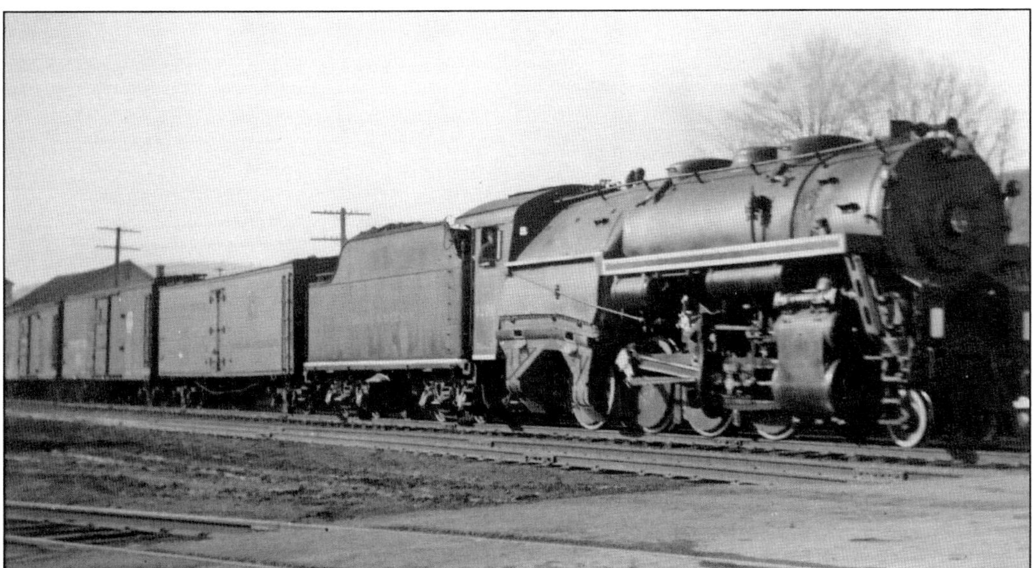

LOCOMOTIVE NO. 1219. D&H locomotive No. 1219, built by Alco in Schenectady, pulls freight cars over a crossing. Built in 1918, the engine received a new all-welded boiler in 1937.

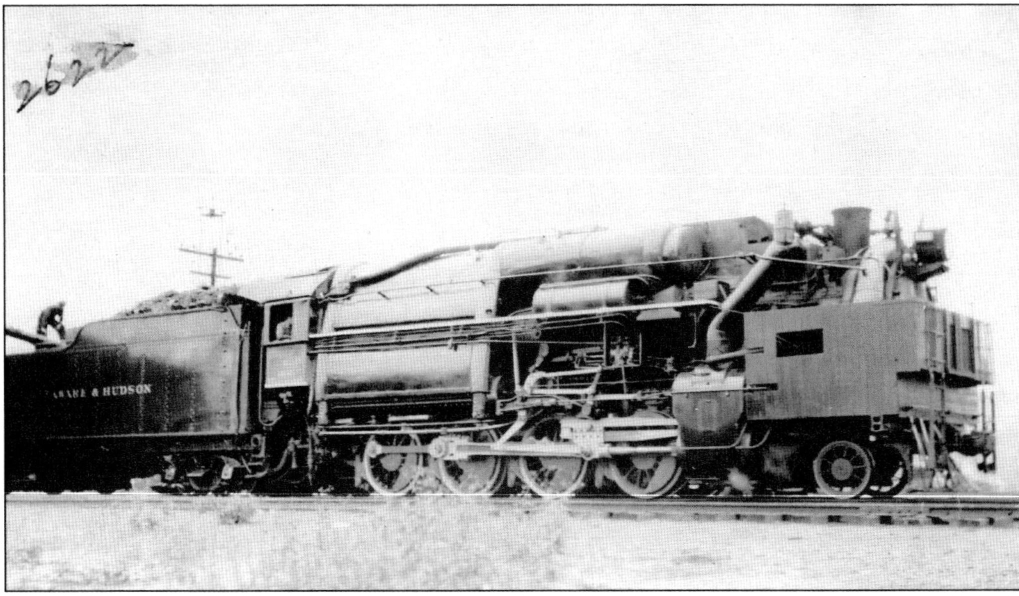

D&H Horatio Allen. Delaware and Hudson locomotive No. 1400 is photographed here in Oneonta on September 7, 1925. It was made by Alco in Schenectady in February 1925. Its total weight was 336,500 pounds. This engine, although no longer around, was important in the early history of the D&H. It was the first of Loree's experimental locomotives.

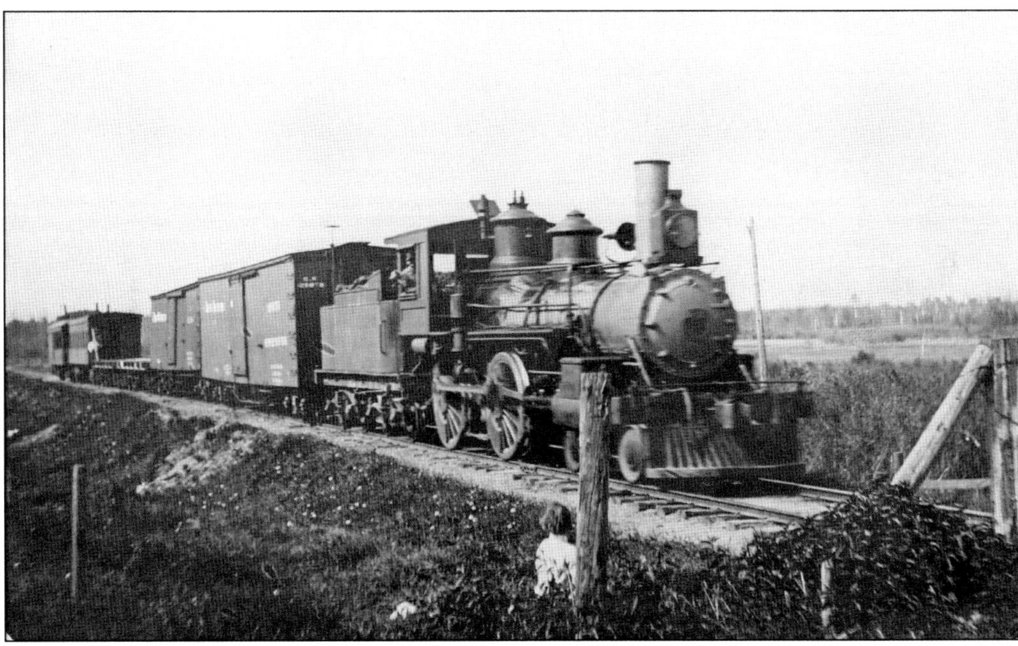

Old-Time Engine. This is an early engine with a smokestack, bell, and "cow catcher." Perhaps it is not traveling on D&H tracks, but the idea of the engineer waving to the little girl standing down the bank is a good one. D&H engineers are always friendly and will wave back to you if you wave at them. It was a wonderful sight for children and adults to view their first train traveling on the tracks.

Nine

Railroadiana

Railroad fever followed the aftermath of the Civil War and rail fans to this day have a certain fascination with train memorabilia, such as ticket stubs, D&H booklets, photographs, books, maps, postcards, old news items, and magazine articles.

The story of the D&H involves many interesting happenings such as this account from a faded newspaper, "At the D&H station at Lookout Point on September 7, 1869, Abraham Richards of Carbondale, Pennsylvania, went to the station to meet his wife and five children. Instead of five there were seven children; his wife delivered twin girls en route."

A news item from the March 5, 1908, *Worcester Times* states, "Engineer 'Al' Gault, who has been off duty for a long time on account of his artificial leg that wouldn't 'track,' recalled Gunmaker Seward, into the case a short time ago. By using a couple of artificial legs and some bicycle supplies they rigged up a leg that is a winner and the jolly (D&H) engineer resumed his grip on the throttle last Sunday."

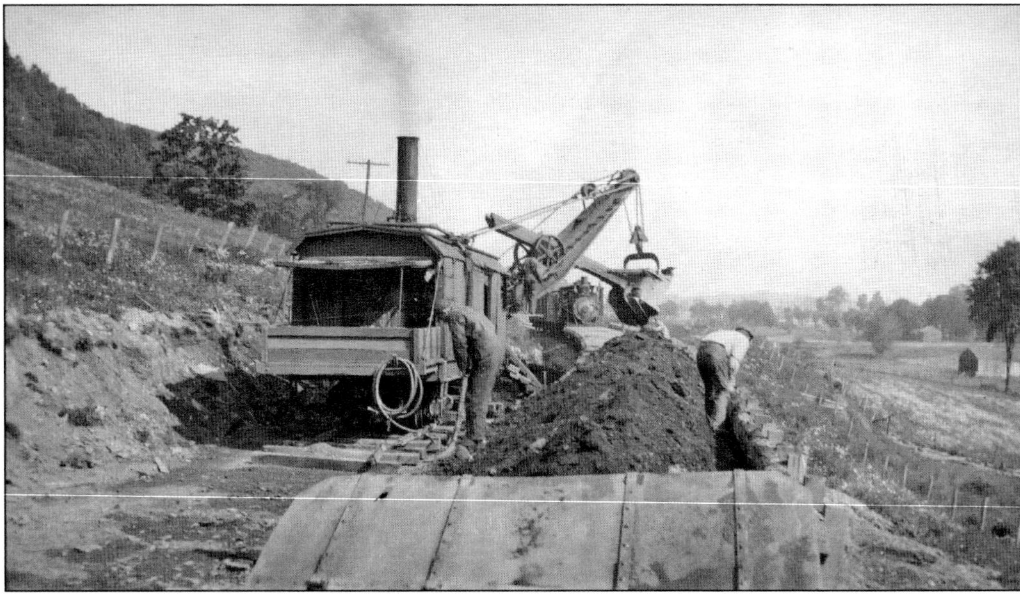

PORTER BROTHERS. A contract to build a third Delaware and Hudson track through Worcester was awarded to Porter Brothers in July 1917. Workmen have unloaded their shovels, graders, and small engines, and construction of a temporary track from a point on the main line will begin. This track will start west of White House Crossing and continue down the hill and across the creek to the site of the new track.

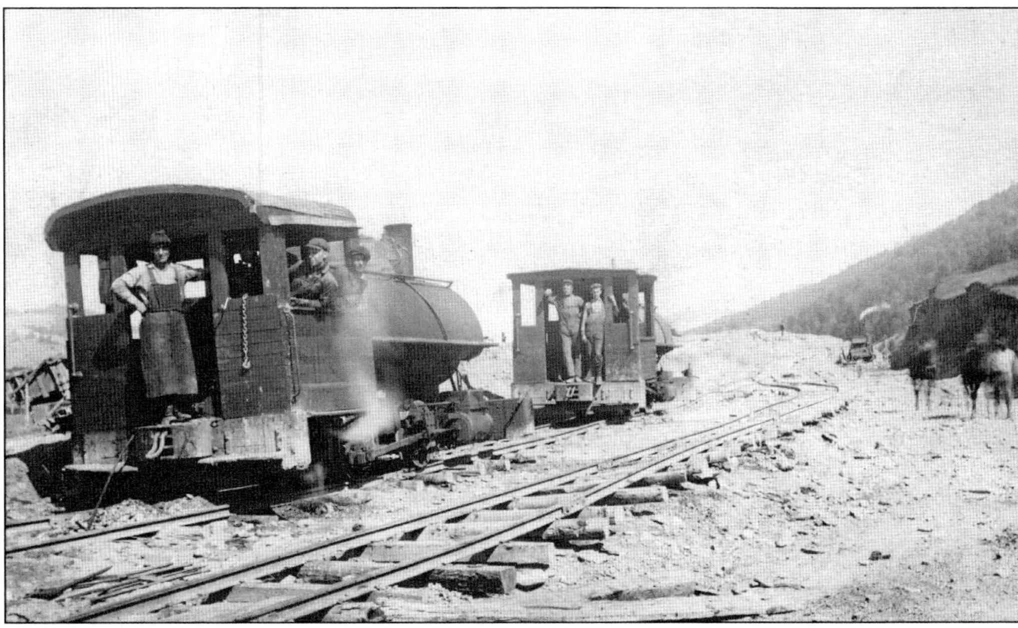

THIRD TRACK. The many passenger trains traveling the rails on the lower track forced freight trains to wait on a siding until the main track was clear, making a third track necessary. From the *Worcester Times* of September 12, 1917, "Last Sunday while working for Porter Brothers two workmen were injured when a work train near Whitehouse Crossing was backing over a trestle that collapsed. Two Swedes were injured, names not available, since they only answer to numbers in the company work."

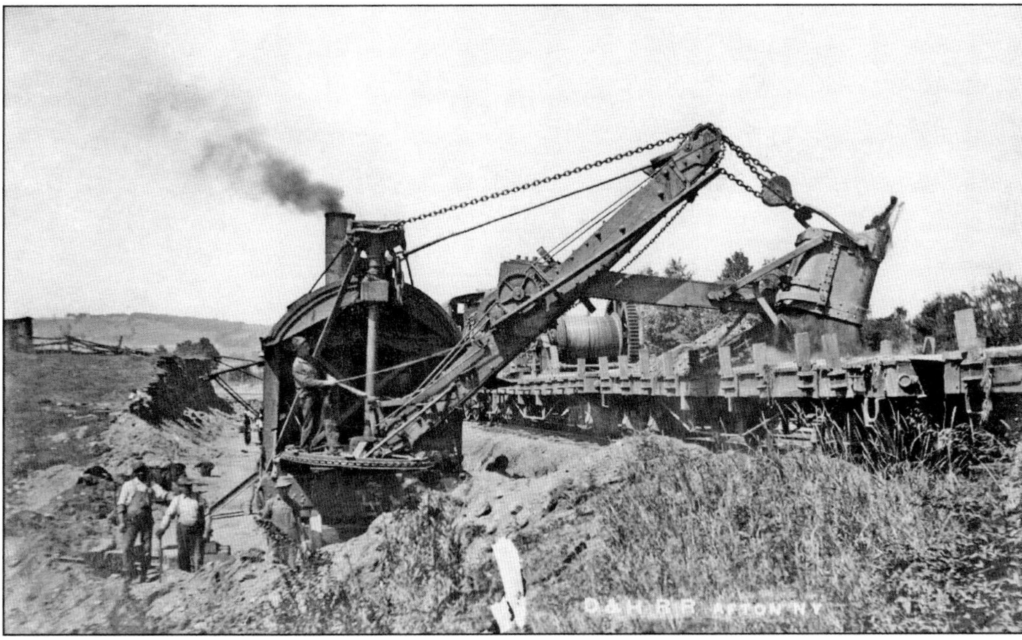

Track Construction. A steam shovel is at the site of early Delaware and Hudson track construction in the Afton area. Men using picks and shovels completed most of the construction of the new track sites. The date on this postcard is November 17, 1911.

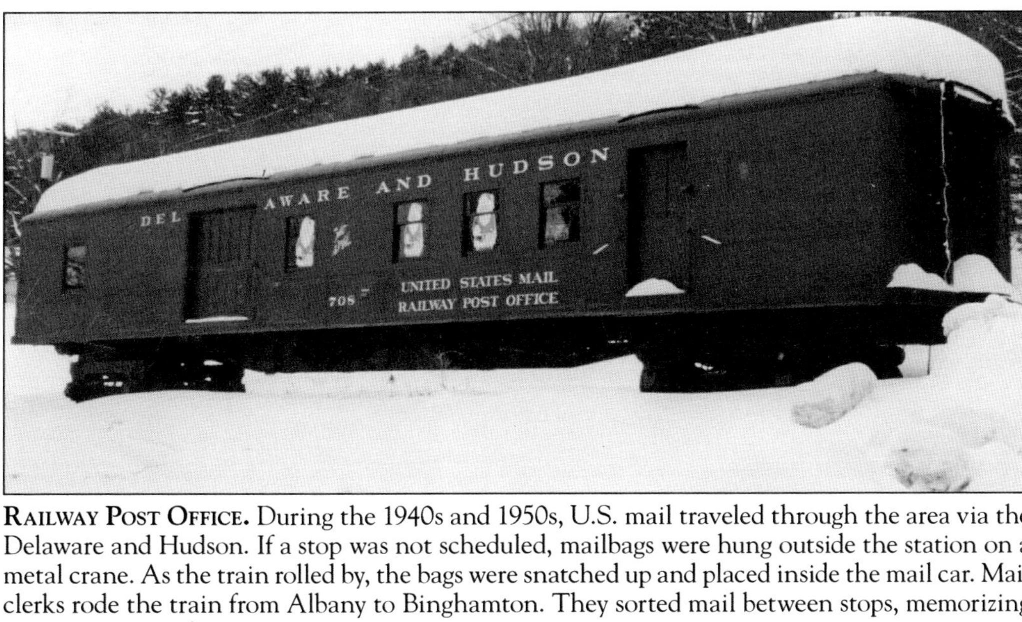

Railway Post Office. During the 1940s and 1950s, U.S. mail traveled through the area via the Delaware and Hudson. If a stop was not scheduled, mailbags were hung outside the station on a metal crane. As the train rolled by, the bags were snatched up and placed inside the mail car. Mail clerks rode the train from Albany to Binghamton. They sorted mail between stops, memorizing names, cities, and towns.

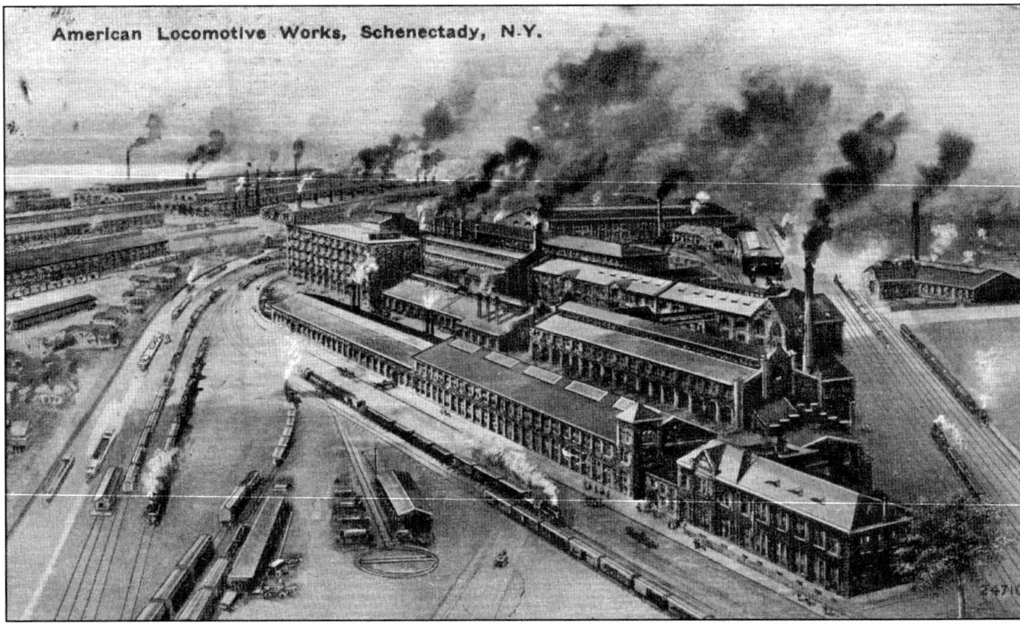

AMERICAN LOCOMOTIVE COMPANY. A 1914 view of the American Locomotive Company in Schenectady shows the extensive span of buildings, tracks, trains, and smokestacks. Many of the Delaware and Hudson Company locomotives were built by Alco, which was formed in 1901 as the result of a merger of several smaller locomotive manufacturers, including Dickson Manufacturing in Scranton, Pennsylvania. The D&H was a longtime customer of Alco.

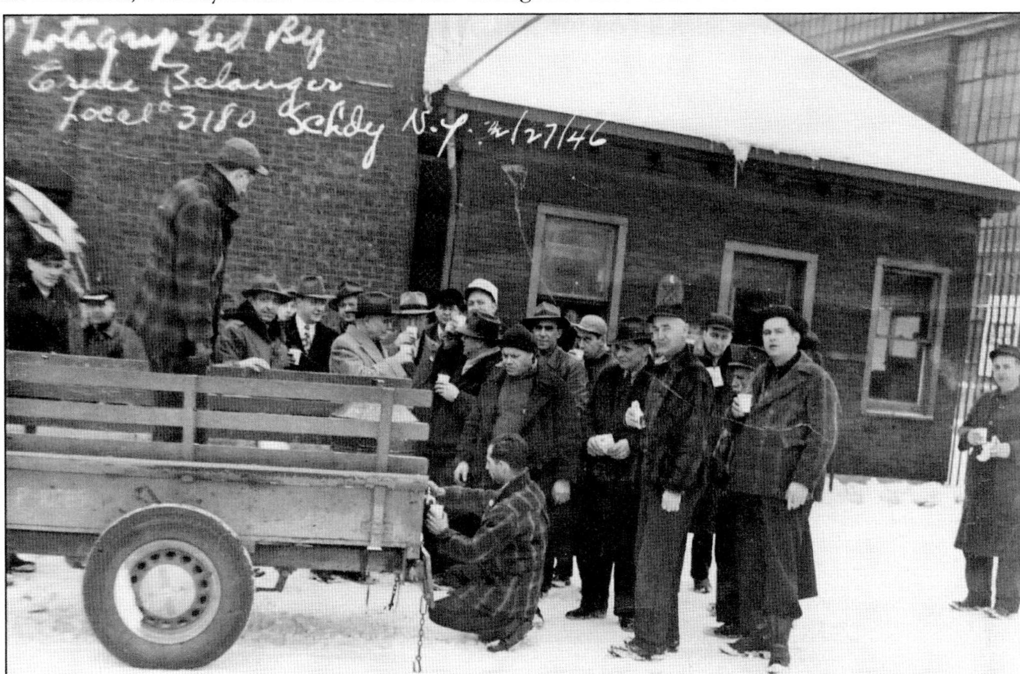

STRIKE AT ALCO. Workers at the American Locomotive Company went on strike on February 27, 1946, at its Schenectady plant. Better working conditions and more pay were some of the grievances. This photograph shows men standing around drinking coffee during the strike.

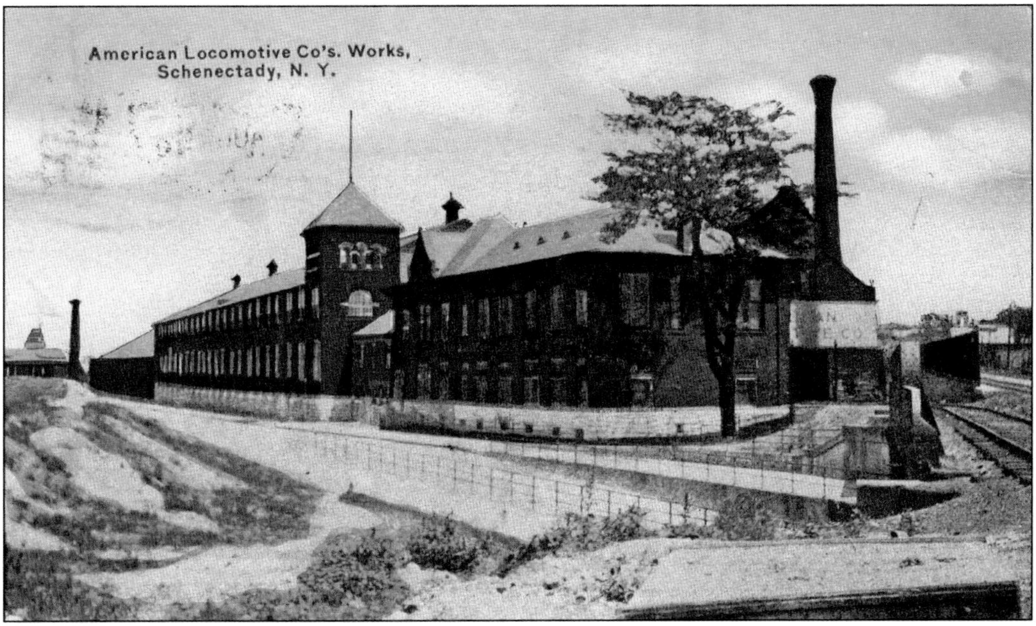

ALCO. This view of American Locomotive Company's building in Schenectady is dated 1910. Alco was the second-largest steam locomotive builder in the United States (after Baldwin), producing more than 75,000. It built many of the largest locomotives ever constructed, including "Big Boy." After the closing of the Schenectady plant, many locomotives designed by Alco continued to be manufactured in Canada and Australia.

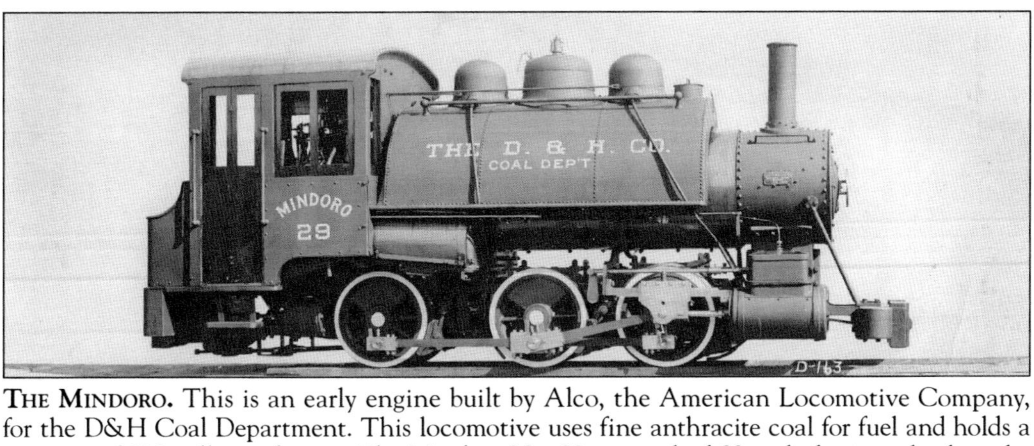

THE MINDORO. This is an early engine built by Alco, the American Locomotive Company, for the D&H Coal Department. This locomotive uses fine anthracite coal for fuel and holds a capacity of 300 gallons of water. The Mindoro No. 29 engine had 33-inch driving wheels and a boiler pressure of 150 pounds.

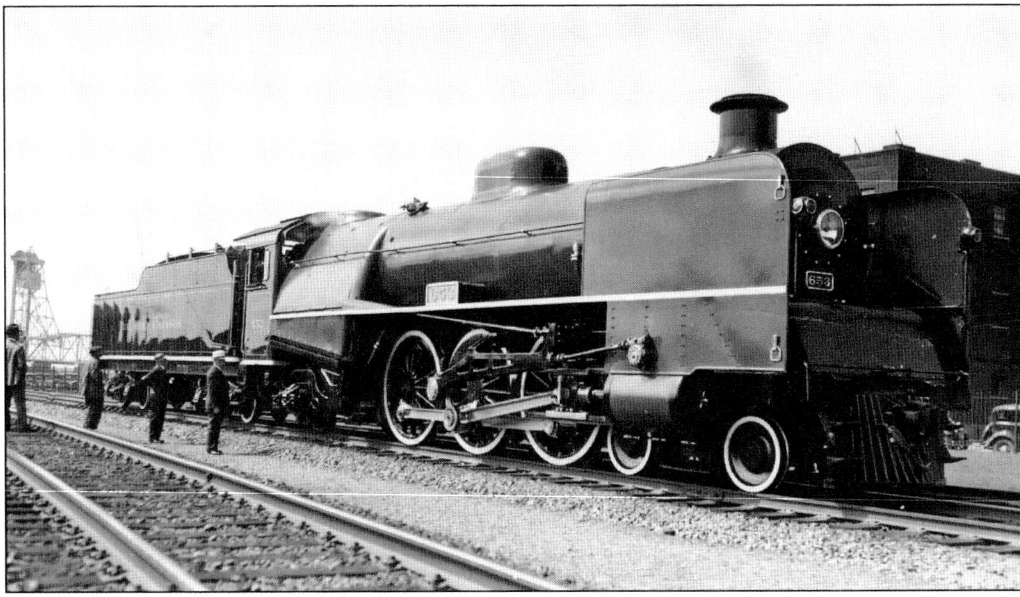

LOCOMOTIVE NO. 653. Locomotive No. 653 is styled with smoke lifters, which give the impression of elephant ears. The smoke lifters and sloping plate running up from the pilot combine to give off an updraft of air. When the locomotive is in motion, the lifters send the smoke higher in the air, improving the engineer's visibility.

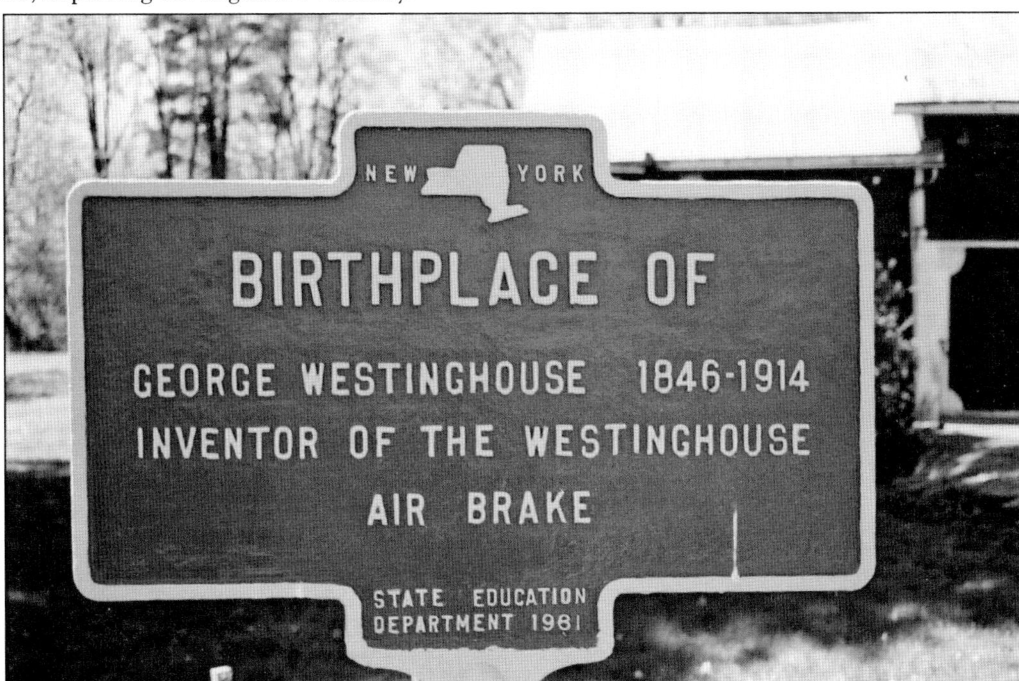

WESTINGHOUSE HISTORICAL MARKER. George Westinghouse Jr. was born on October 6, 1846, in Central Bridge. He became one of the greatest engineers, industrialists, and inventors of his day. He modernized the railroad with his air brakes. Among his 160 patents was the invention of the reverse fail-safe system that remains standard today.

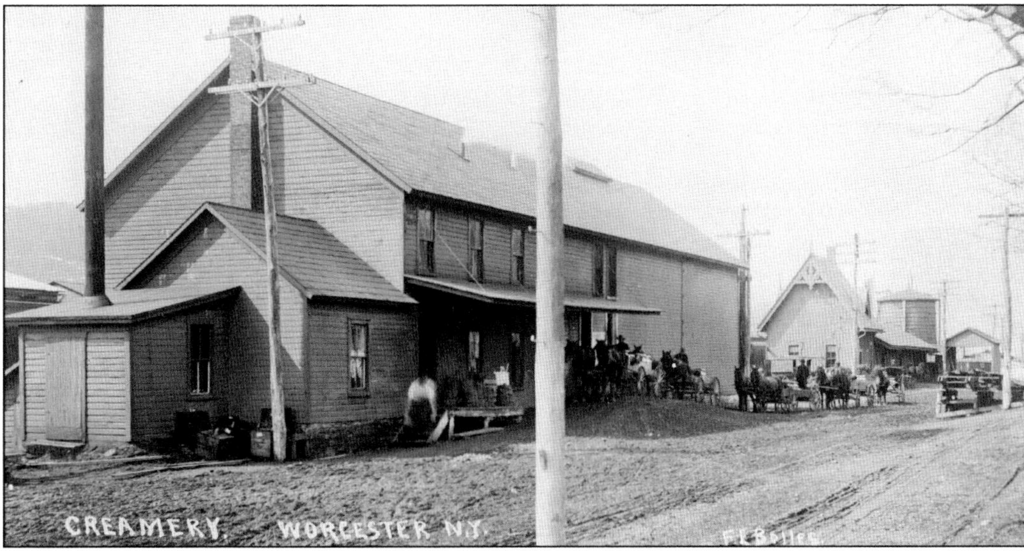

Borden's Creamery. In 1907, the creamery on Depot Street in Worcester came under the ownership of Borden's. When farmers learned that milk would be shipped to New York City on a daily basis, they increased the size of their dairies and brought their milk to the creamery. A huge vat was used to manufacture pot cheese. At one time, 600 pounds of butter and the same amount of pot cheese were regularly shipped to New York City. The Grange League Federation purchased the building for its feed business; it is now used for storage.

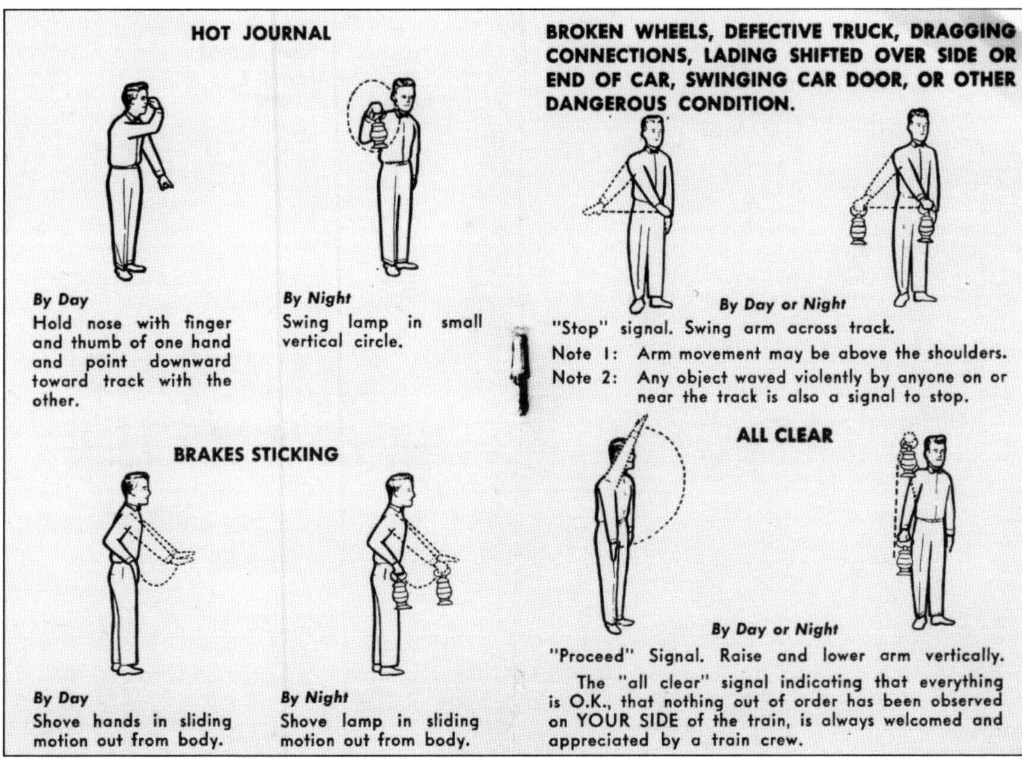

Hand Signals. The D&H printed a small booklet titled "Railroad Hand Signals." The publication states, "A knowledge of these signals may help you to prevent an accident."

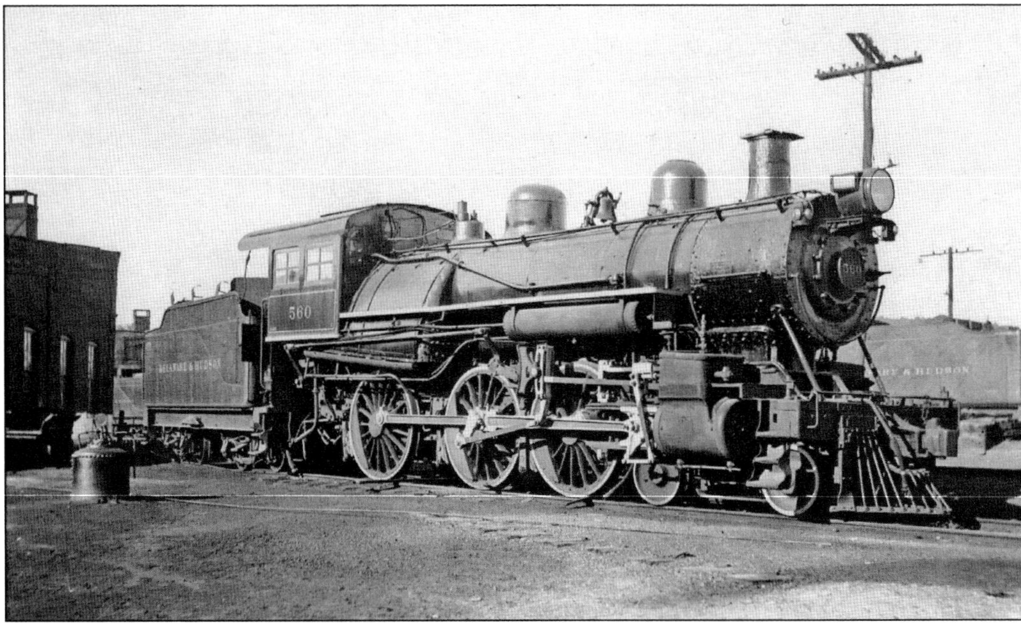

Locomotive No. 560. Delaware and Hudson No. 560 was purchased by the D&H from the Napierville Junction Railway in 1919. Built in 1907 at Alco (Montreal), class D-3 is a 4-6-0 with construction number 43703 and was photographed in Whitehall on August 27, 1925.

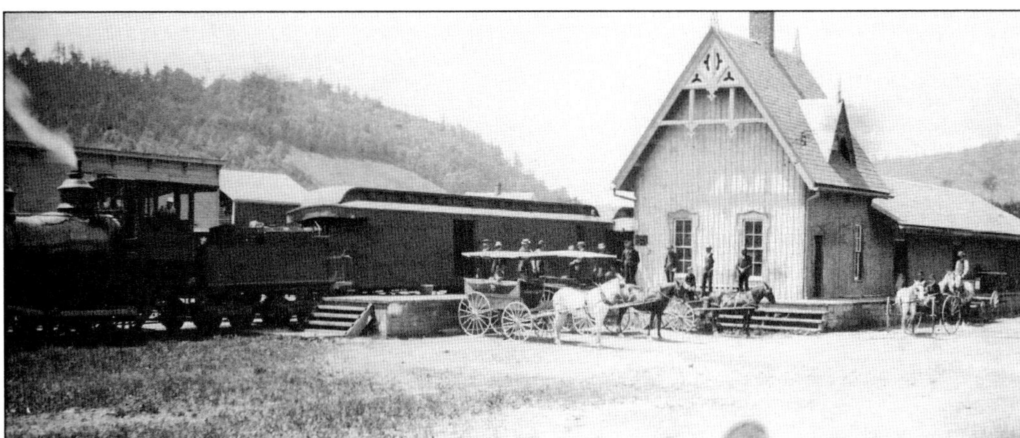

Worcester's First Station. Worcester's original station, built when the Albany and Susquehanna Railroad first came through in 1865, burned in 1879. Farmers stored their hay on the platform around the station, and one day a spark from an engine ignited the straw. This building featured four-over-four divided windows, board-and-batten siding, and decorative scrollwork at the roof's peak. The freight area can be seen to the right.

FRANK M. WRIGHT. According to a news item in the August 4, 1937, issue of the *Worcester Times*, Frank M. Wright, a well-known resident in the village of Worcester, was instantly killed in front of the D&H station at 1:40 p.m. on Monday, August 2, when struck by a southbound milk train. Witnesses say Wright was almost across the track when he saw the train and stepped back between the rails. The newspaper account states, "The engineer, Paul Nashke of Albany, made frantic blasts with the whistle but as Mr. Wright was quite deaf it is possible he did not hear the warning signals until too late."

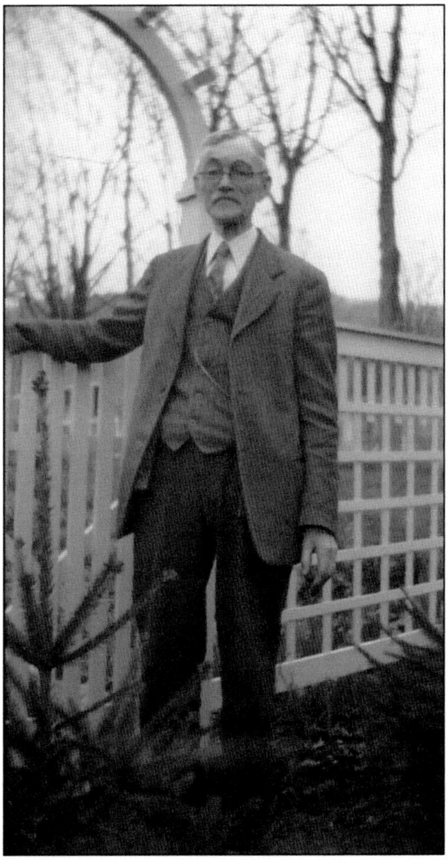

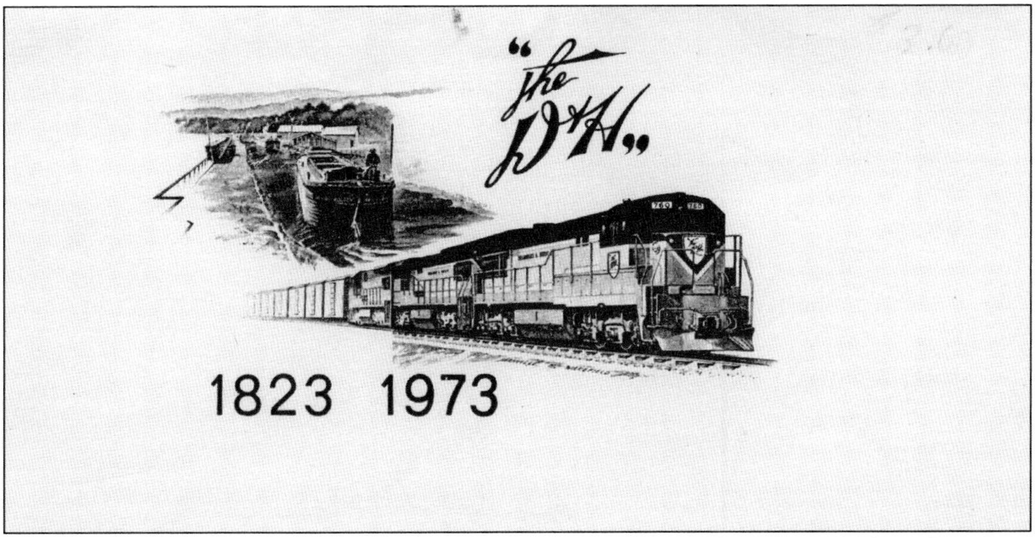

1823–1973. The D&H celebrated 150 years of service to the public in 1973 and was known as America's oldest transportation company at that time. The original D&H Canal Company was chartered in 1823 to operate a barge canal from northeastern Pennsylvania to the Hudson River. The D&H sesquicentennial in 1973 was a milestone attained by few businesses. Railroads played key roles in transporting immigrants to work in local industries.

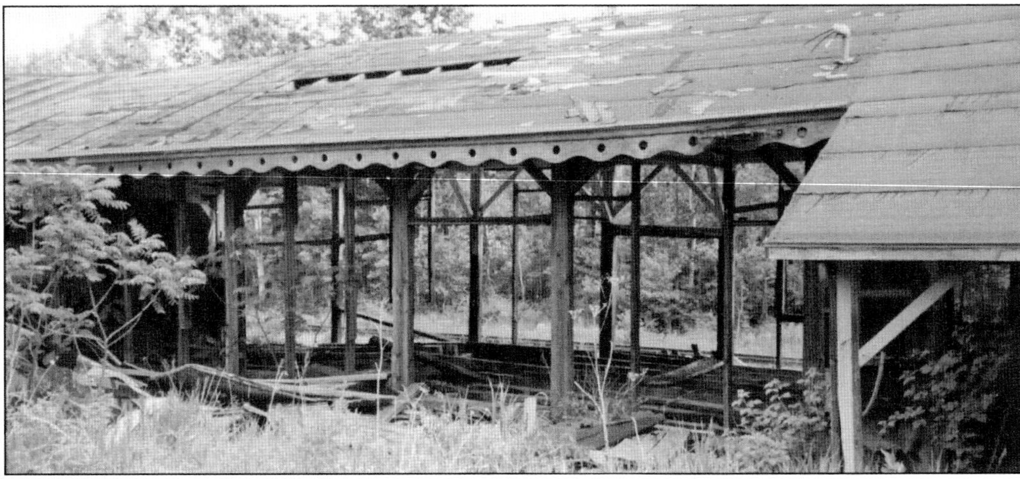

MARYLAND STATION. The Maryland station, built in 1867, has been affected by the ravages of time over 143 years. The structure's frame is still standing, although sheathing and roofing have mostly disappeared. The remaining scalloped edges along the roofline are evidence of the intricate detail that went into building this structure.

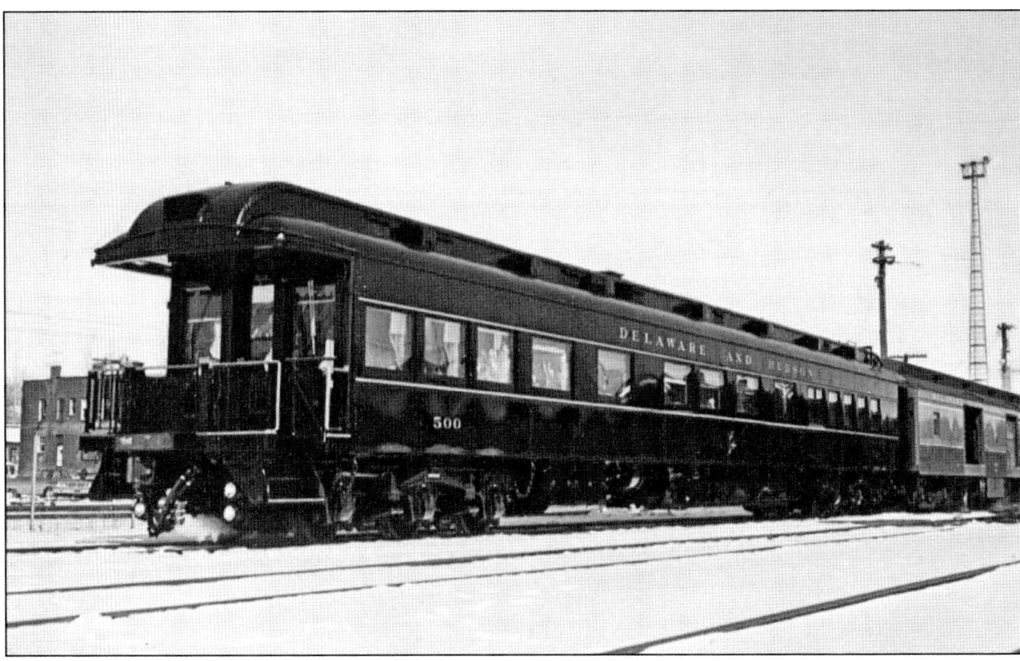

BUSINESS CAR 500. The D&H business car No. 500 was built by Pullman in 1917 for the company's president, L. F. Loree. Cuban mahogany and West Indian satinwood adorned the interior of the car. During the winter of 1967, it was renovated and the exterior was painted berry red. Interior accommodations included a stateroom, drawing room, and bedroom.

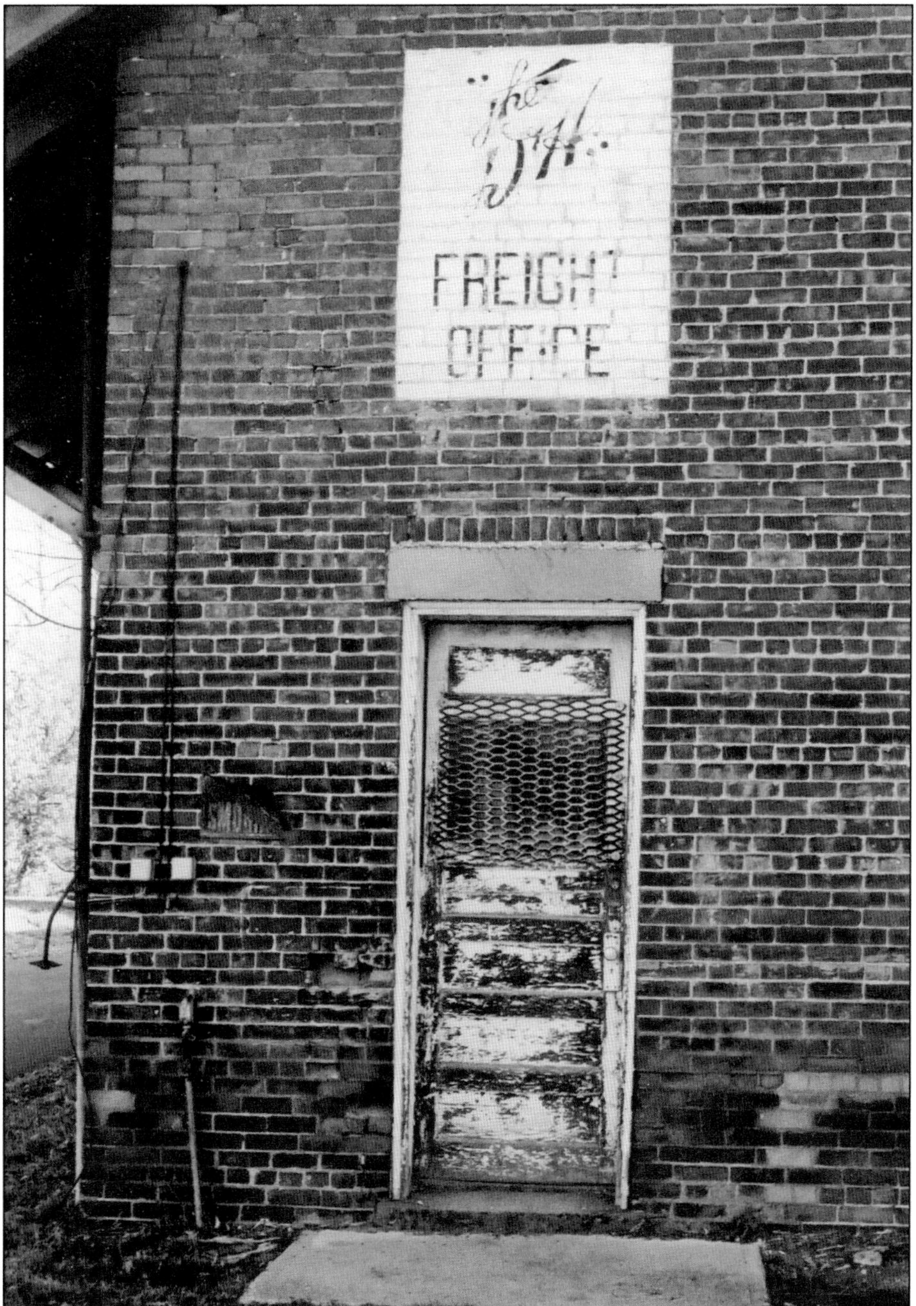

Freight Office. The fading lettering on the former Delaware and Hudson freight office is still visible on the side of this abandoned brick building that was once a part of the busy Cobleskill station. The August 12, 1965, issue of the *Worcester Times* stated that the Public Service Commission authorized the Delaware and Hudson Railway to discontinue resident agency service in Worcester, Maryland, East Worcester, and Schenevus under the jurisdiction of its Oneonta agent. The D&H said that the Western Union business handled by the Worcester agent would be performed in Cobleskill.

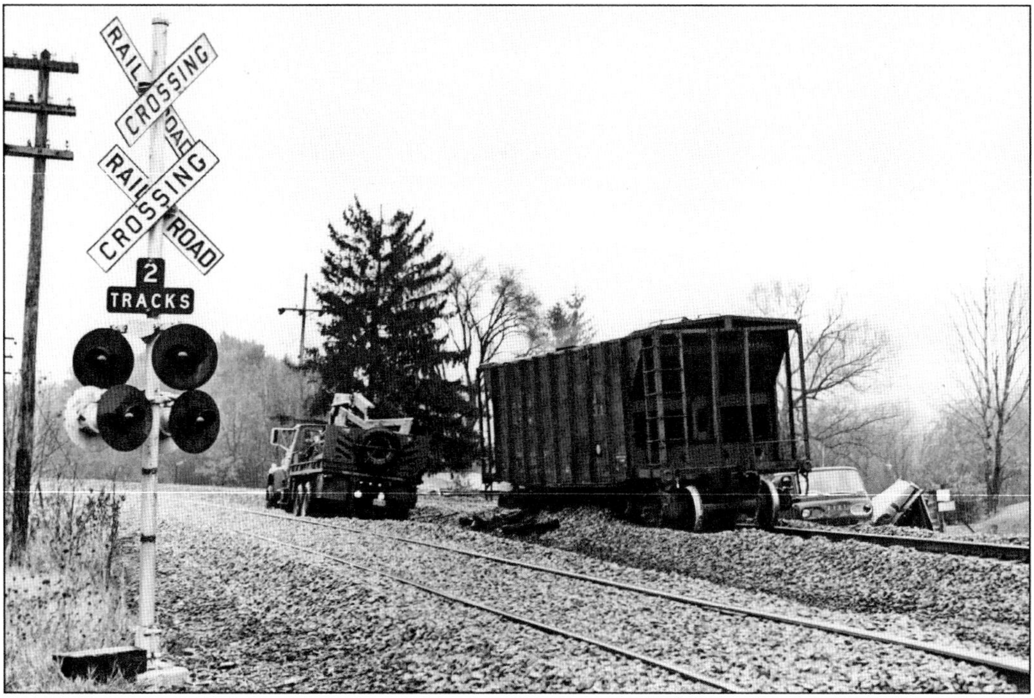

SCHENEVUS DERAILMENT. Two D&H cars derailed on Monday, October 26, 1981, about 200 feet from Farmers Feed Mill in Schenevus. It was reported that workers were placing crushed stones under part of the track to raise the Depot Street crossing for construction at a later date. An empty car slid off the rail, possibly as a result of the extra stones. The first derailment took place at noon, and the second slid off the track at 2:45 p.m. Both cars were back on the track soon.

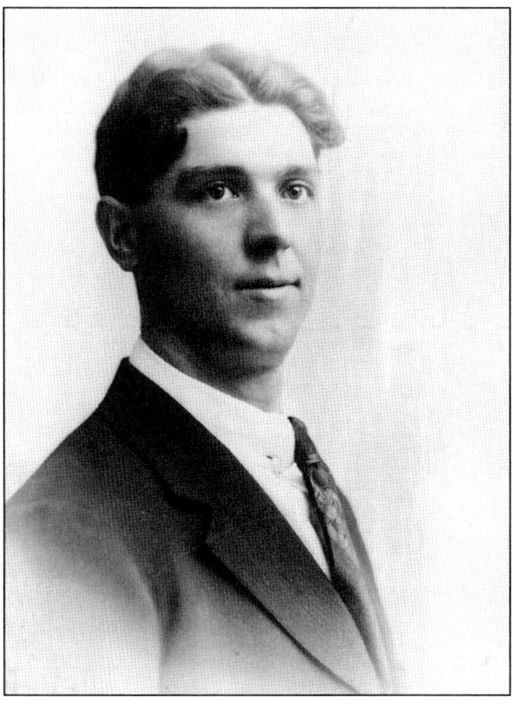

BIG JOHN. During the 1930s and 1940s, John Cicchine, also known as "Big John," faithfully dispatched his duties at the D&H crossing at Depot Street in Worcester. One day, when a locomotive stopped near the crossing, Big John climbed a ladder on one of the cars. The train started moving, and as he descended the ladder, he caught one foot in a rung. The wheels of the train hit his other foot. His leg was amputated below the knee and after gangrene set in, it was cut off above the knee. After he recuperated, Big John could still be seen with his stop sign, standing at the crossing on crutches.

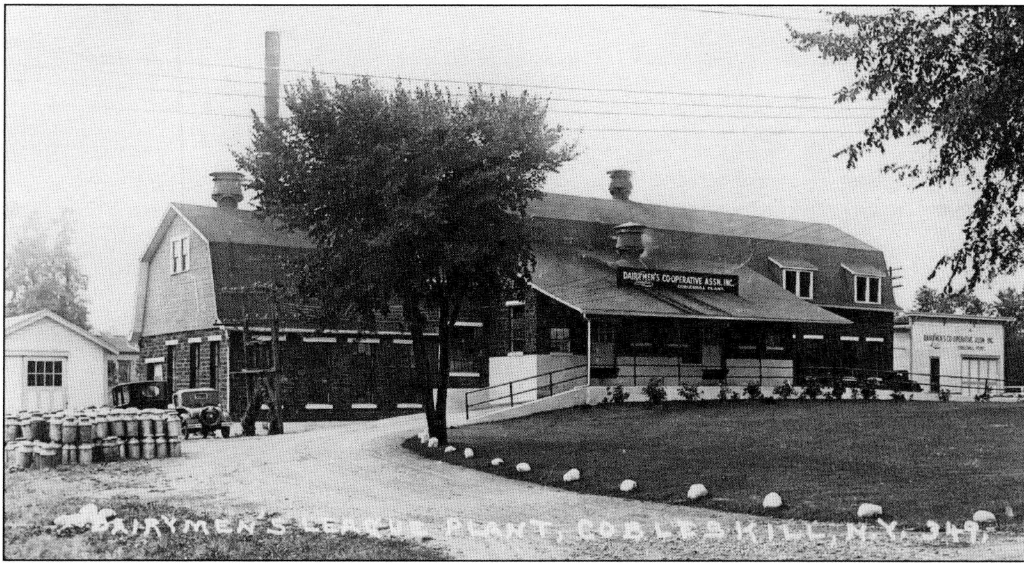

DAIRYMEN'S LEAGUE, COBLESKILL. Every little town had a milk station where farmers delivered their milk. Milk was shipped out by the Dairymen's League in Cobleskill to big cities. The amount of milk was so great that dedicated milk trains were operated. Milk was shipped in bulk-tank railroad cars, and creameries had adjacent ice-storage facilities. In the winter, the Sheffield Creamery in Richmondville stored ice from Schenevus Lake, which was 15 miles away.

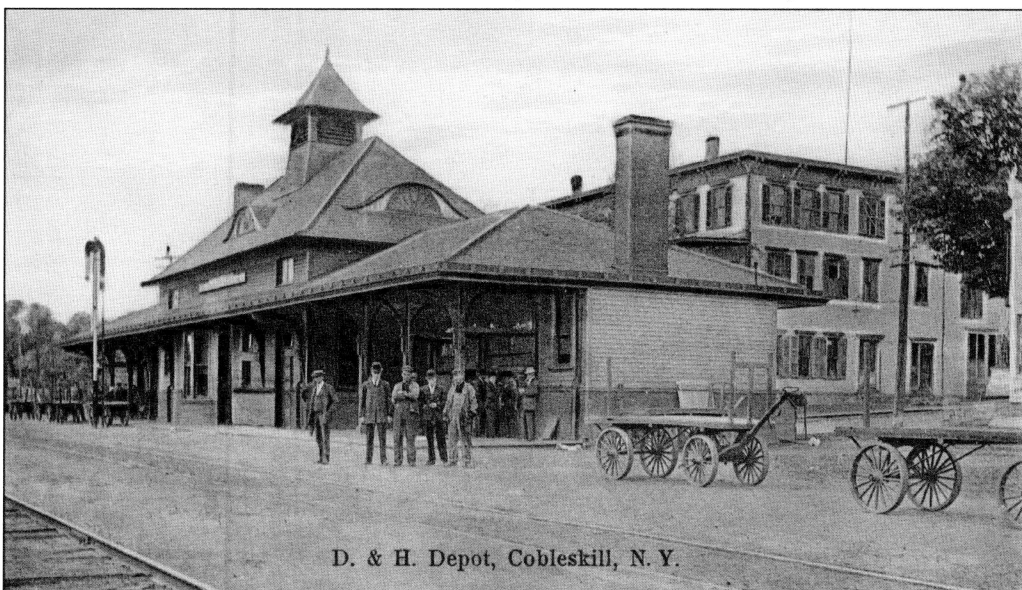

COBLESKILL STONE STATION. The first station in Cobleskill was an old stone structure located where the second one was built. It was constructed in the days of the Albany and Susquehanna (A&S) and torn down to make way for the new one shown here. The stone from the old passenger house was used in the ground walls of this new building. A new freight house was also necessary because of growing traffic on the railroad. The station agent and other employees of the D&H are shown in front of the station. Early locomotives, recognized by the sound of their whistles, bore the names of A&S directors such as Minard Harder and Charles Courter of Cobleskill.

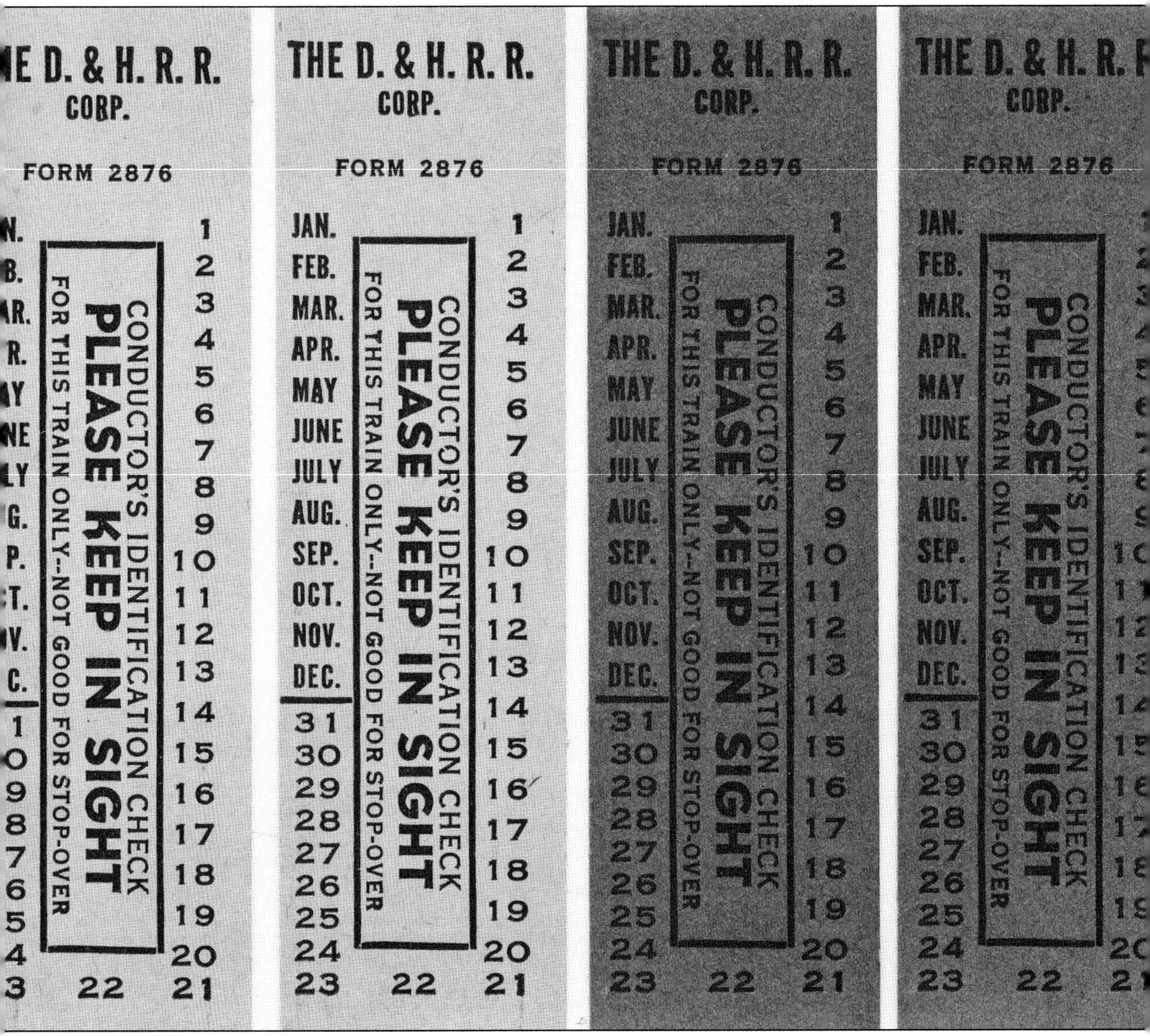

D&H Tickets. Tickets used by passengers riding on the Delaware and Hudson Railway were printed with the months and numbers from 1 to 31. The conductor would punch the tickets, using the correct month and day. The ticket holder was instructed to "keep in sight" for the conductor's identification check.

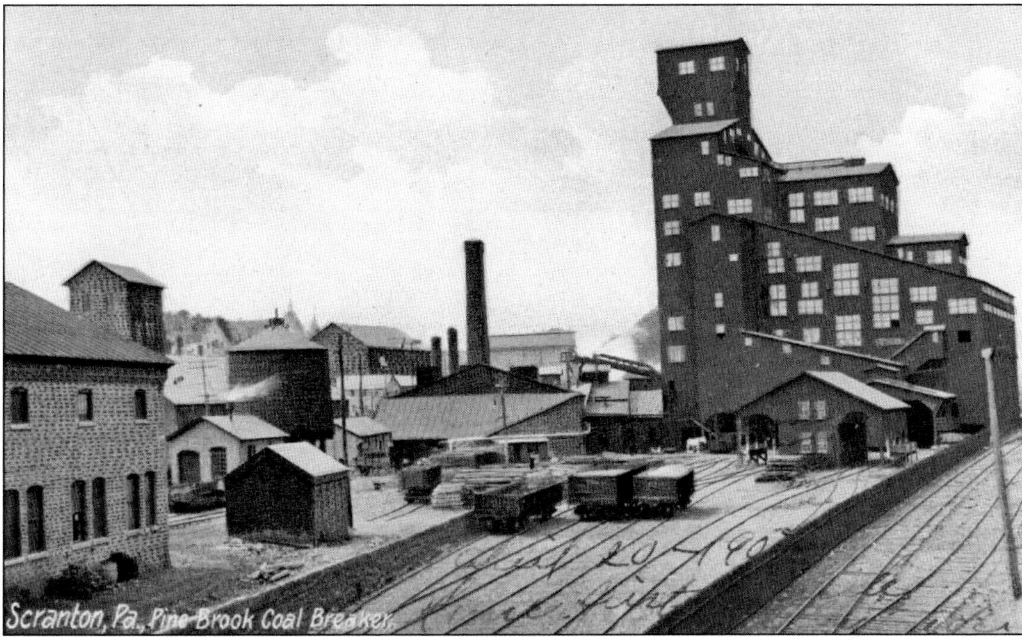

Coal Breaker. This 1907 view is of the Pine Brook Coal Breaker in Scranton, Pennsylvania. Coal breakers, which were located close to an anthracite mine entrance, were where mostly young boys worked all day to break coal into various sizes. This helped to remove impurities from coal, most typically slate. This operation was the forerunner of the modern coal preparation plant.

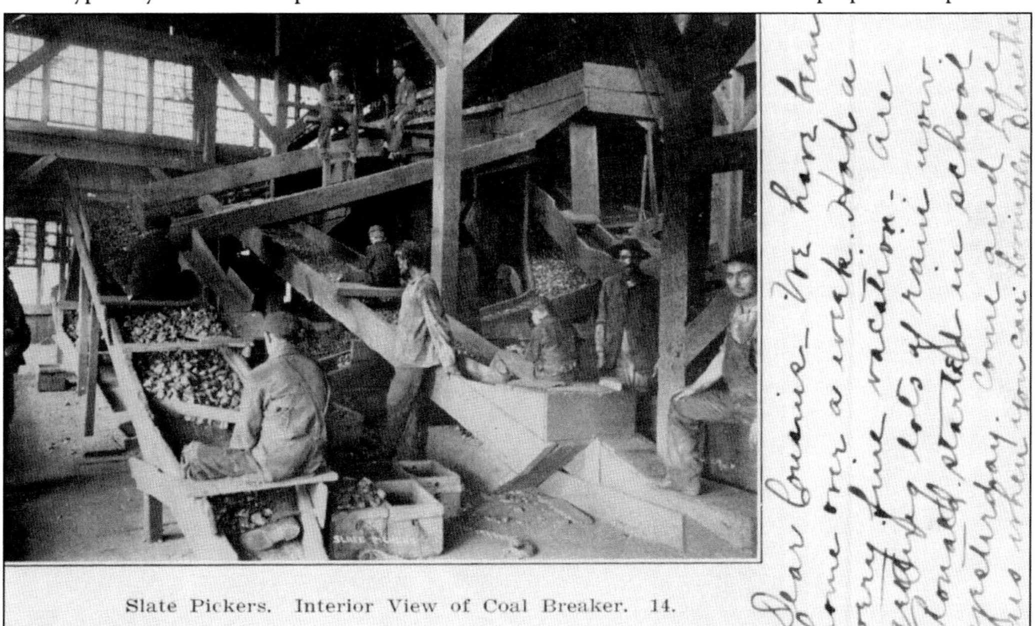

Interior View. Slate pickers at work are shown in this 1901 photograph inside a coal breaker. Coal breakers, which were used at anthracite mines, were in operation between 1800 and the 20th century. Men and boys at work in a coal breaker often suffered the loss of fingers and hands because of fast-moving, coal-laden conveyor belts. The Delaware and Hudson Railway made a lot of income from the anthracite coal business.

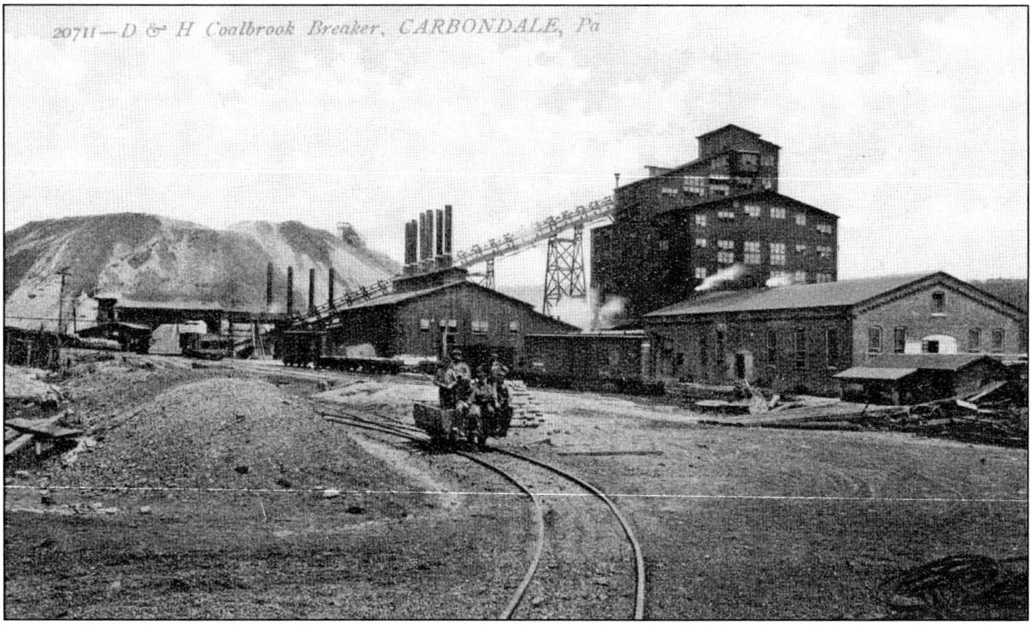

Carbondale Breaker Plant. The D&H Coalbrook Breaker was located in Carbondale, Pennsylvania. The mine is behind the breaker for the convenience of processing the coal. Young boys 12 and older were allowed to work in these breaker plants, even though the work was dangerous. Coal dust and other impurities caused asthma and often resulted in black lung in the workers. This system of processing coal is no longer used.

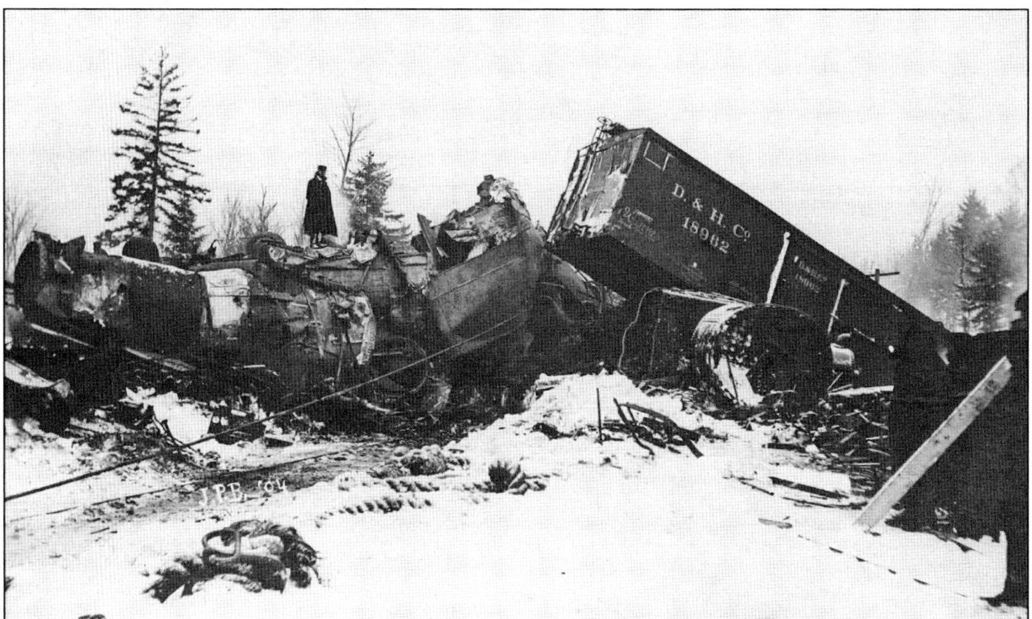

Unidentified Derailment. Photographs of derailments on D&H tracks in the early 1900s seem to be plentiful. This photograph was taken in 1904 at an unidentified location. The boxcar is clearly marked D&H Co. No. 18962. One lone spectator on the ridge surveys the tangled mass of metal thought to be the engine.

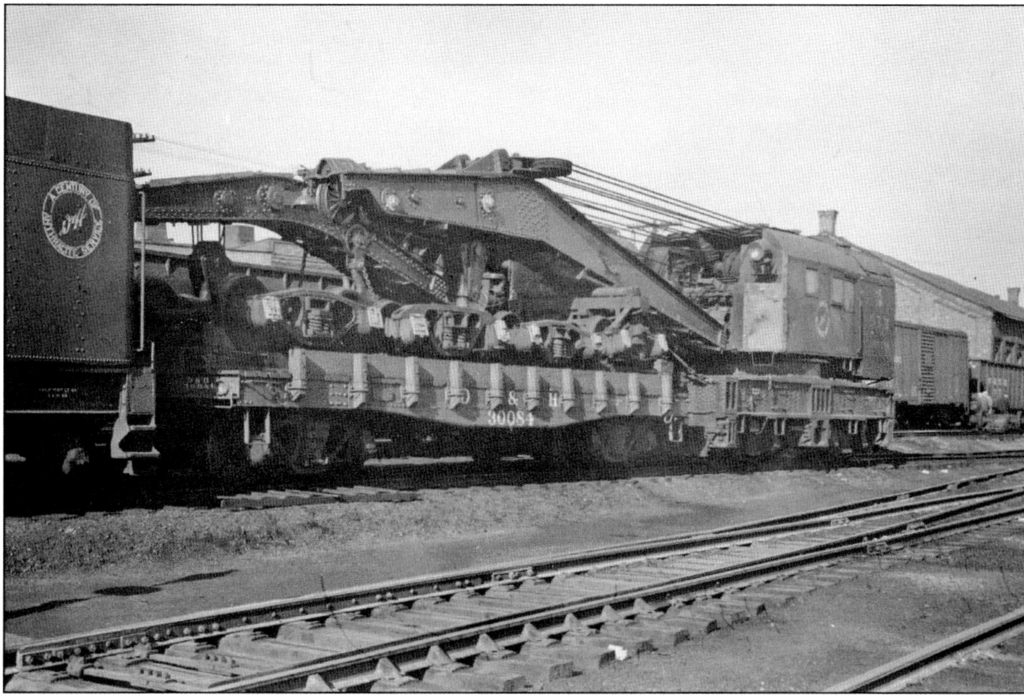

D&H Crane. Flat car No. 30081, with its D&H crane cargo, waits on a siding at the rail yards in Oneonta. The equipment from the 1940s is ready to travel to the scene of a wreck or derailment on the Delaware and Hudson rail line.

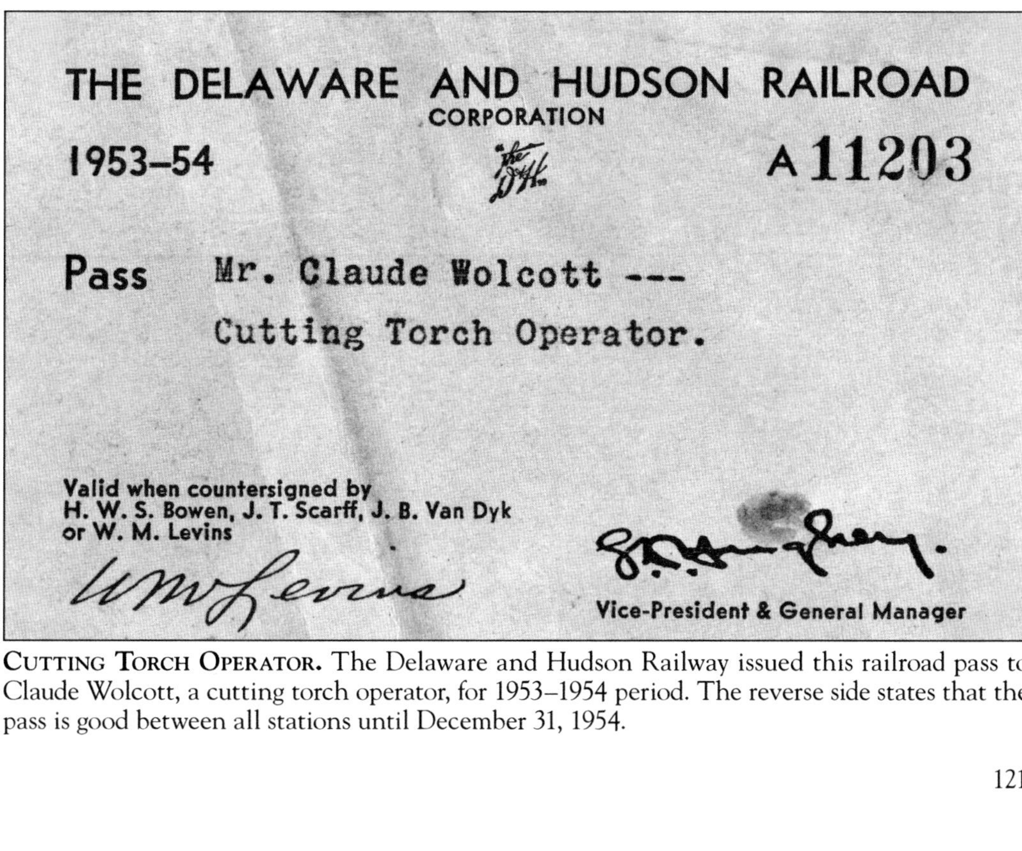

THE DELAWARE AND HUDSON RAILROAD
CORPORATION

1953–54 A 11203

Pass Mr. Claude Wolcott ---
Cutting Torch Operator.

Valid when countersigned by
H. W. S. Bowen, J. T. Scarff, J. B. Van Dyk
or W. M. Levins

Vice-President & General Manager

Cutting Torch Operator. The Delaware and Hudson Railway issued this railroad pass to Claude Wolcott, a cutting torch operator, for 1953–1954 period. The reverse side states that the pass is good between all stations until December 31, 1954.

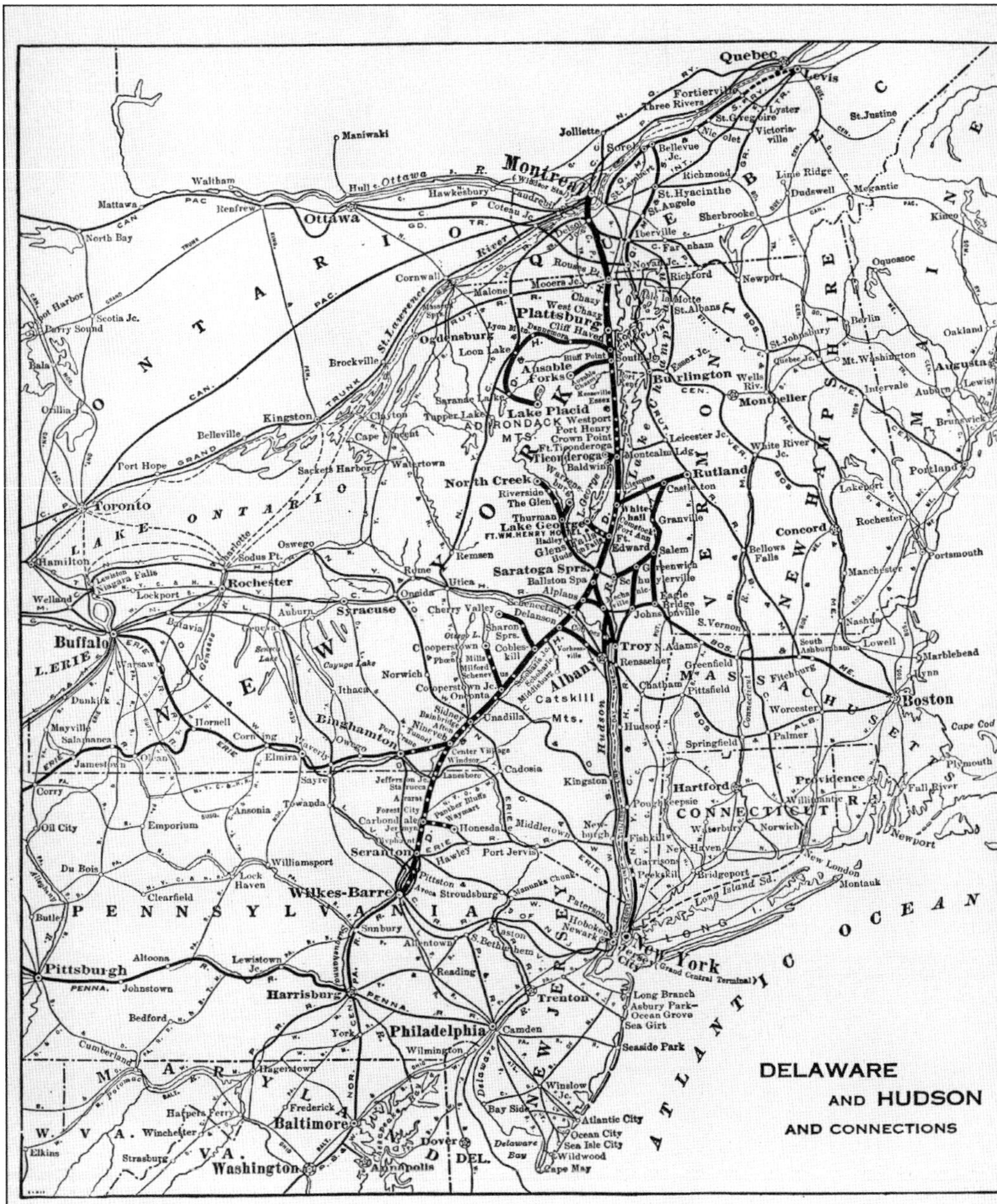

ALBANY TO SCRANTON. This is an old Delaware and Hudson Company map showing railroad connections. The photographs and information in this book cover the Delaware and Hudson area from Albany to Binghamton and the southern tier. The D&H, known as the "bridge line," travels north to Montreal and connects to other rail systems. Many of the vintage photographs in this book cover the Delaware and Hudson in the early 20th century, when coal was hauled along the line and the railroad was in its prime.

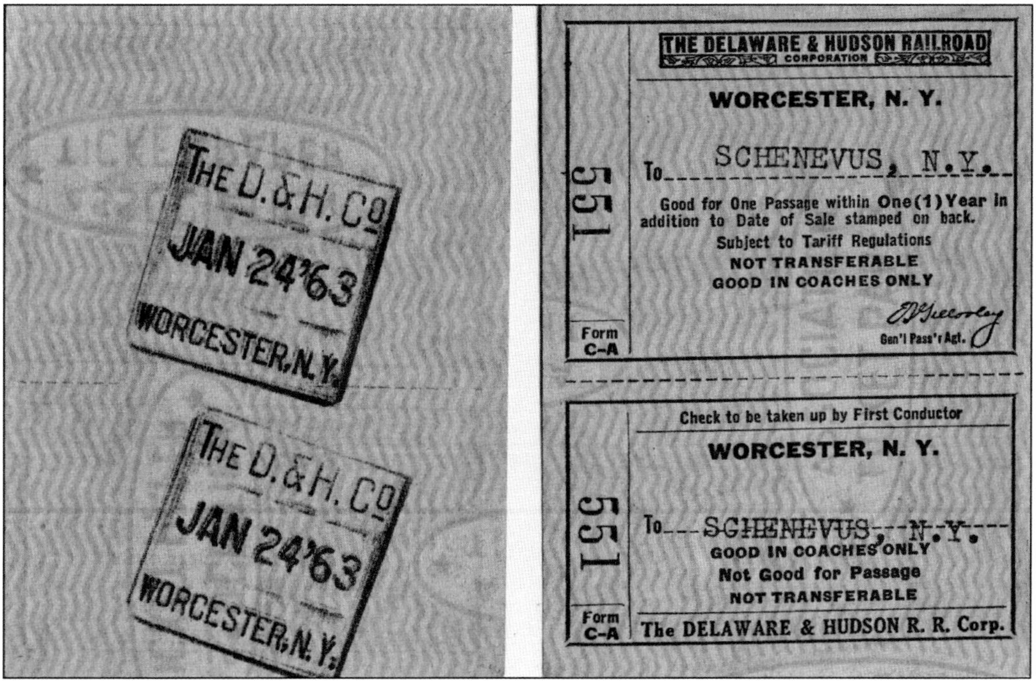

End of an Era. The last D&H passenger train No. 208 on the line between Albany and Binghamton ceased on January 25, 1963. Service was discontinued due to a long history of losing money. A boom in business took place the last week of service for the railroad. Hundreds of schoolchildren, teachers, and adults boarded the train for a ride to the next station, where buses waited to return them to school. Many of the children were experiencing their first trip on a train. The tickets pictured here were used on January 24, 1963, from Worcester to Schenevus and Worcester to East Worcester.

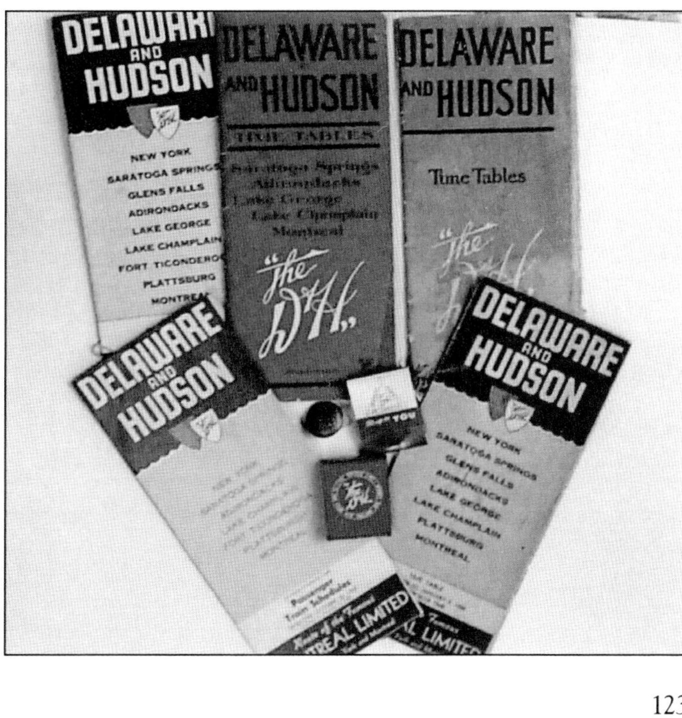

Timetable Collection. A collection of timetables brings back memories of times past and the once-busy train schedules that offered passengers a chance to travel anywhere they wanted to go by connecting to many railroads via the "bridge line."

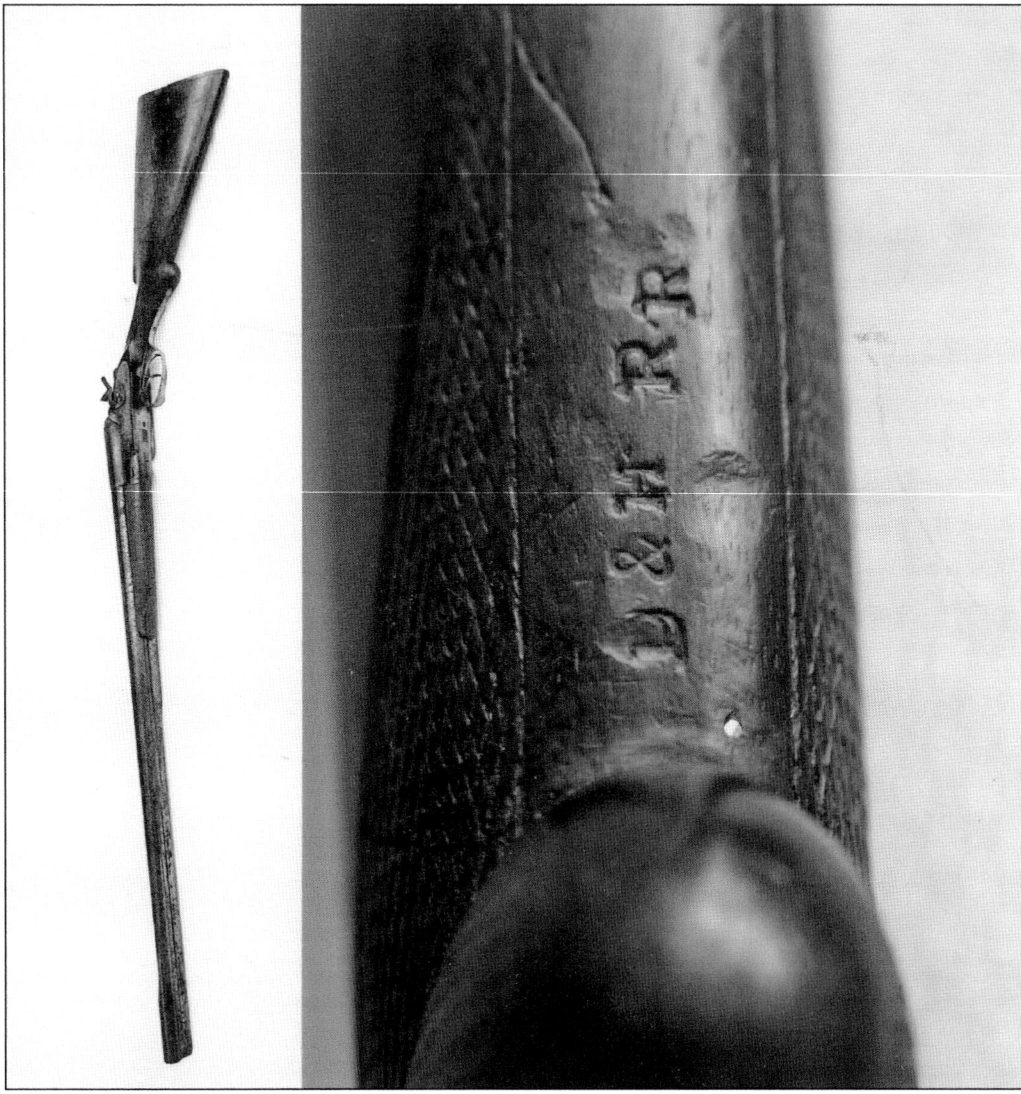

Railroad Security. Over the years, railroad security was of the utmost importance. Railroad police carried some kind of weapon to protect cargo in case of an emergency. This gun was made by Henri Pieper of Belgium and has "D&H RR" imprinted on the gun stock. In the April 2002 issue of the Bridge Line Historical Society *Bulletin*, a column by Stephen T. Wagner stated, "The last train robbery on American rails was probably within the last two hours. Every time a freight train stops for more than five minutes the contents are at risk of pilferage, as well as continuously while cars and containers are in the yard. This is the primary function for railroad police." (Photograph by David Jackson.)

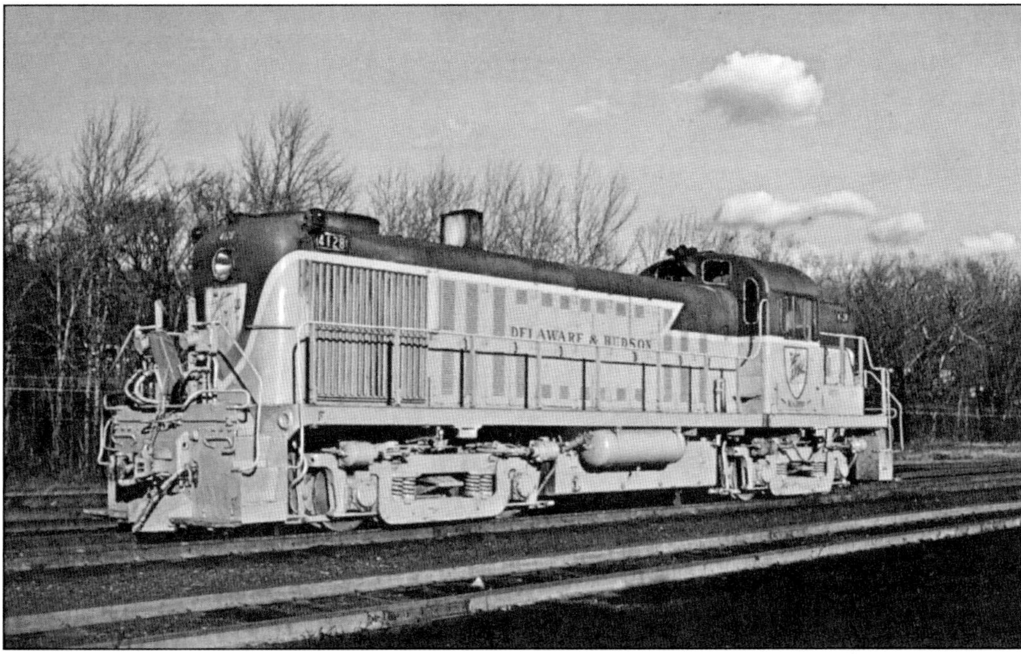

D&H No. 4128. The Alco road switcher represents the type of locomotive in the first generation of dieselization. The No. 4128, an RS-3, had 1,600-horsepower and could be used in multiple with other locomotives. This locomotive, built in August 1953, was the second to the last of the 130 road units that ended the steam age on the D&H. (Courtesy Jim Shaughnessy.)

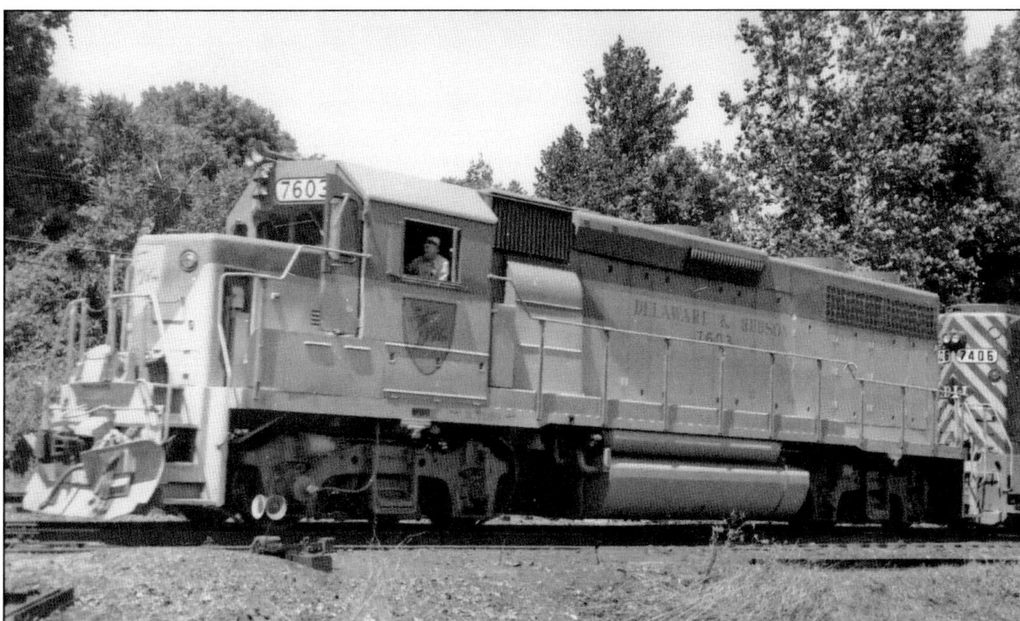

D&H Diesel. This D&H diesel is photographed here in Pennsylvania on July 26, 1976. The diesel, No. 7603, is a GP 39-2. Railroading has come a long way since the D&H first owned the rail line.

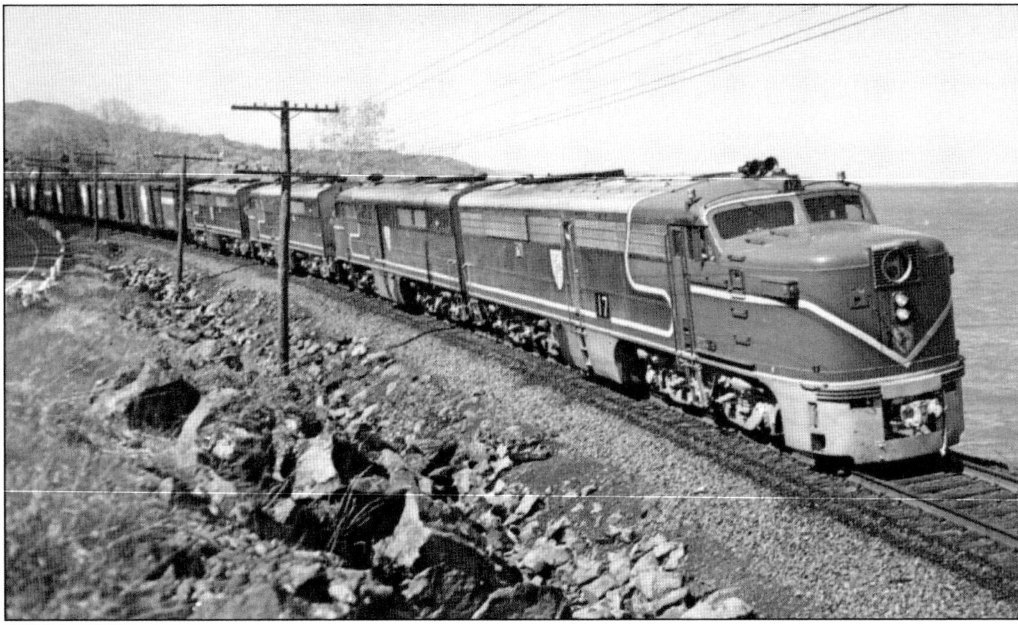

ALCO "PA" UNIT. D&H unit nos. 16, 17, 18, and 19, once the sole survivors of the famed "PA" units, travel along the rails at Lake Champlain. The four locomotives are pulling a line of freight cars, which can now number over 100 on today's rails. These units, built by Alco in 1948 for the Santa Fe Railway Company, were repainted for use by the D&H. (Courtesy of Jim Shaughnessy.)

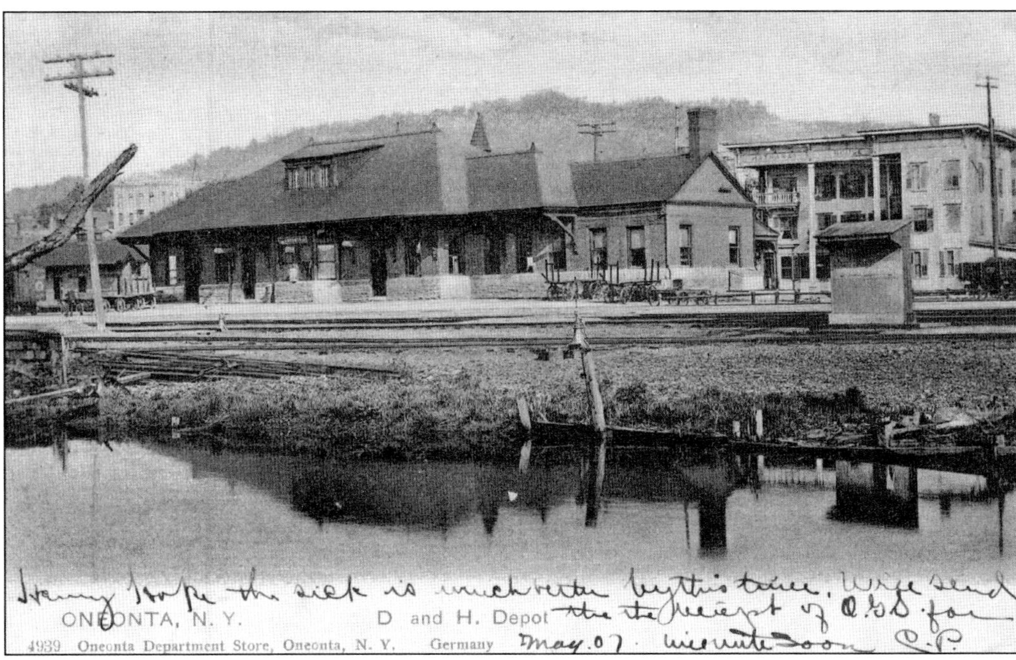

D&H REFLECTIONS. It is appropriate to end this book with one last photograph of the D&H station in Oneonta. Much has happened since Oneonta became known worldwide because of its roundhouse. It is good to reflect on the D&H with photographs, memories, and memorabilia to help keep all that history alive. Let us preserve the past and savor it for future generations.

BIBLIOGRAPHY

Catella, James T. *Our Hometown Railroad.* Main Street Print Shop, 1993.

Dana, Harley Tuttle. *Stray Poems and Early History of the Albany and Susquehanna Railroad.* York, PA: P. Anstadt and Sons, 1903.

Finch, Peter L. "New D&H." *Kaatskill Life.* Spring 1993: 12–23.

Loudon, Jim. *Leatherstocking Rails: A History of Railroading Along the Upper Susquehanna.* Utica, NY: Dodge-Graphic Press, Inc., 2005.

———. *The Oneonta Roundhouse.* Cooperstown, NY: Leatherstocking Railway Historical Society and Leatherstocking Chapter National Railway Historical Society, 1993.

Milener, Eugene D. *Oneonta: The Development of a Railroad Town.* Deposit, NY: Courier Printing Corporation, 1983.

Moore, Edwin R. *In Old Oneonta,* Vol. 2. Oneonta, NY: The Star Job Shop, 1963

———. *In Old Oneonta,* Vol. 5. Laurens, NY: The Village Printer, 1969.

Palmer, Richard, and Harvey Roehl. *Railroads in Early Postcards: Volume One, Upstate New York.* Vestal, NY: Vestal Press, 1990.

Consistent with our mission to preserve history on a local level, this book was printed in South Carolina on American-made paper and manufactured entirely in the United States. Products carrying the accredited Forest Stewardship Council (FSC) label are printed on 100 percent FSC-certified paper.

MADE IN THE USA